Tales of the Rational

Skeptical Essays About Nature and Science

By Massimo Pigliucci

Freethought Press, Atlanta, Georgia

First Edition, First printing, May 2000

ISBN 1-887392-11-4

Printed in the United States of America

Cover: the Lagoon Nebula, where new stars are forming,
photographed by the Hubble Space Telescope (NASA Image
Exchange), Galileo Galilei and Charles Darwin (Perry-Castaneda
Library, University of Texas at Austin). Back cover: Author's photo
by Ed Buckner. Cover design by Massimo Pigliucci

This book is printed using Book Antiqua fonts

Published by Freethought Press,
an imprint of Atlanta Freethought Society
PO Box 813392
Smyrna, GA 30081-8392
http://www.concentric.net/~theafs

To Will Provine, whom I met only once,

but with whom I have been friend forever.

Other books by Massimo Pigliucci:

Il Romanzo della Vita (The Romance of Life), Mondadori: Rome, Italy, 1986

La Via delle Stelle (The Road to the Stars), with Franco Foresta-Martin, Mursia: Milan, Italy, 1987

Phenotypic Evolution: a Reaction Norm Perspective, with Carl D. Schlichting, Sinauer: Sunderland, MA, 1998

Beyond Nature vs. Nurture: the Genetics, Ecology and Evolution of Genotype-Environment Interactions, Johns Hopkins University Press: Baltimore, MD, in press

Contents

Overture: Why I became a skeptic

It was a Sunday afternoon in the late 1970s, I was in my father's apartment in Rome (Italy) and the soccer game on the radio wasn't particularly exciting. So, I picked up a book from his library. He likes having those collections of classic books in which the individual volumes all look the same and that nobody usually ever opens. The book I chose almost at random was Bertrand Russell's autobiography. I started reading it with casual curiosity and did not stop until I went through the whole thing a few days later. If I can single out a defining moment when I became a skeptic, that was the one. Russell's prose was so convincing, so humane, and at the same time so no-nonsense, that there was little arguing about it. For a while I even became a Russell junky and read (with only superficial understanding, since I was only fourteen) several of his books.

But my conversion to skepticism was not complete, it did not happen over the span of a few days, and it wasn't over until several years later. I was brought up Catholic and took first communion mostly because it was the thing to do in a Catholic country where catechism is essentially mandatory in elementary schools. I remember praying to God diligently every evening, usually for mine or my loved ones' welfare, going to church once in a while (especially at Christmas or Easter), and even trying real hard to come up with some "sins" to declare on the rare occasions I went to the confessional. (Though usually I didn't know the words of the prayers that the priest would instruct me to repeat a certain number of times to expiate my bad behavior – a rather embarrassing situation that led to even more penitence.)

However, I also remember my elementary teacher, Mrs. Darmont (she was of French origins) who would make mild fun of the priest who came in the classroom to introduce us to the mysteries of Christianity (no State-Church separation in Italy). Every time he referred to eternal blessing in Heaven (he wasn't strong on Hell), she would add that she was looking forward to such life, but on the other hand there was really no hurry. I suspect that those persistent and good-humored remarks planted the first seeds of doubt in my pliable mind.

My transition from mild Catholicism to agnosticism to atheism took a few years between middle school and the first couple of years in high school. Being in an environment in which most of my high school peers espoused left-wing politics and were generally non-religious probably helped. But I still wasn't a skeptic through and through, since – as unlikely as it may sound now – I believed in extraterrestrial visits to the planet earth as the most likely explanations of UFO sightings.

But to understand that we have to step back several years, to when I was five and my interest in science was first stimulated. It was July 1969 when the Apollo 11 landed on the moon, and I was watching the whole thing on television with my grandparents. I was so excited because my grandfather (actually my grandmother's second husband) was thrilled and communicated his excitement to me. My other grandmother still recalls that I apparently had a good enough understanding of what was going on that I was able to correct her on the proper terminology to use to refer to parts of the lunar Lander – which probably says as much about my obsession for precision as to my interest in science (and perhaps a little bit about an early propensity for lecturing…). My grandpa then gave me my first telescope (little more than a toy) and books about astronomy, and my interest in the field developed for years, to the point of organizing astronomy clubs in junior and high school. Later I seriously considered getting a college degree in physics to become an astronomer, before my interest in biology and genetics took over. Carl Sagan provided some of my first and most influential readings.

Back to UFOs. It seemed to me that simply too many people were claiming to see strange lights in the sky, and even to having close encounters of a varied kind, for the whole thing to be scoffed at as nonsense. I started reading a lot about it, frequenting UFO clubs, and eventually writing on the topic for a couple of magazines. My explanation for why the public doesn't know more about UFOs was twofold: the military is clearly lying because of their twisted idea of national security (I still believe that concerning a variety of much more scary topics), and scientists are simply too complacent and comfortable in their ivory towers (which, now that I am scientist, realize is indeed true in general). However, I was determined to find out the truth in a "scientific" manner. So I kept reading, and even bothered to interview a few witnesses of alleged

UFO sightings, tabulated case histories, and calculated elementary statistics. In other words, I tried to apply the scientific method I had been studying during my readings in astronomy to my not-so-rational belief in aliens visiting the earth.

Why did I believe in such things? Because it was cool! What could be more fascinating than meeting an alien civilization from another galaxy? And wasn't Sagan saying that the galaxy abounds with life? Wasn't Isaac Asimov a scientist *and* a science fiction writer? Clearly, my conception of science and pseudoscience, reality and fantasy, was not well delineated, but the mix made sense to me.

Things changed during my last years of high school for two unrelated reasons: the influence of another teacher, and that of a girl friend who was a lot more rational than I was. The teacher was our philosophy instructor for the last three years of high school and she was quite a character. She would get into the classroom in the morning and we would know that she probably had had breakfast with some alcoholic content, certainly not just milk. She referred to Marx as "Karl," but she was a hell of a teacher and she had an astounding ability to get you (or at least, me) excited about philosophy. Her discussions of the ancient Greeks, the Enlightenment, Schopenauer and Nietzche did in any residual doubts I might have had about religion or God.

The fatal blow to my aliens was dealt by a girlfriend whom I met around that time. She was definitely a no-nonsense kind of girl, and she was very much into astronomy, which is how we met. She was a bit disturbed by my interest in UFOs, but she played along patiently, even trying to help me come up with new rational attempts to investigate the phenomenon. Within a year of our first meeting, however, I had seen the light and all my energy was concentrated on science, with pseudoscience left behind in the dustbin of youthful experimentations. It has been that way ever since.

My newfound position as a skeptic and scientist did not imply any activism though. I wasn't about to try to "de-convert" other people from the errors of their ways. I was too busy going to college, then graduate school, and finally getting a job in the competitive but exhilarating world of academia. Besides, nobody was bothering me, so why waste my time? That changed in the fall of 1995, when I landed a job at the University of Tennessee in

Knoxville. As soon as I arrived on campus, freshly appointed Assistant Professor of Ecology and Evolutionary Biology, an amazing thing happened: the Tennessee legislature, in its infinite lack of wisdom, thought it an appropriate time to discuss a new anti-evolution law, as if the Scopes trial never happened.

I took this rather personally and with a few colleagues and graduate students I founded "Darwin Day," an annual excuse to teach the general public about evolution and perhaps shake a little bit of the intellectual torpor caused in my fellow Tennesseans by a place that has a higher density of Baptist churches than McDonald's (I still have not made up my mind about which one is the greatest evil). Yet, even Darwin Day was a simple intellectual reaction to a bad situation, and certainly something fun to do from time to time, and it would not have changed my life if not for another event that was to happen soon afterwards.

Because of the publicity surrounding Darwin Day I was approached by a local group of skeptics, now known as the Rationalists of East Tennessee. Skeptics? Who are they? Oh yeah, I remembered reading about a publication called the *Skeptical Inquirer* back in my UFOs days, but they were the sworn enemy at that time; those were the closed minded people who wouldn't believe in extraterrestrial visits even if a flying saucer would land in their backyards. Was I interested in going to some of the group's meetings? Not really, not enough time while trying to get tenure and all, and furthermore, are we sure these skeptics are not yet another fringe group of lunatics, perhaps a sort of rationalistic fundamentalists?

Fringe group they are, lunatics they are not. When I finally started to attend their meetings I found lifelong friends, intellectual kinship, and most especially the love of my life. So, here we are full circle. From believer in God to agnostic and atheist, from UFOs buff to scientist, from a "live and let live" attitude to activism that gives additional meaning to my life and makes me feel useful to society. And my intellectual and personal journey is, I hope, only near the beginning.

Acknowledgments. The following pages are an attempt to share some of the thoughts I came across during the last few years concerning varied aspects of science, skepticism, and religion. I have been immensely helped by a number of people whom I would like to thank here. First of all, my wife, Melissa Brenneman, fellow skeptic and humanist, one of the kindest and most thoughtful persons I know. Then all of the members of the Rationalists of East Tennessee, and in particular Sharron and Phil King, Carl and Aleta Ledendecker, and Jerry and Ann Sillman, with whom I spent innumerable hours discussing the very topics that make up this book. A special thank you to my friend Ed Buckner and his wife Diane. Not only have they been always so kind to me, but Ed has indefatigably worked to make this book possible and to make my reasoning as cogent and coherent as he could. I'd also like to thank many fellow skeptics who I met during my travels, who were kind enough to come to Knoxville to share their ideas, or who engaged me in fruitful correspondence: among many others, Michael Shermer, Paul Kurtz, Ken Frazier, Amanda Chesworth, Dan Barker, Andrew Lutes, Herb Silverman, Barbara Stocker, David Schaefer, Barry Palevitz, and Keith Lankford. Many thanks also to James Cherry for providing me with abundant material about creationist Duane Gish and for detailed comments on the effectiveness of my debates, as well as to Jeffery Jay Lowder for like comments on my performance against theist William Lane Craig. They are all a big intellectual family to me, and I am deeply grateful for their friendship and help.

Part I - Philosophical tales

Philosophy is a much maligned enterprise. Most people think of it as the quintessential academic futility, a complete waste of time. Of course, these same individuals do not realize that they have a philosophy too, in fact often more than one. Anybody who has any opinion, however fuzzy, about the great questions of life is more or less consciously espousing a particular philosophy. In fact, one could argue that even if one makes an effort not to follow any philosophy, that is a philosophical position too!

This is certainly not a book on philosophy, but I do touch on many philosophical questions, so it is appropriate to start with three essays dealing with rather philosophical issues. The first entry in this series focuses on the history and use of some terms that permeate the humanist and anti-humanist literature, generally to the great confusion of most readers. If we are to discuss emotionally loaded terms such as humanism, skepticism, or materialism, we better agree on what we are talking about, and my attempt is a beginning in that direction.

The second essay deals with the fundamental difference between methodological and philosophical naturalism: the first one being the most important assumption underlying the scientific method, the second one justifying the use of science to inform philosophical questions. Many people strenuously object to such use, but I think that a philosophy uninformed by scientific findings is bound to be a sterile academic exercise. Science originated from philosophy, and now that it is an independent field of inquiry it can greatly benefit its own intellectual roots—and vice versa.

The concluding essay in this section deals with a rather peculiar idea: that straw men, i.e., simplified or extreme versions of an argument, are actually useful to some extent and do not deserve the bad reputation that they commonly held. At least at the beginning of a discussion, I think it is helpful to clearly delineate the differences between alternative positions, even at the risk of being somewhat naïve about them. It is only further discussion and in-depth analysis that can bring about any compromise between the opposing fields, but such compromise cannot be reached unless one starts with clearly defined alternatives to help anchor the thinking process.

Philosophy can be considered the study of everything, and as such a rather futile enterprise. Or, it can be seen as the mother of all other ways of knowing, including science. As all parents ought to hope, one's children will eventually surpass one's own abilities, partly because they can stand on one's shoulders and see further. It can therefore be argued that philosophy is a doomed discipline, eventually to be replaced by its own intellectual offspring. That may be so, but I would not hasten to close philosophy departments in our universities just yet—we have too much to learn from their practitioners.

Chapter 1 - Rationalism, skepticism, and other "isms": How do we know what's out there, and where "there" actually is

"Can we know the universe? My God, it's hard enough finding your way around in Chinatown." (Woody Allen, Getting Even)

At least some of the readers of this book will consider themselves rationalists, skeptics, humanists, or freethinkers (though others are welcome as well). They will read journals like *Skeptic, Skeptical Inquirer, Free Inquiry, Freethought Today* and *The Humanist*. In fact, many people think of these terms as pretty much equivalent, regardless of their personal feelings about the philosophical positions reflected by these words. In fact, the history and original meaning of many of these philosophical "isms" is quite different, and in some cases radically opposite, to the meaning we may attach to them today. It is important to clear up some of these concepts at the beginning of this book, since they will recur in many of the following chapters. To find out about some of the real or imagined connections among these terms makes for a brief fascinating journey into both philosophy and how the human mind acquires knowledge.

Philosophically speaking

Let us start with **rationalism**. Given the emphasis of modern society on science and rational discourse, who would not be proud of being labeled a rationalist?[1] Yet the founder of rationalism was René Descartes (1596-1650), who conceived it as a way of gaining knowledge without need for experience (Descartes, 1637). *Cogito ergo sum* (I think, therefore I am) was the first rationalistic conclusion Descartes arrived at. Nothing to object to there. However, the *second* "self-evident" conclusion was that God

---

[1] This is, of course, a rhetorical question, since there are many people who are simply horrified by the thought.

exists as well! Ah, now we see that rationalism can be, well, quite irrational... (Interestingly, Descartes deduced the existence of ordinary objects *after* he deduced the existence of God. As Smith [1991] pointed out, there is no fault in being Descartes, but you are certainly to blame if you are a Cartesian.)

Contemporaneously with the development of rationalism, English philosophers such as Francis Bacon (1825) and John Locke (1959) were developing a completely opposite view of knowledge (i.e., a different epistemology), namely **empiricism**. The cornerstone of empiricism is that the best way to learn about the world is to observe it, i.e. to collect data. Modern science clearly originated from 17th century empiricism (although it also incorporates some of the principles of rationalism). The world before the empiricists was a place where magical and mystical explanations reigned supreme, and empiricism's daughter – science – is our main weapon to keep the world a sane place.

Fig. 1.1 – Rene` Descartes (1596-1650): rationalism, but not too much.

Rationalism and empiricism are philosophies at odds with each other, as shown by the bitter controversies between their leading proponents. Yet, most people who consider themselves "rationalists" today also embrace the scientific method. Is reconciliation possible after all? Immanuel Kant (1781) certainly believed so. However, his solution would not appeal to most followers of the contemporary rationalist movement. He proposed that wanting to believe in God is a rational ideal that sheds light on the philosopher's mind, and it is therefore an empirical fact. Furthermore, Kant observed that a great deal of what we perceive about the world (empiricism) is in fact shaped by our minds (rationalism). The generalization of the latter statement led him to the philosophy of *idealism*, which is as far as you can get from modern science.[2]

---

[2] Interestingly, modern science *is* indeed a mixture of empiricism and rationalism, but of a very different flavor from what Kant proposed. Essentially, modern scientists are empiricists who realize that some basic – but

What about **skepticism**? This can be concisely defined as "the idea that something someone thinks is true may in fact not be true" (Stevenson 1998). In some sense, the first skeptic may have been Socrates, who taught his disciples by asking questions aimed at showing them the error of their ways of thinking (the so-called "Socratic method": Taylor 1953). More recently, David Hume has been credited with being the skeptic *par excellence*, though he went so far as to deny the possibility of establishing causal relationships among phenomena, which today is considered the ultimate goal of science. Appropriately enough, the word "skepticism" comes from a Greek root which means "seeking," presumably the truth. As valid and respectable as skepticism may be, it is not a theory of knowledge, but rather a way to reveal that which is untrue. Therefore, it does not strictly speaking have much to do with either rationalism or empiricism as philosophies (although it can make use of either or both). A more modern way to think about skepticism is in scientific-statistical terms, as probabilities to commit one of two fundamental types of errors: rejecting conclusions that are in fact correct (extreme skepticism) or accepting conclusions that are false (extreme gullibility). We will see in Chapter 4 why a good compromise is *not* along the 50%-50% line.

Fig. 1.2 – Leonardo da Vinci (1452-1519), a universal symbol of the Italian Renaissance.

Humanism originated in the 14th century as an effect of the European (mostly Italian) Renaissance. The idea is that what humans think and do has value in and of itself, originally in addition (and today regardless) of what connection there may be to God and her will or intent. As much as the Renaissance and

reasonable – assumptions have to be made from a rationalist perspective. For example, we have to assume that there is a physical world out there, without which the entire scientific enterprise would not make any sense. It is a leap of faith, but a very small one indeed compared to what other alternatives we have.

humanism marked the beginning of the modern era, and therefore the ascent of science, humanism cannot really be considered a philosophy of knowledge, but rather an attitude about the world that proclaims human uniqueness and value. Incidentally,other philosophers had focused on humans in a very similar sense well before the 14th century. For example, the Greek philosopher Protagoras (480-411 BCE) said that "Man is the measure of all things." Protagoras was a sophist (a word meaning "expert," and obviously not modest) and his statement is considered an early example of relativism, the notion that truth is not absolute, but perceived differently by each human being. However, one could hardly come up with a more humanistic statement than the one attributed to him.

Atheism, of course, is not even a philosophy. Rather, it represents a conclusion derived from certain philosophical positions, such as empiricism and naturalism (but not necessarily rationalism, *a la Descartes*). Contrary to popular understanding, an atheist is not someone who believes that there is no God, but rather one who lacks a belief in God (a-theism, without a God). There are several forms of atheism (see Smith 1991), and several reasons to be an atheist (see Chapter 5). Also, Chapter 5 will give readers what I think is a good reason for being an atheist over being an agnostic (literally, one without knowledge, according to the original meaning of the word proposed by Thomas Henry Huxley (1825-1895), but sometimes simply, and unfairly, characterized as an indecisive position for the uncommitted).

Naturalism is for all effective purposes the same as **materialism**. The latter – far from the negative connotation that it has acquired because of its spurious relationship with *Marxism*[3] – is the idea that existence is entirely physical (i.e., there is no metaphysical world). Therefore, all our sensations, including the mental processes through which we acquire knowledge, are based on physical properties of our brains (with all the powers and shortcomings that this implies). From time to time a school of thought emerges that suggests that there is no such a thing as an

---

[3] Notice that materialism is also central to *capitalism*, the economical-political opposite of Marxism. Materialism, therefore, cannot be invoked as a despicable outcome of Marxism any more than it can be used to indict capitalism: it is a premise, not a consequence, of both.

objective reality, and that our perceived universe could in fact be nothing but a figment of our imagination. While logically unassailable, such talk makes my adrenaline levels go dangerously high. The best response I have ever come across is one given by Bertrand Russell, who said that he wished that people questioning reality would get into a car and drive straight into a wall at a speed proportional to their belief that the wall is not real.

Unlike what some people believe, **realism** does not have much in common with naturalism and materialism. Realism states that there are *universals* that exist independently of our minds. It sounds pretty much like materialism, except that said universals are not physical objects, but general *properties* of reality (e.g., "greenness" exists quite independently of any particular thing being green). That realism and naturalism/materialism are distinct is confirmed by the reaction to realism that culminated in William of Ockham's form of *nominalism* (Leff 1975). Nominalism is the contention that universals are simply generalizations of properties of particular objects, that these generalizations are made only by our mind (they are "names"), and they do not exist in the outside world. Ockham's sharpest tool was his "razor" argument. In essence, this says that if two explanations for the same phenomenon rely on a different number of assumptions, we should go with the one that requires the least number of hypotheses (of course, *ceteris paribus* – other things being equal). In other words, the simplest explanation is more likely to be correct. That nominalism, and not realism, is connected to modern science is obvious from the fact that Ockham's razor – now commonly termed "parsimony" – is one of the philosophical pillars of the scientific method.

Finally, we get to **freethought**. This is not a philosophy, but rather an umbrella term that includes a variety of philosophies. To convince ourselves of this, let us just name a few exponents of freethinking. Names that immediately come to mind are David Hume (1740; 1779) and Francois Marie Arouet de Voltaire (1949). But Hume (1740) believed that causality is not necessarily a property of the world, and that we perceive causal connections among phenomena simply because we associate (in our minds) things that happen in a given temporal sequence. This view, as mentioned above, is certainly contrary to the modern foundations of science. Voltaire was a complex figure of his own. He admired

English empiricism and was a witty defender of the power of reason. He was also a *deist*: he believed in the existence of God, but his God is unknowable and promptly retired immediately after having created the world. Voltaire was equally critical of organized religion and of atheism, a position consistent with his philosophical skepticism.

In light of all of the above, I propose that freethinking is indeed the most general label that modern skeptics, atheists, rationalists, scientists, and – to some extent – humanists, can comfortably wear. The fundamentals of the freethought movement are three: the use of logical-empirical means to establish conclusions about the nature of the world; a general principle of tolerance toward the possibly disparate conclusions to which this method can lead human beings; and a partiality to humans as the subjective, not objective, center of our world.

Logic and reality

Most of the above discussion was framed in logical terms, but what *is* logic, anyway? And how does it help us to know what is out there, the chief objective of science and, to a lesser extent, of philosophy? A general discussion of logic and of its relationships to the scientific method and to our quest for truth about the world is not within the scope of this essay, but a sketch is indeed necessary. There are two main ways of proceeding "logically" to acquire knowledge about the world: *deduction* and *induction*. Deduction is the process by which one starts with a number of assumptions and reaches a logically necessary (that is, internally consistent) conclusion from those assumptions. Aristotle's syllogisms are an example of deduction. Perhaps the most famous is:

1. (If) All men are mortal (premise)
2. (Since) Socrates is a man (observation)
3. (Then) Socrates is mortal (conclusion)

From the general premise (1) and the specific observation (2), the conclusion (3) follows logically. Induction, on the other hand, is a method of inferring generalizations from the observations of many instances of particular occurrences. For example, I can predict that the sun will rise tomorrow even without any knowledge of the laws of physics (Hume would have liked this), because it has done so for a long, long time. Induction was canonized as part of the nascent scientific method by Francis Bacon (1561-1626).

Deduction is a more logically powerful method than induction in that its conclusions must be correct (*if* the premises are correct, and that may turn out to be a big "if"). Induction, on the other hand, is prone to error if the conditions that generated a given outcome in the past are significantly altered (in other words, induction can only tell us what will *probably* occur). Take for example the classic tale of the inductivist turkey, narrated by Bertrand Russell. The turkey was brought on a farm and fed in the morning, around 7 A.M. He was a good inductivist, so he would not reach any conclusion about his future in the new place until sufficient observations were collected. After a few hundred days he had notes upon notes recording the fact that he was fed every morning around 7 A.M. However, being an extremely good inductivist, he felt he needed more observations before reaching any general conclusion. Finally, after 364 days of consistent observations he felt confident enough to make a general prediction:

Fig. 1.3 – The dialectic nature of the scientific method as a continuous feedback among observation, deduction (theory) and induction (hypothesis)

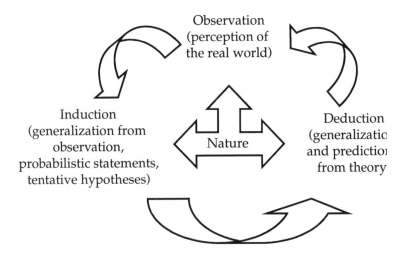

Observation
(perception of
the real world)

Induction
(generalization from
observation,
probabilistic statements,
tentative hypotheses)

Nature

Deduction
(generalizatio
and predictio
from theory

he will be fed again the following morning at 7 A.M. Alas, that day turned out to be Thanksgiving. This cautionary tale notwithstanding, induction is by no means to be underestimated. The entire discipline of statistics is based on induction, since it reaches conclusions based on extrapolation of observations, not on a description of causal mechanisms. And even though statistics can indeed lie (or at least, mislead), a statistical frame of mind has been astoundingly successful in complex sciences such as biology and sociology. Furthermore, induction can aid in generating hypotheses, a cornerstone of the scientific method. Pure deduction is a closed system, which can generate new knowledge only within the strict confines of syllogism-like operations.

Can't we have it both ways? Is there an approach that combines the best of deduction and induction, while simultaneously compensating for each separate method's limitations? As a matter of fact there is one: it is known as *dialectics* (from a Greek word meaning "discussion"), and Socrates is once again due credit for it[4]. Socrates compared alternative ideas by probing into their premises and shifting from one idea to the other in order to see how they held up to criticism. This process of going back and forth is what constitutes a dialectic approach. Sounds familiar? It should, since it is the basis of the so-called hypothetical-deductive method: the scientific method as we know it today.

---

[4] Much later, during the 18th and 19th centuries, Friedrich Hegel first and Engels and Marx later, also used the term dialectics (the latter two authors in the sense of dialectic materialism). Hegel's contribution was in theorizing that an idea, or what he called a *thesis*, can be explored in terms of its opposite, the *antithesis*. The solution to the problem defined by thesis and antithesis can be arrived at through a process of *synthesis* of the two.

Chapter 2 - Methodological vs. philosophical naturalism, or why we should be skeptical of religion

"Question with boldness even the existence of God." (Thomas Jefferson, letter to his favorite nephew, 10 August 1787)

Is religion a legitimate area of inquiry for skepticism? The humanist community answers with a resounding "yes," while the skeptical one is a lot more doubtful (see, for example, several articles in the July/August 1999 issue of *Skeptical Inquirer*, as well as Chapter 6 for a general discussion of the relationship between science and religion). This essay has been inspired by conversations that I had with a couple of friends who happen to be prominently on opposite sides of this divide. Since similar discussions are endlessly carried out between skeptics and humanists as well as among theistic and atheistic scientists, I thought it may be good to summarize the two positions and see where their logical consequences would carry us.

The two main characters whose position I would like to discuss are William Provine, a historian and philosopher of science at Cornell University, and Eugenie Scott, an anthropologist and executive director of the National Center for Science Education. I met them both at the 1998 "Darwin Day" at the University of Tennessee (http://fp.bio.utk.edu/darwin), which set the stage for precisely the discussion on which this chapter is based.

Methodological vs. philosophical materialism

While both Provine and Scott are declared non-theists (the term preferred by Scott) or atheists (Provine's favorite), their positions on the degree of clash between science and religion could hardly be more different. Scott's argument is that science simply does not have anything to say about religion, period. Therefore, scientists should go about their business of investigating natural phenomena and not concern themselves with religious matters of any sort. Needless to say, Scott suggests that this should *a fortiori* be any science educator's behavior in the classroom. As I said, however, Scott is indeed an atheist and a materialist. So, how does she reconcile her theoretical positions with her call for a separation of the two issues in everyday practice?

Scott espouses the view that there is a distinction between *methodological* and *philosophical naturalism*. The first corresponds to what any practicing scientist would do. We *assume* that the world is made of matter, and if indeed there is something else out there, this is simply beyond the scope and reach of the scientific method. The position of philosophical naturalism, on the other hand, is rational, but not strictly speaking scientific. It *concludes* (albeit provisionally) that there is only matter out there, even though we cannot prove this beyond any doubt.

One problem with Scott's dualism is that, even though technically correct, it smacks of political correctness, or at least lacks philosophical courage. When asked how she came to be a philosophical

Fig. 2.1. Intellectual opponents: Eugenie Scott (left) and William Provine (right) at the 1998 edition of "Darwin Day" hosted by the University of Tennessee.

materialist, Scott admitted that this was the result of her knowledge of science. In other words, a scientific understanding of the world leads (not necessarily, but in Scott's, Provine's, and my own case) one to provisionally reject any supernatural force or entity. I think the qualification of "provisional" is important because I do agree with Scott that science cannot conclusively deny the existence of the supernatural. In fact, I would go much further than that: science cannot prove the non-existence of anything at all. All scientists can do is to support positive statements with circumstantial evidence (Lakatos 1974), or disprove them by refutation (Popper 1968). So, we are left with the rather unsatisfactory position that science throws a little bit of light in the abyss of the unknown, but not enough to answer perhaps the most important philosophical question of them all: is there something beyond matter and energy?

Soul? Evolution says no!

Not so for William Provine. His answer is clear: there is nothing out there, we die in the most definitive sense of the word, and there is no point in even asking the question of the ultimate meaning of life. Where does he get this conclusion? From the Darwinian theory of evolution by descent with modification, or so he maintains. According to Provine, not only is there no evidence for anything beyond matter, but the whole essence of evolutionary change should tell us that it is irrational to even look for it. After all, there is an uninterrupted, historical continuity between humans and the rest of the living world. If that is so, we are left with only two possibilities for granting the existence of something immaterial: either we go back to René Descartes' dualism (all living organisms are machines, except humans, that possess not only the *res extensa* but also the *res cogitans* – not only do we have physical bodies, but we possess a non-physical consciousness). Or we assume that *every* living being is made of matter and of spirit, a position that would make even the pope rather uncomfortable (though it is an integral component of some eastern philosophies and of animism).

Provine goes even further, by accusing scientists who cling to a dualistic view either of intellectual dishonesty or of intellectual schizophrenia. Let us see why. The schizophrenic attitude can be traced back to Descartes himself. Although credited with nothing less than the invention of the scientific method (Descartes 1637), the French philosopher recoiled from the implication of his own doing, thereby introducing the above mentioned dualism between the two *res*.[5] Yet, a schizophrenic truly believes in the separation of his two personalities. Where does the dishonesty come into play? The answer, according to Provine, is at least in part the federal funding of scientific research. His thesis is that one of the fundamental reasons that compel most biologists to look the other way and not engage in disputes with religious overtones is simply the fact that the evolution = atheism equation is potentially very

---

[5] To what extent Descartes' position was dictated by his own convictions, by his inability to follow through his own philosophy to its ultimate consequences, or simply by a very rational fear of Church authorities, has been the subject of endless speculations.

dangerous for their pocketbooks (as well as their peace of mind). After all, most evolutionary biology research is funded through federal agencies such as the National Science Foundation (NSF). This is taxpayers' money. What would happen if the taxpayers found out that their money is going to foster atheistic beliefs? Especially given the current conservative (reactionary would be a better word) political climate, it does not take a huge leap of the imagination to see Republican senators and representatives crying foul and axing the already meager NSF budget. Indeed, it is true that NSF does not have a division of "evolutionary biology," while clearly a large portion of its funding for the biological sciences goes to evolutionary research projects under the euphemism of "population biology."[6] Regardless of repeated statements to the contrary, this is *both* a scientific and a political war, and the stakes are as high as the future of education in the most powerful country in the world, make no mistake about it (for more on creationism and its many facets, see Chapters 8, 9, and 11).

On the other hand, Provine's views are an example of philosophical, not methodological, materialism. Scott is correct when she says that you can infer, but not demonstrate, that there is no God, no afterlife, and no cosmic meaning to our existence. Therefore, the real question seems to me to be: what is the limit of science (more on this in Chapters 12-14)? Does science truly confine itself to methodological materialism, and is it therefore silent on everything else? Or, can we use scientific results to make inferences that go beyond a pragmatic approach and allow us to probe into ultimate questions?

You can't have it both ways: methodological naturalism implies philosophical naturalism

I will argue that:

1. It is true that science cannot prove the inexistence of supernatural phenomena or entities; but that,

---

[6] Incidentally, the term "population biology" may be only marginally more politically acceptable than evolution, since to the general public the phrase evokes thoughts of human population control.

2. It is perfectly reasonable to reject such phenomena or entities on scientific grounds (for a specific application of this principle to the question of the existence of God, see Chapter 5).

The first point acknowledges Scott's distinction between methodological and philosophical materialism. As I mentioned above, science cannot prove the inexistence of something. In fact, there are even more strict limits on what science can do. These limits derive from the indispensability of falsifiable hypotheses[7] (not always easy to formulate), and from the necessity of enough empirical evidence to actually test such hypotheses. For example, in the case of the origin of life (Chapter 12), or the origin of the universe itself, the questions may be scientifically approachable, and it certainly is possible to derive falsifiable alternative hypotheses. However, we may never have sufficient data to actually test and reject (or provisionally accept) some of the hypotheses that have been proposed. Unfortunately, the universe is not constructed in such manner to leave abundant clues for the scientifically minded Sherlock Holmes, whether we like it or not.

The second point is, obviously, the most controversial. My reasoning (as well as Provine's) is that you cannot pick and choose your philosophy depending on the situation. A methodological materialist who is not a philosophical materialist is basically saying that he believes in matter and only matter... *most* of the times! But if you grant the possibility of a god messing around with the universe once in a while, where do you get the assurance that that god is not doing it every day, every minute, in every place of the universe? Furthermore, I think that Scott's position betrays a misunderstanding of the nature of science. Science is not about proving things; it is about constructing workable causal models of

---

[7] A falsifiable hypothesis, according to Popper (1968) is a conjecture that can—in principle—be refuted. As such, it constitutes a scientific (testable) hypothesis. If a hypothesis is not falsifiable, i.e., if there is no way to disprove it, then it is not science. For example, if I say that I can guess *some* of the cards being picked at random from a deck because of my psychic powers, I am not making a scientific statement, since it is obvious that I would get some cards right simply by chance. However, if I specify a percentage of cards that I will guess correctly, and this percentage is statistically above the one expected by chance, then my claim is falsifiable (and, in this case, it would be demonstrated to be false).

reality. For a scientist to reject the supernatural, god, and (therefore) ultimate meaning in life is perfectly logical. The reason for this is that all such rejections are implicitly understood as provisional, and they are necessary to construct the best hypothesis consistent with the data. Since there is no evidence of any god or supernatural design in the universe, the *scientifically-informed* conclusion has to be that there is none (unless and until such conclusion is falsified by the available evidence). Once one understands that science is not about definitive proofs but about reasonable working models (or proof beyond currently reasonable doubt), the distinction between methodological and philosophical materialism gets very much blurred. And by the way, falsification of the naturalist paradigm is indeed possible (contrary to what creationist Phillip Johnson maintains: Johnson 1997). The ongoing controversy over the so-called anthropic principle is a case in point. Should we conclusively determine that the probability of existence of our universe is infinitesimally small, and should we fail to explain why physical constants have assumed the quantities that we observe, the possibility of a designed universe would have to be seriously considered.[8]

The peculiar thing is that most practicing scientists and educators, including Scott, apply exactly this reasoning every day of their lives. Suppose you have a graduate student who comes in with the results of an experiment and a series of alternative explanations for the observed data. If one of the explanations is "God did it," you will reject it on the grounds that there is no evidence of such supernatural intervention, as well as because it is no explanation at all. In other words, it is a characteristic of the scientific method to reject explanations based on unnecessary hypotheses, as well as hypotheses that carry no explanatory power. Such rejection, of course, does not equate to saying that there is no god. It simply means that our provisional model of the universe is consistent with the idea that there is no god, and we will go with that for now. Should new evidence emerge, a true scientist would reconsider his working model and, if so compelled by the nature of reality, would change it accordingly.

---

[8] For a fascinating introduction to the current state of the Ultimate Theory in physics and its cosmological implications, see the book by B. Greene, *The Elegant Universe* (1999).

This discussion about methodological and philosophical naturalism may sound very much academic and abstract, except that it has already had a profound impact on the U.S. national policy on the teaching of evolution adopted by the very influential National Association of Biology Teachers. In 1998, the NABT was pressured into changing its definition of evolution by conservative Christian theologians Alvin Plantinga and Houston Smith, an unprecedented act of interference of religion in public education. The controversy (see Appendix to this chapter) raged around the fact that the original NABT definition included the words "unsupervised" and "impersonal" to describe the process of evolution. These were seen as unscientific statements, because nobody can prove that evolution is indeed unsupervised or impersonal (methodological naturalism). Yet, every textbook and professional publication in evolutionary biology makes precisely that assumption (philosophical naturalism) – otherwise the whole (astoundingly successful) explanatory framework of evolutionary biology (and in fact of science itself) would be a joke!

The distinction between methodological and philosophical naturalism, therefore, misses one important component of the scientific method: science is an enterprise based on (reasonable) philosophical assumptions, not just a collection of facts. Two of these assumptions are particularly relevant to our discussion. First, William of Ockham (1285-1349), who incidentally was a scholastic theologian, proposed what is now known as Ockham's razor (see Chapter 1): "It is vain to do with more what can be done with less." In other words, supernumerary hypotheses (such as the existence of god) are to be avoided if we can explain the same facts with fewer assumptions. Second, David Hume (1711-1776; also see Chapter 1), the arch-skeptic, said that "extraordinary claims require extraordinary evidence" (Hume 1992). This is exactly the position of skeptics of the paranormal, astrology, alternative medicine, and so on. It is difficult to see why such a basic precept of science should not be extended to religion.

I think that part of the problem resides in a matter of semantics. When a scientist says "there are no flying horses" she doesn't mean that she has exhaustively searched the entire universe to incontrovertibly verify that fact. The sentence just means that we assume there is no Pegasus (the flying horse of Greek mythology) because we have a good theory of mammalian anatomy and of flight, and the two do not make it likely for animals like the mythical stallion to exist. There is always the possibility that we will observe one on some remote area of the globe, or find its fossilized remains, or discover it on another planet. Until then, however, I bet on Provine, dollars to doughnuts.

Appendix - The NABT controversy on the definition of evolution

Below is an open letter that I prepared for the National Association of Biology Teachers and that was sent to the NABT Board in 1998, together with the signatures of the people listed at the end of the letter. Afterwards, a committee of some of these people, including evolutionary biologists William Provine (Cornell), Richard Lewontin (Harvard), Douglas Futuyma (Stony Brook), Bryan and Deborah Charlesworth (Edinburgh), Nick Barton (Edinburgh), Chris Simon (University of Connecticut), Mitchell Cruzan (University of Tennessee), David Rand (Brown University), Linda Maxson (University of Iowa), and me, worked on a new definition that was submitted to the Board. The new definition read:

"The diversity of life on earth is the outcome of evolution: a natural process of temporal descent with genetic modification that is non-directional, except for human intervention, and is explicable by principles of physical and biological science including natural selection, changing environments, chance, and historical contingencies"

The Board considered and rejected our proposal. To this day, Christian conservatives are responsible for defining evolution to biology teachers across the nation.

Open letter to the National Association of Biology Teachers, to the National Center for Science Education, and to the American Association for the Advancement of the Sciences

Object: recent changes in the wording of the NABT's definition of the word "evolution"

To whom it may concern,

It has recently come to our attention that the NABT, with the support of the NCSE, has changed its statement defining what evolution is. This change apparently was at least in part the result of pressures from the Christian Fundamentalist movement. We strongly urge your organizations to reconsider such a change, and to defend scientific and educational principles in the face of public or partisan pressure of any kind.

Our feeling is that this was an unfortunate decision, that can potentially mislead the American public and that yields undue authority to the already overwhelming political and religious pressure over science that has been mounting in this country in recent years. The NABT and the NCSE, as well as the scientific community at large, have an inalienable right and a peremptory duty to defend rationalism and open inquiry. The proposed change of the statement simply betrays such high ideals at their core. The significance of the change is far greater than just dropping two controversial words, since it represents the first wedge of a movement intended to surreptitiously introduce religious teachings into our public schools.

The original NABT statement

The original NABT definition of evolution was crafted in 1995 as a "Statement on the Teaching of Evolution." The first item on the list of "tenets of science, evolution and biology education" read:

> The diversity of life on Earth is the outcome
> of evolution: an *unsupervised, impersonal,*
> *unpredictable* and *natural* process of

> temporal descent with genetic modification
> that is affected by natural selection, chance,
> historical contingencies and changing
> environments

While the customary modern definition of evolution in graduate level textbooks is more akin to "changes in allelic frequencies in a population" (D. Hartl & A. Clark, 1989—*Principles of population genetics*, Sinauer), the above quoted statement very accurately portrays the broader meaning that evolutionary biologists attach to the term. Furthermore, since the NABT was looking for a definition that could be understood by the general public and applied by biology teachers nationwide, references to specific subject matters such as population genetics are ineffective.

The modification and how it came about

The 1995 NABT statement apparently offended some religious fundamentalists and other creationists, chiefly among them Berkeley lawyer Phillip Johnson (author of *Darwin on Trial* and other misleading literature on evolution). Apparently, Johnson and others have claimed that the statement implies that evolutionary theory is an ideological statement, since the words "unsupervised" and "impersonal" automatically exclude any divine intervention. This was explicitly suggested by a letter to the NABT by Alvin Plantinga, John A. O'Brien Professor of Philosophy at Notre Dame University, and Huston Smith, Thomas J. Watson Professor of Religion at Syracuse University. Notice that neither of these is a biologist.

Smith's and Plantinga's concern was that the NABT wording "... gives aid and comfort to extremists in the religious right for whom it provides a legitimate target. And, because of its logical vulnerability, it lowers Americans' respect for scientists and their place in our culture. If the words 'impersonal' and 'unsupervised' were dropped from your opening sentence it would help defuse tensions that, as things stand, are causing unnecessary problems in our collective life."

As a consequence of this upheaval, the NABT agreed to reconsider the wording of the controversial statement, and did so at its 1997 meeting. The Board voted to retain the original statement, on the sound reasoning that Smith's and Plantinga's assertion that the wording "contradicts the beliefs of the majority of the American people" is irrelevant. Scientific definitions, according to the Board, are independent of public opinion. But things did not end there. In the face of mounting pressure, the Board was reconvened at the end of the meeting, a few days later. The outcome of the new discussion was that:

> 1) The extant wording that included "unsupervised" and "impersonal" apparently was miscommunicating both the nature of science and NABT's intent;

> 2) The deletion of those two words would not affect the statement's accurate characterization of evolution, and affirmation of evolution's importance in science education.

Eugenie Scott's comment on the NCSE web page (http://www.natcenscied.org/) was that the new NABT statement (http://www.NABT.org/positions.html) was the result of "a statesmanlike decision that better fulfilled [the NABT] goal by reducing a potential source of conflict in the classroom."

Why it was a bad move

Apparently, the feeling at the NABT meeting was that the organization and the American public (mostly, the Christian Right) had a miscommunication problem. The NABT did not want its statements to include theological positions—rightly so. This politically correct attitude, however, does not serve science very well. We do not disagree that science, and evolutionary biology in particular, cannot prove or disprove the existence of *some* kind of God. On the other hand, the reason the American public perceives a direct conflict is because indeed evolution denies many attributes of various forms of the Christian God. In this, fundamentalists and the American public at large are smarter than most scientists give them credit for. It is time for the scientific community and for educators to simply face this fact and move on, regardless of the consequences and predictable social outcry.

In fact, Scott's statement that the NABT move was an example of "statesmanlike decision" is particularly illuminating of the fear of scientists and educators to face political and religious pressures. It is the same "statesmanship" that prompted the National Science Foundation to actively delete any appearance of the word evolution in the layman abstracts of research proposals in evolutionary biology funded by the Federal Government. Furthermore, the NABT change promptly backfired, culminating in a *New York Times* article declaring that creationists had won intellectual recognition. This was, and still is, followed by creationist propaganda using the change in the statement as a powerful weapon for their religious agenda.

As for the two points raised at the final NABT Board meeting, let us analyze them in some more detail. The words "unsupervised" and "impersonal" were taken as miscommunicating the nature of science. Not really. Science is based on a fundamental assumption: that the world can be explained by referring only to natural, mechanistic forces. Johnson is quite right in affirming that this is a philosophical position. He is wrong when he suggests that it is an unreasonable and unproven one. In fact, every single experiment conducted by any laboratory in any place on Earth represents a daily test of that assumption. The day in which scientists will be unable to explain natural phenomena without referring to divine intervention or other supernatural forces, we will have a major paradigm shift—of cataclysmic proportions.

The second point of the Board's deliberation is that dropping the contentious words does not affect the accuracy of the portrayal of evolution to the American public. Really? The NABT leaves open the possibility that evolution is in fact supervised in a personal manner. This is a prospect that every evolutionary biologist should vigorously *and positively* deny. All we know so far about the evolutionary process tells us that there is no supervision except for the action of natural selection. Furthermore, a personal involvement would imply some "person" who would take care of directing the evolutionary process one way or the other. The fossil record, as well as the importance of random events such as catastrophes, mass extinctions, and genetic drift, assure us that such a personal involvement has not happened. Unless, of course, the person in question is supervising evolution in a way to perfectly mimic an unsupervised, impersonal process. A possibility, the latter, that is outside science, but that has been repeatedly invalidated on philosophical grounds ever since David Hume and well before Darwin.

In conclusion, we reiterate that evolution indeed *is*, to the best of our knowledge, an impersonal and unsupervised process. Scientists are always open to revise their positions if new compelling evidence surfaces, so that creationists can be reassured that the incriminated words will be dropped if demonstrated to be inconsistent with reality. Until then, please leave the job to scientists and educators, not to lawyers, theologians, and politicians.

Signed,

Massimo Pigliucci, Associate Professor of Ecology and Evolution, University of Tennessee, Knoxville

Clifford C. Amundsen, Assoc Prof, Botany and Ecology and Evolutionary Biology, University of Tennessee, Knoxville

Guido Barbujani, Dipartimento di Biologia, Universita' di Ferrara, Italy

Nicholas H Barton FRS, Institute of Cell, Animal & Population Biology, University of Edinburgh, United Kingdom

Alfredo Bezzi, Department of Earth Sciences, Genoa University, Italy

Luigi M Bianchi, Science and Technology Studies, Atkinson College, York University, Canada

Ian A. Boussy, Associate Professor of Biology, Loyola University of Chicago

Melissa Brenneman, Librarian and Computer Sciences teacher, Knox County Library System, Knoxville, TN

Brian Charlesworth, Royal Society Research Professor, Institute of Cell, Animal and Population Biology, University of Edinburgh. President-elect of the Society for the Study Evolution

Deborah Charlesworth, University of Edinburgh, United Kingdom

Lounes Chikhi, The Zoological Society of London, Institute of Zoology, London, United Kingdom

James T. Collins, Instructor of Biology, Kilgore College, Kilgore, Texas

Justin D. Congdon, Senior Research Ecologist, Savannah River Ecology Laboratory

Mitchell Cruzan, Assistant Professor of Ecology, University of Tennessee, Knoxville

Veronique A. Delesalle, Department of Biology, Gettysburg College, Pennsylvania

Paulo de Oliveira, Dept. Biologia, Universidad E'vora, Portugal

DeWeese, "layperson," University of California, Santa Barbara

Thomas J. DeWitt, Research Assistant Professor, Center for Ecology, Evolution, & Behavior, Thomas Hunt Morgan School of Biological Sciences, University of Kentucky, Lexington

Michael Dohm, Department of Biology, University of California, Riverside

M.Tevfik Dorak, M.D., Lecturer in Haematology, University of Wales College of Medicine, Cardiff, United Kingdom

Holly Downing, Department of Biological Sciences, University of Wisconsin-Whitewater

Shannon Eaker, PhD student in the Biochemistry, Cell, and Molecular Biology Department, University of Tennessee, Knoxville

Simon Emms, Department of Biology, University of St. Thomas, St. Paul, Minnesota

James C. Estill, University of Tennessee, Department of Botany, Knoxville

Mark Fishbein, Department of Botany, Washington State University, Pullman, Washington

Else Juliette Fjerdingstad, Assistant Research Professor, Institute of Zoology and Animal Ecology, Lausanne University, Switzerland

Ejnar Jules Fjerdingstad, Ph.D., Former Associate Professor of Anatomy, University of Aarhus, Denmark

James A. Foster, Department of Computer Science, University of Idaho, Moscow

Gordon A. Fox, Dept of Biology, San Diego State University, California

Aurora Fraile, Professor Titular, Depto de Biotecnologia, E.T.S.Ingenieros Agronomos, Madrid, Spain

Geist, Ph.D., Professor Emeritus of Environmental Science, The University of Calgary, Canada

Bernard Godelle, Ancien ilhve de l'Ecole normale supirieure de Paris, Mantre de confirences`, l'Institut national agronomique de Paris-Grignon

Peter Gogarten, Professor of Molecular and Cell Biology, University of Connecticut, Storrs

Sean Graham, Research Fellow, Department of Botany, University of Washington, Seattle

Jane Gray, Professor, Department of Biology, University of Oregon, Eugene, Oregon

Correigh M. Greene, Animal Behavior Graduate Group, Section in Evolution and Ecology, University of California, Davis

Ann Grens, Ph.D., Assistant Professor of Developmental Biology, Indiana University, South Bend

Christopher P. Grill, Ph.D. candidate, Center for Ecology, Evolution, and Behavior, University of Kentucky, Lexington

Louis J. Gross, Professor of Ecology and Mathematics, University of Tennessee, Knoxville

Marjorie Gurganus, PhD, Postdoctoral Researcher, Max Plank Institute for Chemical Ecology, Jena, Germany

David S. Guttman, Ph.D., Research Associate, Department of Molecular Genetics and Cell Biology, University of Chicago

Judy Jernstedt, Associate Professor, Department of Agronomy and Range Science, University of California, Davis

Hossein Jorjani, PhD, Department of Animal Breeding & Genetics, Swedish University of Agricultural Sciences, Uppsala

Suzanne Koptur, Associate Professor, Department of Biological Sciences, Florida International University, Miami

Anna Korn, M.A., Berkeley California

Darren Kriticos, Ecologist - CRC Tropical Pest Management, Gehrmann Labs, University of Queensland

Matthew P. Hare, Ph.D., Department of Organismic and Evolutionary Biology, Harvard University Biolabs, Cambridge, Massachusetts

Carla Ann Hass, Ph.D., Biology Department, Penn State University, University Park, PA

Wendy Hein, Center for Ecology, Evolution, and Behavior, University of Kentucky, Lexington

Guy A. Hoelzer, Department of Biology, University of Nevada, Reno

John H. Hornberger, Jr., Animal Behavior Graduate Group, University of California, Davis

David Hosken, Zoologisches Museum, Universitat Zurich-Irchel, Switzerland

Delbert W. Hutchison, Department of Biology, Washington University, St. Louis, Missouri

Gerald H. Learn, Research Associate, Department of Microbiology, University of Washington, Seattle

Martin J. Lechowicz, Department of Biology, McGill University, Montreal, Canada

Carl Ledendecker, Knoxville-TN Montessori Teacher

Richard C. Lewontin, Alexander Agassiz Professor of Zoology, Museum of Comparative Zoology, Harvard University, Cambridge, Massachusetts

Robert Loest, Ph.D., IPS Advisory, Inc., Knoxville, Tennessee

Patrick Lorch, Biology Department, University of Toronto at Mississauga, Ontario, Canada

Andrew Lowe, IACR-Long Ashton Research Station, Bristol, United Kingdom

John M. Lynch, Academic Associate, Interdisciplinary Humanities Program and Department of Philosophy, Arizona State University

James Lyons-Weiler, Doctoral Program In Ecology, Evolution, and Conservation Biology, University Of Nevada, Reno

Paul Mack, Department of Genetics, University of Georgia, Athens

Anna Maleszyk, Ph.D. student at the University of Tennessee Knoxville

Carlo C. Maley, Massachusetts Institute of Technology

Malpica Ph.D., Senior Research Fellow, Instituto Nacional De Investigaciones Agrarias, Departamento de Proteccion Vegetal, Madrid, Spain

Stephanie Mariette, Laboratoire de Genetique et d'Amelioration des Arbres Forestiers, INRA, Cestas, France

Linda Maxson, Dean, College of Liberal Arts, University of Iowa, Iowa City, Iowa

Amy McMillan, University of Kansas Graduate Student at the University of Southern Maine, Gorham

Allen J. Moore, Department of Entomology, University of Kentucky, Lexington

Phillip A. Morin, Ph.D., Associate Director of Population Genetics, AxyS Pharmaceuticals, Inc., La Jolla, California

Paulo Gama Mota, Professor Auxiliar in Animal Behaviour and Evolutionary Biology, Departamento de Antropologia, Universidade de Coimbra, Portugal

Eric S. Nagy, Department of Biology, University of Virginia

Gavin Naylor, Assistant Professor, Iowa State University

Isabel S. Novella, Department of Neuropharmacology, Division of Virology, The Scripps Research Institute, San Diego, California

Theodore J. Nusbaum, Ph.D., Department of Ecology and Evolutionary Biology, University of California, Irvine

John Pastor, Professor, Department of Biology, University of Minnesota, Duluth

Professor Emeritus Hugh E. H. Paterson, University of Queensland, Australia

Javier Paz-Ares, Centro Nacional de Biotecnologia, Campus de Cantoblanco, Madrid, Spain

Devon E. Pearse, Graduate Student, Department of Genetics, University of Georgia

Dmitri Petrov, Ph.D., Junior Fellow, Harvard University Society of Fellows, Cambridge, Massachusetts

David Rand, Associate Professor, Department of Ecology and Evolutionary Biology, Brown University, Providence, Rhode Island

Rosemary J. Redfield, Department of Zoology, University of British Columbia, Vancouver, Canada

Susan Elise Riechert, Professor of Ecology and Evolutionary Biology and Distinguished Service Professor, University of Tennessee, Knoxville

Thierry Rigaud, Universite de Poitiers, Laboratoire de Biologie et Genetique des populations de Crustaces, Poitiers Cedex, France

Jaime Rodriganez, Departamento de Mejora Genetica, INIA, Madrid, Spain

Alex Rosenberg, Professor of Philosophy, winner of the Lakatos Prize for distinguished contributions to the philosophy of science, Honors Program, University of Georgia, Athens

Ilik J. Saccheri, Department of Ecology and Systematics, University of Helsinki, Finland

T.P. Salo, Professor Emeritus, Biochemistry, University of Tennessee, Knoxville

Samuel M. Scheiner, Department of Life Sciences, Arizona State University West, Phoenix

Johanna Schmitt, Professor, Department of Ecology and Evolutionary Biology, Brown University, Providence, Rhode Island

Andrew Schnabel, Assistant Professor of Biology, Department of Biology, Indiana University South Bend

Niall Shanks, Ph.D., Associate Professor of Philosophy, Adjunct Professor of Biological Sciences, East Tennessee State University.

Ann Sillman, Maryville, Tennessee, Retired Respiratory Therapist

Gerard I. Sillman, Maryville Tennessee, Retired Systems Analyst

Jonathan Silvertown, Reader in Biology at The Open University, United Kingdom, Executive Editor, Journal of Ecology

Chris Simon, Department of Ecology & Evolutionary Biology, University Of Connecticut, Storrs

Suzanne Southerland, Ecology and Evolutionary Biology Alumnus, University of Tennessee, Knoxville

Steve Trewick, Department of Zoology, University of Otago, Dunedin, New Zealand

Evelyn Tsang, Evolutionary Molecular Biology, MSc, McGill University

Robert van Hulst, Chairperson, Biology Department, Bishop's University, Lennoxville, Canada

Marta L. Wayne, Department of Genetics, North Carolina State University, Raleigh

Gunter Wagner, Professor and Chair, Department of Ecology and Evolutionary Biology, Yale University

Niklas Wahlberg, Department of Ecology and Systematics, Division of Population Biology, University of Helsinki

Jeffrey D. Wall, Graduate Student, University of Chicago

Jake Weltzin, Assistant Professor, Department of Ecology & Evolutionary Biology, University of Tennessee, Knoxville

Renate A. Wesselingh, Postdoctoral Research Associate, Department of Genetics, University of Georgia, Athens

Lorne Wolfe, Assistant Professor, Department of Biology, Georgia Southern University, Statesboro, Georgia

Helen J. Young, Biology Department, Middlebury College, Vermont

Chapter 3 - In defense of straw men

"Delight at having understood a very abstract and obscure system leads most people to believe in the truth of what it demonstrates." (G.C. Lichtenberg, 1742-1799, Aphorisms)

Straw men have a bad reputation. According to the Merriam Webster's Collegiate Dictionary (10th edition), a straw man is a "person set up to serve as a cover for a usually questionable transaction." Not exactly a respectable job. Metaphorically, a straw man is a way to caricature your opponent's argument in order to be able to quickly dismiss it, or to poke easy fun at it. If you are a scientist, you surely don't want to be accused of having made up a straw man. Even if you are right, the other side will get a lot of mileage simply out of pointing that to the audience (and, incidentally, in so doing building *another* straw man to substitute for your own actual arguments). Yet, I have to lament the increasing rarity of straw men in modern discourse. Don't get me wrong. I do not think that it is fair to caricature someone's ideas so that you can shoot them down at will. On the other hand, there is an opposite danger intrinsic in the attitude that ideas and theories are complex, multifaceted, and to some extent *vague*. While it is too easy to hit a target you yourself designed and placed in the best possible range, it is unfairly difficult to hit one that keeps shifting position and whose contours are fuzzy and tend to blend into the background.

To see what I mean, let us discuss three examples of newly proposed scientific theories that can (and were) originally described as "pure" opposites (the straw man model), and that later on became more fuzzy. In the first example, the fuzziness was limited in scope and did not invalidate the antithesis to the old paradigm the new theory was meant to replace. In the second case, the increasing vagueness of the new proposal made it very difficult to distinguish it from some forms of the opposing view. In the latter instance, what materializes is a politically correct "compromise" between the two views. But is such a compromise a reflection of the complexity of the real world, or is it rather an example of intellectual waffling that only confuses our understanding of reality? The last example is one that has been around for some time, and it simply refuses to go away. In that case, my thesis is that in fact both theories are wrong, but that the proposed compromise completely misses the point.

Case 1: Ptolemy vs. Copernicus

As it is well known, throughout the Middle Ages people believed that the earth was at the center of the universe and that everything else, including the sun, rotated around it. This view of the universe was codified by the Greco-Egyptian astronomer Ptolemy (also known by his latinized name, Claudius Ptolemaeus) in the 2nd century CE. In his 13-volume *Almagest* he explained the apparent movement of the planets, the sun, and the moon in the sky with a complex system of concentric spheres known as epicycles. The system was not exactly an example of mathematical elegance, and it was rather difficult to apply in practice to calculate the actual positions of the various celestial bodies. All of this notwithstanding, it worked – more or less. You can think of it as a cumbersome algorithm that will give you sufficiently approximate answers, even though it did not reflect at all the actual structure of the universe (but Ptolemy, of course, didn't know this).

Then, in the 16th century, along came Nicholas Copernicus, a Polish astronomer who in his book *De Revolutionibus Orbium Coelestium* single-handedly dethroned man from the center of creation, relegating the earth to being just one among several planets, all dutifully orbiting the central sun. Now, the original version of Copernicus' theory can be squarely opposed to the old Ptolemaic system, in the classical "straw man" fashion. The two theories' fundamental tenets are simple to characterize, and are indeed in sharp opposition to each other. Regardless of the details, one can say that the essential feature of the Ptolemaic system was that the earth was immobile and everything else rotated around it; similarly, it is not unfair to claim that the essence of the Copernican revolution was to completely revert the order of things and put the sun at the center. Everything else, in both theories, was just an accessory to make the calculations turn out reasonably well. Neither man would probably have objected to such a "straw man-like" summary.

However, things soon became more complicated. You see, Copernicus thought (mistakenly, as it turned out) that the orbits of the planets were circular. The main reason that brought him to this conclusion was tradition: the circle has always been considered a perfect geometric figure, so how could celestial bodies follow anything but a perfect path in the heavens? But if we assume that that is indeed the case, calculations of the positions of the planets in the sky following the Copernican system are not much better than similar calculations based on the Ptolemaic system. Is the Copernican theory nothing more than another, more or less useful, algorithm to solve a practical problem, while the true nature of the structure of the solar system remains hidden forever?

Fig. 3.1 – Nicholas Copernicus, who single-handedly dethroned man from the center of the universe.

Obviously not, but to see that we had to wait for Johannes Kepler who, in 1609, published *Astronomia Nova*. A textbook example of the synthesis of a previous theory (Copernicus's) and painstakingly accurate new observations (mostly carried out by Kepler's mentor, Tycho Brahe), *Astronomia Nova* proposed the radical idea that the planets rotate around the sun on *elliptical*, not circular, orbits. Furthermore, each planet traces an ellipse of a different shape from that of any other planet. The whole system is only constrained by the fact that the sun has to occupy one of the foci of each ellipse.

Overall, the Copernican-Keplerian theory is quite different from the original version, but the same straw man applies. One of the two fundamental tenets of the theory is still that the earth rotates around the sun, not vice versa. Now, however, a second crucial component is added, that the orbits be elliptical instead of circular. This addition notwithstanding, nobody can accuse the new theory of becoming fuzzier, because the modification introduced by Kepler does not represent a regression toward the Ptolemaic model. Indeed, it moves the theoretical edifice further away from Ptolemy's thinking by adding one more distinctive element to the new conception. In this example, the "simplistic" characterization of the opposing viewpoints sharply defines the two camps and helps focusing on their fundamental differences. There is no attempt at compromising.

Case 2: Darwin vs. Eldredge & Gould

Quite a different case is provided by the controversy that took evolutionary biology by storm in 1972 when two young paleontologists, Stephen Jay Gould and Niels Eldredge, proposed what appeared to be a major challenge to the Darwinian theory of evolution. One of the main tenets of Darwin's idea of descent with modification (Darwin 1859) is that evolution is a gradual phenomenon. *Natura non facit saltum* (nature does not do jumps) is the way he put it. Darwin got the idea from the principle of uniformitarianism that was a cardinal point of Sir Lyell's *Principles of Geology*, one of the books that inspired the young British naturalist during his voyage on the *HMS Beagle*.

Fig. 3.2 – Charles Darwin dealt another blow to humankind's pride by demonstrating that we are derived from "lower orders of animals." The concept still encounters remarkable resistance in some segments of modern society.

The notion was that past events are explainable in terms of the same processes seen in action today, in a sort of cautious back-extrapolation. For example, in the past mountains were formed and eroded slowly, by exactly the same geological and atmospheric phenomena that are raising and eroding mountains now. Analogously, Darwin thought, since we observe natural selection acting today on small variations present in natural populations, it is an accumulation of many such small steps that must have brought into existence the bewildering variety of life forms we currently observe.

Fig. 3.3 – The difference between the classical Darwinian theory (left) and the punctuated alternative proposed by Eldredge and Gould (right) in terms of rapidity of evolutionary change. A, B, and C represent three related species, and the lines indicate the relationships among them (e.g., B is more closely related to C than either is to A, which split earlier from the common ancestor of the other two). Classical Darwinism proposes that the divergence is gradual, as indicated by the sloped lines connecting the species: the less vertical the lines are the slower the pace of evolution. Punctuated equilibrium predicts that divergence between species (measured by the degree of morphological dissimilarity) is geologically very rapid, so much so that it may appear instantaneous in the fossil record (vertical lines).

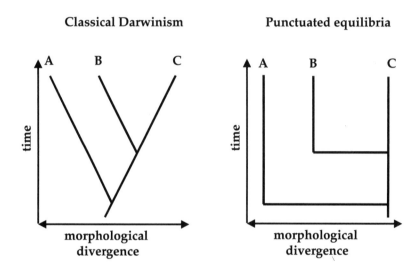

Then Eldredge and Gould came along, claiming that – on the contrary – evolution proceeds by a syncopate alternation of brief bursts of change alternated with long periods of stasis, a pattern ever since known as "punctuated equilibria" (Eldredge and Gould 1972). A fundamental distinction between classical Darwinism and punctuated equilibria is found in the way the two schools interpret the fossil record. For a classical Darwinian, such record is highly imperfect due to the vagaries of fossilization processes and of the geological circumstances that have to occur in order for us to actually recover a given fossil. Therefore, gaps in the fossil record are interpreted as missing pieces of information. To a punctuationist, on the other hand, the information is far less incomplete than previously thought and the gaps are "real," i.e. they are witnesses of the sudden periods of morphological change associated with speciation (origination of new species). The fossil record can therefore be interpreted almost at face value.

If the difference between the two visions of evolution is presented in this "straw man-like" fashion, then it's pretty clear that we are talking about two completely distinct *modes* of evolution, and real organisms can do either one or the other, but not both (of course, *some* groups of plants or animals could follow one mode, and some the alternative one, but not both simultaneously). Therefore, all we have to do is to graph the amount of change in a given lineage against time, and we will immediately see if Darwin or Eldredge & Gould were on the mark.

Except that when we do this, we find that there is a continuum of possible graphs, with some lineages showing clearly punctuated patterns, others unmistakably falling into the gradualistic framework, and several cases right in between the two extremes. One of the solutions that have been presented for this dilemma is that "rapid" vs. "gradual" is actually a matter of scale. For one thing, the pace of evolution cannot be measured in absolute time, since organisms with a longer generation time tend to evolve more "slowly" (i.e., it takes them more absolute time to develop the same number of generations of a rapid-cycling species). More importantly, what is "rapid" from a paleontological perspective (i.e., when measured over millions of years) may still appear quite "slow" at the neontological level (i.e., if one considers organisms currently living, since it would take thousands of generations to accomplish the "rapid" shift postulated by Eldredge and Gould's theory).

Many paleontologists have accepted this scale-dependent compromise because otherwise it is hard to find a known evolutionary mechanism that would cause *really* rapid evolutionary change (i.e., almost instantaneous). As a matter of fact, such a "jumping" theory of evolution had been proposed twice before, by Richard Goldschmidt (1940), and independently by George Gaylor Simpson (1944) during the early 1940s. But both previous incarnations of the idea had been rejected because of their inherent contradiction with what we know about genetics and natural history.

Here is where the utility of the straw man is most clear. If we "reconcile" punctuated equilibria and gradualism on the ground that they are really the same thing seen through different temporal lenses, we reject a straw man characterization of either theory. However, in so doing Eldredge & Gould pay the price of being entirely reduced to a footnote to Darwin.[9] Only if we stick to the "hard" distinction between the two alternatives do we have truly competing hypotheses, either of which can be firmly rejected by comparison with the available evidence. Making a "straw man" out of Darwin and Eldredge & Gould makes possible to have them compete in the arena of scientific explanation. Otherwise, they merge into each other in a fuzzy unified whole into which one of the two almost completely disappears from sight.

Fig. 3.4 – A simple example of emergent properties in nature: the physics and chemistry of water is not the simple sum of the physics and chemistry of its constituent atoms. Notice, for example, how water molecules can form complex structures by aligning their positive and negative charges (that attract each other) and keeping charges of the same sign at a distance (since they repel each other). O = oxygen; H = hydrogen. Plus and minus indicates electric charge. Atoms not in scale.

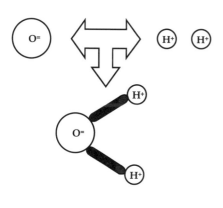

Case 3: the eternal nature vs. nurture debate

So much has been written about the relative contributions of nature and nurture in shaping organisms' morphology and behavior, that I will discuss it here only very briefly. The two "straw man-like" positions in this case are: 1) behavior (for example, the degree of intelligence in human beings) is mostly a result of genetics; *ergo* there is no point in bothering too much with improving the environment (such as spending money on education). Or, 2) behavior is mostly caused by environmental circumstances,

---

[9] Incidentally, not too bad of a fate.

therefore any claim about genetic differences smacks of racism, sexism, or some other kind of "ism."

Now, even the staunchest supporters of either side will start by acknowledging that *of course* there is a little bit of both going on. Nevertheless, the two straw men are clearly defined: either the environment is responsible for the lion's share of the explanations of human behavior, or the genes are. These extreme positions are easy enough to test and refute or confirm. In fact, a whole branch of biology, quantitative genetics, has been erected for the expressed purpose of untangling genotypic from environmental effects.

The problem emerges when we find out that there is a third possibility: environments and genes may interact in a way that is not simply additive. In other words, the behavior in question may be due not only to somewhat separable genetic and environmental components, but also to a degree of interdependence between the two. From a biological standpoint, this is due to the fact that the action of a particular gene can be triggered and modulated by an environmental stimulus; simultaneously, one of the consequences of that gene action can be to modify the original environmental conditions, or at least the way they affect the growth, development, and reproduction of the organism. The outcome of all this is what is sometimes termed an "emergent property." The simplest example of an emergent property is water: its physical-chemical behavior is not reducible to the simple sums of the physical-chemical behaviors of the atoms of oxygen and hydrogen that make up water. The reason is that water's properties depend on the exact interaction of hydrogen and oxygen (chiefly from the fact that the resulting molecule has a triangular shape with two poles of opposite electric charge).

The existence of so-called "genotype-environment interactions" undermines both straw man positions. If indeed the interaction is what is most prevalent (as seems to be the case: Pigliucci in press), then either extreme does not make sense and should be rejected. However, notice that this case is different from the gradualism vs. punctuationism discussed above. Here the "middle of the ground" is not a compromise at all, and it does not merge the two opposite viewpoints: on the contrary, it denies both. Once again, however, the rejection of the original position(s) is possible only because they were clearly and unambiguously stated.

A different way out would be to waffle on the exact percentage of a given behavior that is attributable to either genes or environments. This would truly make the theory fuzzy, cause the boundary between the alternatives to get blurred, and result in some sort of political compromise that has no scientific meaning whatsoever (because, unless one specifies more or less exactly the percentages in question, any quantitative prediction based on the theory would be impossible).

Lakatos and the structure of theories

The point of this discussion is to highlight the necessity to clearly define any given theory or statement. Only an unambiguous assertion can be confirmed or refuted, the two processes by which science and rational thinking progress. Obviously, the more rigidly defined the theory is (the more "straw man-like"), the less likely it is to accommodate the realities and vagaries of the outside world.

This tradeoff, however, should not be surprising. Any theoretical scientist faces the same problem whenever she produces a new mathematical model of the world. A mathematical model is by necessity a restricted and unambiguous version of the real thing. As such, it has the advantage that its simple structure can be explored at will, and can be tested against reality. On the other hand, the mathematical model is by definition incomplete. If you wish, this same relationship exists between a map and the territory that the map is supposed to represent. If you make the map *too* simple, you will miss many fundamental aspects of the area you are interested in. On the other hand, you cannot make the map as detailed as the entire territory actually is, because you would need a map as large and complex as the real thing, which would take away the whole point of any model: achieving a reasonable (and useful) simplification of a complex problem.

Any scientific theory, and in fact any rational statement about the world, is not different from a mathematical model. It can be expressed in non-mathematical language, but it should aspire to the same level of precision and testability. Otherwise, we fall into fuzzy thinking[10] and more or less uncommitted and useless statements. Incidentally, the tendency of common language to fall into this kind of problem is exactly why mathematics is so appreciated as a scientific tool. It isn't really that the book of nature is written in mathematical terms: there is no book written nowhere by anyone. Rather, a mathematical language seems to be more accurate in getting through whatever it is that nature is telling us.

From a philosophy of science viewpoint, this discussion leads to conclusions similar to those reached by Imre Lakatos (1974). According to Lakatos, any reasonable scientific theory (and, I am implying here by extension, any significant statement about the world) is made of three components: the hard core, the protective belt, and the positive heuristic. The hard core constitutes the fundamental identity of the theory. If this is rejected, the whole theory dies. In the case of the Copernican theory, for example, the hard core is the straw man-statement that the earth rotates around the sun, not vice versa. The protective belt is made of corollary statements that do not alter the central message, but allow for expansions and for a closer match with reality. For Copernicus, this was Kepler's contribution about the actual shape of planetary orbits. The positive heuristic is made of all the new predictions that the theory can generate, and against which it will be tested in the future. In the case of the Copernican system, the future positions of the planets, or the occurrence of solar and lunar eclipses.

My general contention is that a theory that is fuzzy enough to allow for too much waffling and compromise (i.e., it cannot be characterized by a straw man) lacks an identifiable hard core. As a consequence, it is not a scientific theory, and it does not permit us to make any progress in our understanding of the universe. Think about that the next time that someone is accusing you of making a straw man of his views.

---

[10] In the pejorative sense of the word, nothing to do with recent developments of information theory that go by the same appellative (Kosko 1993).

Part II - Tales of science and religion

Science and religion have had, and probably always will have, a rather peculiar relationship: on the one hand, people's physical welfare depends on good science; on the other hand, many perceive their psychological well being as inextricably related to their religious beliefs. Furthermore, the two are at odds in terms of their intellectual underpinnings, with science based on evidence and critical thinking and religions established on faith and dogma. This has generated endless tensions at least since the beginning of modern science in the 1500s, tensions that continue to this day.

There has been quite a concerted attempt lately, on the part of both religionists and some scientists, to reconcile the two fields, as well as to reinterpret instances of past conflict (such as the burning at the stake of Giordano Bruno, or the prosecution of Galileo) as rather exceptional "incidents" in an otherwise peaceful coexistence. I think that both the current conciliatory mood and the historical revisionism are misguided attempts that will bring no good in the long run. The most one can say about science and religion is that they are to be pursued separately, and that any reconciliation of the two is best left to the mental gymnastics of individual human beings. I do not see what science has to gain from being reconciled with a system of superstitious beliefs that stands for the exact opposite of free inquiry. Similarly, it seems to me abundantly evident from past history that religion has always lost ground whenever directly confronted with scientific findings, and that it would therefore be wise for religionists to shy away as much as possible from any engagement with science. Any claim to the effect that religion has nothing but to look forward to new scientific discoveries is simply bad rhetoric.

I included four essays in this section, starting with one refuting the logic underlying the infamous Pascal's wager, a longstanding argument in favor of believing in God whose compelling force has been in my opinion grossly overestimated. The idea is that if you don't know if God exists or not, you are better off assuming that he does, since the potential payoff of such belief vastly outweighs the consequences of adopting the opposite strategy. Besides the fact that I am not at all sure that God would be so easily fooled into accepting bet-hedgers in Heaven, this is the same argument by which lotteries make a lot of money out of naïve individuals whose main strategy for a comfortable retirement is to attempt to buy the winning ticket.

The second essay in this section is my best shot so far against the existence of a supernatural deity. I try to make a distinction among different kinds of gods, and to show that they either do not exist, or that if they do they are inconsequential to our lives. I bring science into this discussion because I think that the blanket statement that science cannot address the problem of God's existence is actually incorrect, and that science can indeed inform some of our discussions on this matter, as it can inform—without necessarily resolving them to everybody's satisfaction— many other philosophical problems.

The third essay in a sense expands on the theme of science, religion and skepticism by attempting a comprehensive classification of different ways of thinking about religion and the natural world, while in the process discussing the limits of the skeptical position. My attempt revolves around the idea that opinions on these matters are defined by a complex landscape outlined by the degree of contrast between science and religion (which varies depending on how one sees either) and by the very concept of God (which also varies dramatically according to different religious beliefs).

The final essay in this part of the book deals with what I think is a legitimate question that any skeptic should consider: regardless of the truth of religion, can one make the argument that it is good for society because of its positive influence on the morality or psychological well being of human beings? I take as my starting point an article published by the conservative Heritage Foundation to explore in detail such dilemma. Perhaps not surprisingly, I come out strongly on the side of a negative answer.

Chapter 4 - A refutation of Pascal's wager and why skeptics should be non-theists

"Man is obviously made for thinking. Therein lies all his dignity and his merit; and his duty is to think as he ought." (Blaise Pascal, 1623-1662, Pensées)

One of the most popular arguments of people who believe in a God and would like to make an "irrefutable" case for their beliefs is the (in)famous "Pascal's wager." Within the skeptic and humanist communities, one of the most delicate, politically wide-ranging, and emotionally charged debates concerns the question: should a coherent skeptic also be an atheist (or at least agnostic)? This chapter attempts to discuss a fundamental link between the two issues while making use of an essential component of the scientific method to solve both. I will discuss a broader series of reasons for rejecting theism in Chapter 5 and return to the wider spectrum of positions about the relationship between science and religion in Chapter 6.

Blaise Pascal was a mathematical genius of the 17th century, and in every sense the father of modern probability theory. He was also a deeply religious man, follower of the Jansenist movement, a French Christian sect that emphasized personal holiness and especially predestination. In his *Pensées (Thoughts)*, published posthumously in 1670, Pascal mounted a philosophical defense of faith as a fundamental mean of understanding the universe. The so-called Pascal's wager is a unique blend of theism and probability theory, that is – in my opinion – an archetypal example of that contradiction between mysticism and rational thought that was so characteristic of the origin of modern science. The same mix was typical of all the path-breaking thinkers in equilibrium between the old medieval set of assumptions about the universe and the forthcoming Enlightenment, from Descartes to Newton, from Copernicus to Galilei. As in the case of Descartes, we can say that there is nothing wrong with being Pascal, but it surely does not make sense to be a "Pascalian."

The wager consists of the following simple argument. We do not know if God exists, therefore, we are faced with an arbitrary choice of believing in him or not. If we do not believe, we can live whatever life we please on earth, but we are faced with potential eternal damnation afterwards. If we believe, we will forgo some earthly pleasures on the short run, but we may gain an everlasting reward after we die (of course, it is unknown why God should restrict our pleasures under threat of eternal torment, but that is another question). Pascal's conclusion, based on his budding probability theory, is that we should obviously go for the latter choice. The potential reward is infinite, while the sure loss is meager indeed (at least, so it seemed to a 17th century conservative Christian). What is wrong with Pascal's wager? If you think about it, his argument is the same that modern lottery agents use to convince you to buy their tickets (scaled down, obviously, since the reward is very high, but not infinite, and the material loss is much smaller than your entire life). The reason Pascal's wager does not work is the same reason why you should never plan your retirement on winning the lotto.[11] For the wager to work, Pascal has to make a fundamental (not explicitly stated) assumption: that the *a priori* probabilities of God's existence or inexistence are the same, a Solomonic 50-50. But if the

Fig. 4.1. French philosopher Blaise Pascal (1623-1662), a mathematical prodigy who – together with Pierre de Fermat - formulated some of the basic principles of modern probability theory. Among other things, he invented the first mechanical calculator and was able to relate the level of mercury in a column to the external barometric pressure. Religiously, he was a Jansenist, and therefore a believer in absolute predestination. On the other hand, he believed in human progress through science and empirical investigation. Go figure.

---

[11] Although in November 1999 newspapers around the United States have published the astounding statistics that 25% of the American public thinks that playing the lotto is in fact a better retirement strategy than tax-deferred investment plans. Even Pascal would have been horrified by this widespread lack of understanding of probability theory.

probability of winning the lotto were indeed 50%, you would be a fool *not* to plan your retirement on it! The reason you do not do it is exactly because you know that while the reward may be very high, the likelihood of actually getting it is incredibly small (minuscule would be a more appropriate adjective).

Now, how do we attach an actual probability to the existence (or lack thereof) of God? Clearly, we cannot do it in the way a statistician would like to do it, because we have no data from repeated or controlled experiments (i.e., we do not have the luxury of observing several universes, some with and some without Gods, and then calculating their relative frequencies. Neither do we have a theoretical model predicting the likelihood of godless universes – although Stephen Hawking may have gotten something very close to the latter: Hawking 1993). It is equally clear that we can easily find human beings willing to attach either extreme value to such probability: staunch atheists will estimate it at zero, while equally stubborn theists will assure you that it is 100%. So, isn't Pascal's assumption of 50-50 a reasonable alternative after all?

Of course not. All of the above simply means that humans disagree profoundly, and that we have no clear experimental evidence one way or the other. However, if we cannot think in quantitative terms, perhaps we can achieve a qualitative estimate. After all, we do not need to know *exactly* what our odds of winning the lotto are; all we require to make our decision is to know that they are very, very small. There are two orders of reasoning that would lead me to conclude that the probability of the inexistence of God is in fact exceedingly small. First, every time we consider a God with physical attributes, that is one that actually *does* something in the universe (as opposed to the unfalsifiable but sterile deistic position: see Chapter 5), science invariably tells us that that God does not exist. We thought that God caused lightning, now we know better; we attributed to him a worldwide flood that modern geology says never occurred; and so on and so forth. Second, even a much reduced version of God (either the deistic one, or the so-called "God of the gaps"[12]), assumes the

---

[12] Deists, such as another French philosopher, Voltaire, basically say that God created the universe and then retired. The God of the gaps is invoked by some moderate creationists, who point to any piece of incomplete modern scientific

existence of the supernatural, that is of something we have absolutely no evidence of, that is not necessary to explain the world, and quite plainly is the result of wishful thinking on the part of a pathologically insecure humanity. Either way, we cannot prove the inexistence of God (or of anything else, for that matter, see Chapters 2, 5 and 6), but we are certainly warranted – at this stage of our quest – to conclude that its likelihood is astoundingly small. If that is correct, than Pascal's wager reduces to the general case of lottery tickets: you shouldn't buy either.

Fig. 4.2. The relationships among type I error (the likelihood of rejecting a truth), type II (the likelihood of embracing a falsehood), and the logistic problems imposed by larger and larger sample sizes. There is an inverse proportionality both between the two types of errors and between these and the sample size of an experiment. Alas, these relationships make it impossible to reach certain (or even very highly probable) conclusions on anything.

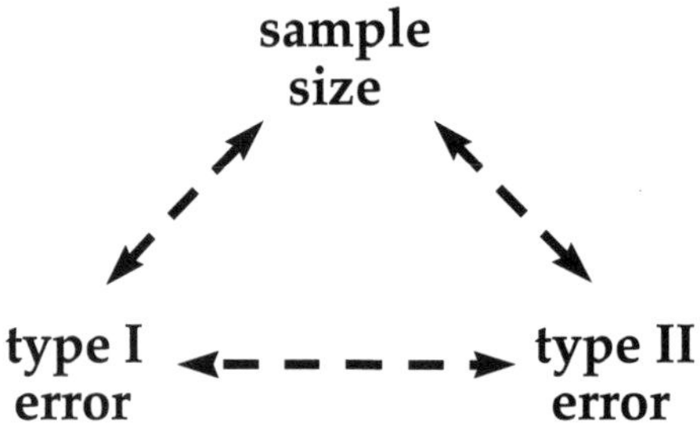

sample size

type I error **type II error**

Two fundamental types of mistakes

What does that have to do with the relationship between theistic belief and a reasonable intellectual commitment to skepticism? To get to the second part of my argument we have first to briefly discuss a fundamental concept of modern statistics (and therefore, ironically, an intellectual grandchild of Pascal): the difference between type I and type II errors in hypothesis testing (we have informally encountered them in Chapter 1).

It is a basic tenet of modern quantitative science (such as most of biology, for example), that there is no way to get to prove or disprove any particular hypothesis with absolute certainty. All

knowledge to carve some possible space for a supernatural intervention. The first God, even if he existed, would not give you the kind of reward Pascal was after; the second one is simply another word for "I don't know," and it is bound to shrink farther and farther as long as science will progress in its understanding of the natural world.

that statistically-based hypothesis testing can offer is "a very likely maybe." That is, of course, a source of comfort, not despair, for scientists. After all, actually *knowing* the probability of being correct (or wrong) while making a decision is much better than basing your choice on the flip of a coin. It also follows from elementary statistical theory that every time we accept a hypothesis we may be committing what is know as type II error: we may in fact being embracing the wrong conclusion. On the other hand, any time we reject a hypothesis on the basis of a statistical test, we may be committing a type I error: shutting the door to a correct answer.

In an ideal world, we would like to reduce both kinds of errors to zero, of course. Alas, only religion promises (and cannot deliver) as much. In science, you can arbitrarily reduce the likelihood of type I errors, but in so doing you will have to face an equally dramatic increase of type II errors, and vice versa. There is a third option, in that it is indeed possible to minimize (but never annihilate) both kinds of error by correspondingly increasing your sample size, that is the number of observations or data points you rely upon when making whatever decision. In other words, the only way to make more informed decisions is, well, to increase the amount of information at your disposal. This, of course, is only apparently a way out: increasing the amount of available information carries logistical problems, since the cost of an experiment (or whatever other way to accumulate knowledge) is usually proportional to the amount of information one wishes to gather. Especially in this era of budget-minded everything, it seems unlikely that even decisions associated with substantial human costs (such as the efficacy of a new AIDS drug) are going to be funded at an adequate level to dramatically reduce the errors associated with hypothesis testing (see figure 4.2).

Now, type I or II errors can, and are, committed regularly by *any* person who makes decisions, not just by scientists. Which is why this discussion is vital for everybody. Not only do you have a certain likelihood to fall prey to either kind of error while you make more or less important decisions in your life (like which car to get, or whom to marry), but these problems are very much at the forefront of social policy and, therefore, of politics. For example, let us consider the debate on capital punishment. The liberal position that this should be abolished corresponds to an attempt to minimize type II error: liberals don't want to risk putting to death innocent people (accepting a falsehood). Of course, by so doing they will inevitably free some real criminals (rejecting a truth) and the likelihood of both outcomes will decrease only if we spend more money researching each case. The conservative choice of retaining the death penalty, of course, is in accordance to a desire to reduce type I errors (freeing criminals); but this too comes with a price, namely the probability of frying an innocent on the electric chair. (Incidentally, one cannot think of liberals as always reducing type II errors and conservative preoccupied with type I mistakes: on fiscal policy, the liberal spending mentality corresponds to funding all that is worth, and in so doing giving money to some useless projects – a minimization of type I errors. On the other hand, the fiscally conservative approach wastes less money, but it also ends up not funding worthy causes – a type II error)

So, the real question is: which kind of error should we attempt to minimize within the limits posed by the logistics of the situation? Wisdom (1997) schematized the situation by suggesting the existence of two fundamental types of personality among humans, the "gullible" and the "skeptic." Gullible people essentially put a premium onto minimizing type I errors: they are terrorized by the idea of rejecting an important truth; therefore they lower their standards of acceptance in order to reduce such possibility. Of course, in so doing they also end up believing a lot of baloney. Skeptics, on the other hand, are folks who really would like to avoid embracing false truths, so they concentrate on minimizing type II errors (an approach, incidentally, that is hardly worth of Hell, even if God does exist). Contemporary society (at least in theory) shuns the gullible and rewards the skeptic. Yet, as Wisdom points out in his article, this was not always the case. In fact, for most of human history, "gullible" people have made up the respectable part of society (together with that other apparently necessary component, the oppressed), while skeptics were burnt at the stakes.

The question that faces every skeptic and scientist (and that indeed should face *every* human being) is then: what is it better, to reduce type I or type II errors? If the choice were only a matter of personal preferences, then I'm afraid that the current social status of scientists is usurped, and that skeptics should not feel too good about themselves because they think they have a better philosophy than gullible people.

But there is one powerful argument that takes us out of this conundrum, an argument that – I am sure this comes as no surprise to the reader – favors the skeptical position by a long shot. A rather negativistic way of putting it would be that there are many more falsehoods than truths out there. A more accurate statement would be that since there is only one reality, there are many more wrong than correct hypotheses about that reality. In other words, if you accept that reality is not just a figment of your imagination, and that in fact you can "know" something about it, you also concur with the conclusion that only one small subset among a series of hypotheses to explain that reality is correct. Ergo, the majority of hypotheses out there are false. As in the case of Pascal's wager, it is a better strategy to attempt to reduce type II error because the actual probability of mistake is not 50-50, but very much skewed toward falsehood.

Where does that leave the debate about theism within the skeptical and humanist communities? Let me first clarify that this is not, and should not be, a debate about rights. Everybody has the right to believe whatever mix of ideas she feels comfortable with, no matter how contradictory these ideas are (furthermore, just as an exercise in humbleness, one would be better off to remember that regardless of how careful we are in reducing type II errors, we still probably believe a lot of nonsense, unless we embrace the nihilist and intellectually sterile position of the original skeptics such as Socrates, who knew he knew nothing: Stevenson 1998). This said, one can still argue that some beliefs are mutually contradictory, or at least logically inconsistent. I think that a theistic skeptic falls just into this kind of situation (see Chapter 6).

Theism is a form of belief in the supernatural, that is a form of mysticism. By the same argument I used in the beginning against Pascal's wager, we can conclude that – while a supernatural realm *may* exist – it certainly is very, very unlikely. Therefore, in believing in the supernatural, one behaves like a gullible person (in the benign sense of someone who reduces type I errors), not as a skeptic. Hence, a logically consistent skeptic should be either an atheist or, at most, an agnostic. The usual objection to this conclusion is the so-called "empirical" evidence that many skeptics are also theists.[13] However, this is no objection at all, in that it only shows that humans have an uncanny ability to simultaneously hold to beliefs that are mutually incompatible. But we didn't really need another demonstration of *that*, did we?

---

[13] Anthropologist Eugenie Scott used this argument in a private conversation with me, and Stephen Gould published an entire book partially based on this premise. I therefore call this the "Scott-Gould fallacy." Scott is a good sport, and I am sure she will not get offended. I cannot vouch for Gould.

Chapter 5 - A case against God: science and the falsifiability question in theology[14]

Napoleon: "But Messier de Laplace, what about God?"
Laplace: "I have no need of that hypothesis."
(Apocryphal quote attributed to astronomer Pierre Simon Marquis de Laplace while explaining his theory of the origin of the solar system to Napoleon)

By all accounts, scientists are human beings. This apparently trivial observation carries a lot of explanatory power when it comes to rather unscientific practices many scientists willingly engage in. It is this same truism that led Kuhn (1970) to propose the idea that the scientific enterprise is mostly determined by the social context in which it happens, a position termed "rationalist relativism" by Casti (1989). Even though Kuhn then searches for ways to establish which of a series of paradigms is "better," his philosophy of science fundamentally transcends any idea of an objective and knowable external reality. Pushing the envelope just a bit further leads to the absurd position of Paul Feyerabend (1975), an irrationalist relativist who claims that there is no such thing as the scientific method, and that science has the same ontological status as astrology and mysticism.

As a practicing scientist, I obviously couldn't disagree more with either Kuhn or Feyerabend. I am certainly not to deny the fact that science is a human activity, and as such quite clearly subject to the full spectrum of human weaknesses, including irrational and emotional thinking, if not downright fraud (Gould 1996). Nevertheless, science remains by far the single most successful set of tools to learn about the natural world and to predict its behavior. Furthermore, science is the only human activity with a built-in system of self-correction when tested against the vagaries

---

[14] A version of this article has been published in *Skeptic*, volume 6(2), pp. 66-73, 1998. This is the "original director's cut."

of the real world (unlike astrology, mysticism, or philosophy of science for that matter).

This is why, for example, scientists are so stubbornly opposed to equal time for the teaching of creationism and Darwinism in biology courses. Creationists appeal to the "democratic" soul of the American public: if there are two alternatives, let's hear both of them and let the market decide which one is best. But the best science, unlike what Kuhn might think, does not proceed by consensus and advertising, and certainly not by granting equality among theories. That is why the equal opportunity teaching is sheer nonsense. We teach what we currently think is the best of our understanding of the universe, not a plethora of half-baked or outdated ideas given just for the sake of "equality." Accordingly, we do not teach on equal basis the Ptolemaic and the Copernican systems, because we know better.

Similarly, scientists are willing to leave their ivory towers to engage in public battles against irrational beliefs such as astrology, alien abductions, telepathy, mental metal-bending, prophecies, homeopathic medicine, therapeutic energy, ghosts, and all sorts of other ancient and modern myths. Did I say *all* sorts? Well, not really all. One island of irrationalism has held out very well, almost untouched by the otherwise overwhelming triumph of the scientific method. And it isn't a small island, either. It's that huge, mysterious, and fascinating continent called religion. To put it as philosopher of science Will Provine (1988) did, if you are a scientist and you go to Church you "simply have to check your brains at the Church door." In the following, I shall explore why this is the case by examining two examples of scientists dealings with religion. I will then attempt a brief discussion of the dynamics of this phenomenon, as well as suggest a couple of modest proposals as possible solutions.

Scientists still *don't* believe in God

Edward Larson, a science historian at the University of Georgia, and Larry Witham, a *Washington Times* reporter, published a peculiar commentary in the April 3, 1997 issue of *Nature* (Genoni 1997; Larson and Witham 1997). The title of the article was "Scientists are still keeping the faith." The story reports a study carried out by the two authors to replicate a classical survey performed by the psychologist James Leuba in 1916. Leuba set out to test the hypothesis that the more people were educated, the least likely they were to believe in God. He therefore asked 1,000 American scientists about their beliefs and his results confirmed the idea that scientists as a group are much less likely to believe in God than the public at large. Leuba attributed this to the scientists' better education, and ventured to predict that with the passing of time and the presumed increase in the education of the general public, religious beliefs would become more and more rare.

Larson and Witham attempted to replicate Leuba's study as closely as possible. For example, they considered the same number of scientists, divided among biologists, physicists, and mathematicians; they got their sample from the same source used by Leuba, i.e., the directory published in *American Men (and Women) of Science*. The attempt to repeat the original conditions met with some problems, as freely admitted by the authors themselves. For example Leuba's sample of one thousand scientists

Fig. 5.1. A comparison of the likelihood of believing in God between the general public and scientists, the latter category then subdivided into mathematicians, biologists, and physicists. Adapted from Larson and Whitam (1997).

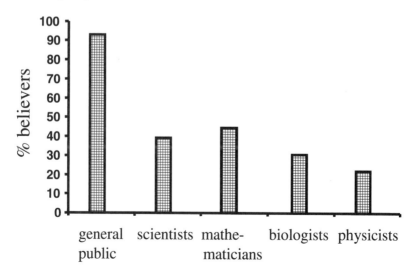

represented about 20% of the available entries, while an equivalent sample today constitutes about 3% of the total; this increases the likelihood of statistical errors in comparing the two samples. Furthermore, Leuba distinguished between "great" scientists and "ordinary" ones, finding that the belief in God was markedly lower within the first category. Such a distinction is no longer reported in *American Men and Women of Science*, presumably because of political correctness. Even though it would certainly be possible to rank the scientists based on a number of criteria (time allocated to teaching vs. research, number and quality of publications, and so on), Larson and Witham did not feel compelled to mirror the original research *that* closely.[15] There is also some discussion about the way the questions were actually phrased. Larson and Witham attempted to follow Leuba's definition of God as "hearing prayers and giving immortality." They felt, however, that several interviewees would have answered differently if given a less traditional, more "modern" (I would say more vague) definition of God. Perhaps. Unfortunately, the choice here is either to replicate a fundamental study conducted 80 years earlier, or to start from scratch. And most of the appeal of Larson's and Witham's attempt lies precisely in the comparison with Leuba's.

The results are summarized in Figure 5.1, with an additional column showing the level of belief of the general public. I am reporting here only the answers to the question "do you believe in a personal God?" We will get to the other two questions below. The results were as clear as astounding, but their interpretation is more than open to alternative views. The fact is, scientists did not change their opinion that much in the intervening period between the two surveys. True, physicists have supplanted biologists as the leading group of atheists, but Leuba found in 1916 pretty much the same percentages reported in Figure 5.1 . Larson's and Witham's conclusion, as evident from the title of their paper, is

---

[15] They later on published a follow up in which they queried outstanding scientists, defined as those who are members of the National Academy of Sciences (Larson and Witham 1998; Larson and Witham 1999). The results did indeed mirror Leuba's once again, with an even lower percentage of scientists believing in God than the American psychologist originally reported in his survey: today, only about 7% of greatest scientists believe in a personal God.

that scientists *kept* their faith after 80 years. My conclusion would be that scientists were still by and large *without* faith. Why?

One, as Figure 5.1 clearly shows – and as was reported by Leuba – scientists have a dramatically lower probability of believing in God than the general public, and this fact has remained unchanged throughout the past 80 years. It seems much more logical to use the general public as a "control" group and claim that the control and the "treatment" have maintained the original status (believers and non-believers respectively), rather than twisting things around by asserting that scientists "held" onto a minority position within their own group!

Two, Leuba's original hypothesis is very difficult to test by a simple repetition of his experiment. His contention was that people with more education would be less likely to believe in God. Since scientists tend to be among the best educated people (especially about the realities of the physical universe), Leuba's decision to poll scientists was logical, and his results are consistent with the hypothesis. However, to repeat the test 80 years later is quite tricky. One of the underlying assumptions here is that knowledge has accumulated, and education improved, *for scientists across the board*. But this can be questioned. While our knowledge of the physical universe has indeed improved during the 20th century, the level of general education of most scientists is probably comparable to, or at least not dramatically different from, what it was 80 years ago. Our general vision of the universe has not changed that dramatically (as opposed to what it was, say, in Galileo's time). We already had the theory of evolution, astronomy had long ago swept the earth from the center of the Universe and of the galaxy, and the old age of our planet was becoming accepted knowledge when Leuba conducted his research. Quantum theory and molecular biology have since revolutionized physics and biology respectively, but did they really add much to an educated person's understanding that there is little place for God in the real universe?

Furthermore, Leuba's original projection was based on the reasonable assumption that the education of the general public will steadily progress and that therefore everybody will eventually consider God on the same level with astrology or telepathy. There are two problems with this line of reasoning. First, even though more people than ever are attending college (at least in the Western world), belief in astrology, parapsychology and all sorts of other superstitions or pseudo-sciences is at an all-time high. Clearly, there is not much of a correlation between the level of general (as opposed to *scientific*) education and the ability to discriminate between fiction and reality. As for scientific education, while this reportedly went up during the 1960s and 1970s as a result of a national effort to catch up with the Russians in the space race, any science college teacher can testify that today's standards are not quite what we would like them to be (Edmunson 1997).

Also, what does it actually *mean* to be "more educated"? My experience with the American educational system is that this translates into acquiring very specialized knowledge in a particular field, usually a practical one such as business administration. What causal and therefore predictive link could possibly exist between knowing how to improve your company's bottom line and deeper insights into the ultimate questions of "life, the universe, and everything" (Adams 1986)? I am not faulting Leuba for this at all. He approached the problem from the optimistic viewpoint of one who was witnessing the fruit of Darwin's and Freud's work. The education he had in mind truly was universal, wide-ranging, and presumably would indeed lead to a better general understanding of who we are and were we come from. That vision was incomparably more "liberal" than the liberal education that has been under such intense fire in the United States since the Republican party and the Christian Right have become more powerful (Shorris 1997).

In the 1997 survey scientists were also queried about their belief in human immortality (a corollary of most religions). The result was clearly along the lines of Leuba's predictions: the percentage of believers decreased from 51% to 38%! A third question probed the desire for immortality. While 34% of Leuba's interviewees had answered that they would like to be immortal in some sense, about 10% of modern scientists did. Therefore, even though the answer to the main question has indeed not changed appreciably, there is plenty of support for the conclusion that the belief in a personal God *with the attributes and corollaries of mainstream religion* has been significantly eroded among scientists (but not the general public). Overall, it seems that the same low proportion of scientists believes in God, but that their concept of such an entity has become more refined and abstract (usually the first step toward atheism: Smith 1991).

Given all of the above, I feel justified in reversing Larson's and Witham's interpretation of the results. Instead of concluding that scientists are "keeping the faith" (thereby insinuating that it isn't such an irrational thing to do), I would suggest that the two surveys dramatically point to a general failure of our educational system. We are not becoming more educated; we are simply acquiring more *knowledge*. There is a fundamental difference between the two.

Ironically, Leuba's research contributed to this sad state of affairs. His findings were one of the sparks that started Williams James Bryan's crusade against the teaching of evolution in the 1920s, that culminated in the infamous Scopes trial in Tennessee in 1925 (Larson 1997; Webb 1997). Beginning with that landmark case, the battle has been waged incessantly, with mostly symbolic and legal (but not substantial) victories for rationality. For example, considering just what happened in Tennessee, let us remember that Scopes *was* convicted, that the overturning of his conviction was on technical grounds only, and that the law was not repealed until the 1967 challenge brought by sixty Tennessee teachers and the National Science Teachers' Association (NABT). Furthermore, the Tennessee legislature tried again to curtail the teaching of evolution as recently as 1996, once more failing on a matter of technicalities and finances, not because of any strong message from the public (educated or otherwise)! (Larson 1997; Webb 1997)

Should scientists mess with religion?

The answer to this question is a resounding "No!" from one of the leading biologists and skeptics of the century, Stephen Jay Gould of Harvard. Before I try to show the fallacy of his position, let me make one point extremely clear. I *do not* belong to the fashionable category of Gould-bashers. I have the utmost respect not only for his scientific achievements, but also for his stated political and philosophical positions. Nevertheless, I think the author of "Ever Since Darwin" really got it wrong this time.

Gould published an article in *Natural History* (Gould 1997) in which he promulgated his NOMA principle (for Non-

Overlapping Magisteria).[16] The cardinal points of the principle can be summarized as follows:

1. The net of science covers the physical universe and what it is made of (facts).
2. The net of religion extends over questions of moral meaning and value.

Simple enough. But as H.L. Menken, the caustic journalist who covered the Scopes trial said: "For every complex problem, there is a solution that is simple, neat, and wrong." The NOMA principle is not really new. In 1923, as a response to the first manifestations of the fundamentalist movement that lead to the Scopes trial, the moderate Presbyterian pastor James Vance cosigned a widely publicized statement with 40 others, including the Nobel laureate Robert Millikan and the famous biologist Henry Fairfield Osborn (Larson 1997). The document called for entirely separate spheres of influence of science and religion: science would deal with "the facts, laws and processes of nature," while religion would address "the consciences, ideals and aspirations of mankind." Much further back in time, Italian humanists used a prototype of NOMA during the Renaissance, with horrible results in the case of Giordano Bruno, and modest ones in that of Galileo.

Gould's NOMA principle came out of his (and a few other biologists') enthusiasm for the fact that the pope finally acknowledged that Darwin may be right after all (John Paul II 1997). The Catholic Church historically maintained an antagonistic stance towards evolution, perhaps best summarized by words written in the *Humani Generis* (On Human kind) encyclical by pope Pius XII in 1950. While acknowledging the possibility of evolution, he stated:

> "Some imprudently and indiscreetly hold that evolution ...explains the origin of all things ...Communists gladly subscribe to this opinion so that, when the souls of men have been deprived of every idea of a personal God, they

---

[16] He then expanded his discussion to book size with *Rocks of Ages* (Gould 1999). However, his argument in the book is essentially the same, and I refuted it in detail in an article published in *Skeptical Inquirer* (Pigliucci 1999).

may the more efficaciously defend and propagate their dialectical materialism."

As modern Protestant fundamentalists put it, evolution is the root of the tree of evil. As he did with Galileo a few years earlier, Pope John Paul II (not otherwise known as a liberal) attempted to correct this posturing when he wrote in *Truth Cannot Contradict Truth* (in a message to the Pontifical Academy of Sciences that does not have the authority of an encyclical):[17]

"Today ... new knowledge has led to the recognition of more than a hypothesis in the theory of evolution. It is indeed remarkable that this theory has been progressively accepted by researchers, following a series of discoveries in various fields of knowledge. The convergence, neither sought nor fabricated, of the results of work that was conducted independently is in itself a significant argument in favor of the theory ... However ... the moment of transition to the spiritual cannot be the object of this kind of observation."

Notice that this is by no means a sweeping triumph for evolutionists. Quite the contrary, it's a Pyrrhic victory.[18] In essence, John Paul is actually violating Gould's own NOMA principle, in that he advocates a special divine intervention for a fundamental step in human evolution (the appearance of consciousness, which I am equating with his vaguely defined "spirituality", since there can be no spirituality without consciousness).

There are plenty of other things that are dissatisfactory in NOMA. First of all, religions (at least most Western religions and Islam) actually *do* make plenty of claims about the physical nature of the universe, and these are not restricted to the spiritualization of the human soul. If we take Christian fundamentalism, for one,

---

[17] The same Pope later expanded his thoughts on the relationship between religion and science in *Fides et Ratio*, published in 1999. See Chapter 6 for more details.

[18] Pyrrhus (319-272 BCE) was the king of Epirus and had the rare distinction of defeating the Roman army at Heraclea and Asculum. However, the victory came at such a staggering cost that there was not much to celebrate about. The Romans, incidentally, won all their territories back.

we are faced with all sorts of bizarre claims about evolution, the origin of life and the universe, the age of the Earth, and so on (e.g., Gish 1995; Jennings Bryan 1996; Al-Najjar 1998; Ham 1998; Yahya 1999). Each one flies straight into the face of all modern scientific disciplines. And please, do *not* dismiss religious fundamentalism (either of Christian or Muslim flavor) as a fringe movement: it is shaping American politics and everyday life, as well as entirely controlling a number of countries in the world, especially in the Middle East. But even outside fundamentalism, let us remember that the Catholic Church sequentially denied the fact that the earth is a sphere, that it rotates around the sun, and that all living beings originated from a single ancestor by evolutionary processes. The fact that church leaders have progressively retreated from extreme positions only means that they found themselves in increasingly indefensible territory on each of those specific cases: several battles have been won, not the war.

Secondly, the NOMA principle's abdication of moral questions to religion implies that morality is somehow not to be subjected to one of the fundamental processes of scientific investigation: self-correction. As fundamentalist Danny Phillips once put it, "Science changes every day, and for us starting believing in something that changes every day, over something that's stood fast for over 3,000 years; that's hideous, and we don't need to do that" (quoted in the newsletter of the Rationalists of East Tennessee, March 1997; see http://www.korrnet.org/reality). But it is science, in the form of cultural anthropology, which clearly shows us that moral beliefs are relative,[19] they depend on the cultural context, and – above all – they *evolve*. So, why relinquish our right to rationally discuss and modify moral beliefs to an authority that doesn't have a shred of supporting physical evidence to submit? More importantly, this authority *prides* itself on not changing its views regardless of science or society at large.

Gould's NOMA gives religion total control over moral issues and over matters of value. But is alleged divine inspiration the only source of morality for humans? Setting aside despicable

---

[19] I am not talking here of complete moral relativism in the sense of anything goes, but of the more subtle and rational idea that many moral precepts are in fact arbitrary and driven by the particular times and culture one happens to live in.

trends toward "natural morality" and "Social Darwinism" (Miele 1996), do we not have a multi-millennial history of thinkers and philosophers who engaged in in-depth discussions of human morality? Is Kant's moral imperative necessarily given by God? And what about Plato, Aristotle, or Bertrand Russell? In fact, the argument can be easily made that divine laws as they are expressed in the Bible or the Koran are simply the canonization of human agreements and social contracts, girded with super-human aura to make them more easily enforceable.

Lastly, I will take exception to Gould's implied dichotomy between the physical and the psychological/spiritual spheres. As a biologist, he should know better. Think for a moment about the evolution of emotions. As Darwin (1890) showed, it is easy to realize that the psychological, moral, and ethical characteristics of humans are in fact the product of evolution. They are an epiphenomenon of the complexity of our brains, intertwined with our meandrous history as primates and hunter-gatherers. My conclusion is that *there is no real distinction* between the two spheres that Gould so neatly and Solomonically partitions between science and religion. They both are legitimate subjects of rational investigation, and our best hope for a better society and human condition is the application of reason and self-correction in both areas.

God as a falsifiable hypothesis

Before we can discuss what, if anything, science has to say about God, we need to be clear on what we mean by that term. According to "The Encyclopedia of Philosophy" (Edwards 1967) there are three conceivable kinds of gods: the *metaphysical* God, the *infinite anthropomorphic* God, and the *finite anthropomorphic* God.

A metaphysical God is one that does not have any relationship whatsoever with the physical world. This kind of God is usually invoked by believers to explain the existence of evil, which is patently incompatible with any kind of omnibenevolent and omnipotent anthropomorphic God. The argument is that "good" and "evil" are human concepts that do not apply to God. We can dismiss this kind of God on two grounds: first, it is unintelligible. What does it *mean* to have a God that does not reflect any human value? Second, it is psychologically useless. Let us not forget that the main reason people believe in a God is to gain comfort about the meaning of the world. But a metaphysical God cannot offer such comfort at all, and therefore loses any function in a human society. That is why very few people, if any, today believe in a metaphysical God.

An anthropomorphic God can be either infinite or finite. The infinite version is the most popular one. It corresponds to the Christian tradition of an omnipotent entity. The finite version is a somewhat "minor" God (called the demiurge by some Greek philosophers: Jaeger 1947). We can dismiss the idea of a finite God, since most people throughout the world – and especially in western societies – would not subscribe to it for the same reasons that they would be unsatisfied with a metaphysical God. Interestingly, the reason to propose an imperfect God is psychologically the same one for purporting the metaphysical version: to explain the baffling presence of evil in a world that clearly is not "the best of all possible worlds" (Voltaire 1759).

What about the most common and psychologically satisfying God of them all, the omnipresent, omniscient, omnipotent, infinite anthropomorphic God? The first question to answer about this kind of God is: should we take an atheistic position, or be more moderate and maintain agnosticism? Atheists have a bad reputation, sometimes being described on the same terms as fundamentalist Christians, Jews, or Muslims, as intolerant, narrow-minded individuals that are sure about things no one can be sure about. Yet, my position here is that an infinite anthropomorphic God can be treated as a hypothesis about the physical universe, a situation that gives atheism an edge over simple agnosticism.[20]

Let me clarify this point. Even though believers – especially when cornered by obvious unpleasant realities of the physical universe (Gould's "facts") – maintain that belief in God requires faith, and it is therefore immune from any contingent or scientific investigation, they don't really mean it. Fundamentalists, for one thing, freely claim that God created the universe in so many days,

---

[20] Notice that this does not apply to other kinds of Gods, a rhetorical trick used by Christian apologists such as William Craig (see Chapter 10).

in a specific sequence of events, and not long ago. They further claim that this God handcrafted all species of living organisms, and that he literally runs the everyday affairs of the universe. Otherwise, prayers would not work. These statements are obviously falsifiable (and false)! But even non-fundamentalists tend to think of God as somewhat interacting with the physical universe (if not, what would be the point of having a God?). If he is not literally running it, he certainly originated and designed it (at least by "picking" the right physical laws: this is sometimes pompously referred to as the "strong anthropic principle" – Tipler 1995). So, God interacts, to a more or less limited extent, with the physical world. Which means that God is somewhat *a part of* the physical universe. By this definition, the existence of God is a question within the realm of scientific investigation.

Now, if we admit that God can be thought of as a hypothesis about the real world, then we have to clarify what we mean by the terms hypothesis and theory. A hypothesis is a specific prediction made within a general theoretical framework. Unfortunately, there are two kinds of usage for the word "theory," one scientific, the other vernacular:

1) In science, the usefulness of a theory lies in its ability to explain and make specific predictions about observable phenomena. Such a theory may produce a set of hypotheses that in turn can be verified or falsified (i.e., rejected: Popper 1968). A scientific hypothesis can be investigated by empirical means. For example, modern astrophysicists have proposed a complex theory about the origin of the universe, known as the "Big Bang." One of many predictions of the Big Bang scenario is that the universe should still be permeated by a background radiation, a sort of leftover heat from the initial explosion. This hypothesis is subject to empirical investigation. Indeed, the background radiation was discovered by radiotelescopic observation in the 1960s (Hawking 1993), and it matches perfectly (i.e., quantitatively) the theoretical predictions. Notice that this does not mean that the Big Bang theory is "true," only that it is more consistent with available data than any alternative proposed so far.

2) In layperson's terms, the word theory implies a diminutive or derogative tone (as in "it is *just* a theory"). This kind of theory

is made of a series of vague statements that cannot be tested scientifically and it is therefore truly outside the realm of science. For example, "God created the universe" is a vague statement, with no real explanatory power, since it simply substitutes one mystery (the origin of the universe) for another, less parsimonious one (where did God come from, anyway?).

The agnostic position is simply that the second kind of theory, being outside the realm of scientific inquiry, cannot be proven false or true, and therefore cannot be rejected – as the atheists would do. But this is a gross philosophical and logical mistake. This equates rejection with disproof. Simply put, we do not need to disprove many things that we reject outright as silly or inconsequential. For example, as we have discussed in Chapter 2, we reject the existence of flying horses *a la* Pegasus not because we have *proven* that they do not exist (since to do so would require a thorough search of the whole universe), but because their anatomy flatly contradicts everything we know about vertebrate evolution (and a few aspects of aerodynamics, too). Notice that this skeptical position is always open to revision, should a flying horse suddenly appear within visual range. Analogously, atheists are not stubborn unbelievers (or at least, they shouldn't be). Most of them would readily convert if given a decisive proof of the existence of supernatural entities.[21] Even believers use the rational argument, paradoxically against other believers! Why is it that a Christian (or

Fig. 5.2. Galileo Galilei (1564-1642), the Italian physicist and mathematician who helped remove the earth from the center of the universe and suffered the consequences at the hand of the Catholic Church.

---

21 Incidentally, this is the reason I don't like the TV series *X-Files*: it is not because it portrays paranormal phenomena as real. After all, it is a work of fiction, and one knows that she is supposed to suspend her disbelief when watching such things. Rather, the annoying aspect is the portray of the skeptic investigator: given all the evidence that gets thrown in her face at every episode, she is a hopelessly close-minded person, not a true skeptic.

any rational person today) does not believe in Zeus and Apollo and cheerfully dismisses them as fantasies? Because they are vaguely defined entities that are very unlikely to ever have been historical figures, despite the fact that the ancient Greeks didn't feel that way!

In summary, if the God hypothesis is simply a vague statement, it can be at least provisionally rejected as silly and unnecessary even though technically we cannot prove God's non-existence. If, on the contrary, it is meant as a relatively precise statement about the physical world, then we can investigate God's existence with the well-established hypothetical-deductive method. How do we do that? By enumerating the supposed attributes of such a God and treating them as testable hypotheses.

For example, one of the most powerful of the theses used by theologians in pre-Darwinian times was the argument from intelligent design (Paley 1831, more on this in Chapter 9). It went like this: the universe, living beings, and especially humans are so complex and perfectly put together that this must be the making of a creator. It is astounding that this same reasoning is still at the center of modern controversy thanks to some amazingly uninformed books published recently (Behe 1996; Dembski 1998), coupled with rampant die-hard ideological blindness, and notwithstanding the fact that Hume had demolished the argument even before it was advanced by Paley (Hume 1779). This is even more extraordinary since Darwin himself cleverly (and purposefully) turned the argument around by painstakingly demonstrating that the universe is not perfect at all (Darwin 1859; Dawkins 1996). Take the human eye, one of creationists' favorite examples. It is well known that we have a blind spot in our eyes. It is caused by the fact that the blood vessels and nerves serving the eye are positioned in front of the optical components inside the retina. This is a rather annoying feature, which a competent engineer would have certainly avoided. In fact, cephalopods (i.e., squids, octopuses, and the like) have their eye (that evolved independently from the vertebrate's) built the other way around, so they don't have to suffer from this inconvenience. The only possible conclusions are: a) God didn't design the thing; b) God is pretty sloppy and not worthy of all our unconditional admiration; or c) God likes squids a lot better than humans. Take your pick.

Here are some other scientific or simply logical reasons not to believe in an anthropomorphic God, based on actual statements about the physical world that are an integral part, of or are implied by, most modern religious beliefs. The list is far from exhaustive, and its sole point is to make the argument that logic and science can indeed say a lot about *specific* gods purported by different religious sects.

- *Statistics* vs. God. There is a very clear inverse relationship between the amount of human knowledge and the credit (or blame) we are willing to give God for direct intervention in the universe: the more we know, the less we attribute to supernatural causes. Any scientist faced with such a remarkably consistent trend would not hesitate much to extrapolate just a bit and declare God very likely non-existent.
- *Astronomy* vs. God. Biblically-derived cosmologies put the earth at the center of the universe, and imply that the sun rotates around our planet. As it is well known, Copernicus (1543) and Galileo (1632) took care of that hypothesis and of any possibility that the sun ever "stopped."
- *Geology* vs. God. The earth is definitely and significantly older than the few thousand years allowed by western religions (even eastern ones don't come much closer: Dalrymple 1991).
- *Biology* vs. God. Biology is rich with challenges to established religions. The neo-Darwinian theory of evolution is probably the most powerful blow of them all, but the demonstration from modern molecular genetics that humans and chimps are very closely related and almost identical is another. Current biodiversity studies clearly cast a dark cloud (pun intended) over the story of Noah's Ark. Tons of ink have been spent publishing calculations of exactly how many animals Noah could possibly fit in his Ark. Given modern estimates of the existence of millions of previously unknown species, as well as paleontological studies (the dinosaurs and the ammonites clearly didn't make it on Noah's vessel), I think this is yet another myth we can safely relegate to allegory and not literal (or even approximate) truth.
- *Anthropology* vs. God. Religions are historical products of changing human cultures. They come in a variety of flavors,

often making very different claims about the nature of God and the universe. How are we supposed to choose the right one? Be careful, because every religion will send you straight to hell if you make the wrong choice. Furthermore, religions are born, evolve, and die, as demonstrated by the extinction of the ancient Greco-Roman gods, or by the varied history of the text of the Bible itself. Therefore religion, and the belief in any particular God, is a relative concept, subject to historical accidents. A very shaky basis indeed for an eternity-long commitment (see Chapter 4). Indeed, I find the position of many Christian theologians on morality very peculiar. They suggest that we need a God because we cannot do without an unchanging moral code (see Chapter 10). Without God, the argument goes, all morality would be empirical and relative. Should we then conclude that modern Christian ethics is based on the same bloodthirsty logic that fills the Bible with rape, murder, and genocide? I didn't think so.

If after all this anybody still *wants* to believe in a logically inconsistent and physically impossible God, that person of course *does* have that right. Naturally, the same person also has the right to believe in voodoo, astrology, telepathy, and alien abductions – but with no more claim to the truth. Atheists are not in the business of telling people what they can or cannot believe (unlike most religious fundamentalists), but simply what makes sense, according to the best of our knowledge, to believe or not believe. The astonishing thing is that most people do not hesitate to believe in a completely self-contradictory God and allow such belief to guide their entire life; on the other hand, the same people demand highly logical and empirical standards when they make such relatively inconsequential choices as buying a car.

Why do scientists offer the other cheek?

If the idea of an anthropomorphic God can be considered a testable statement about the physical world, and therefore amenable to scientific investigation, why is it that the overwhelming majority of scientists avoid the whole affair, claiming like Gould does that it isn't science's business to mess with religion? Why is it that we do not feel compelled to actively fight ignorance and superstition in all of its forms, as our role as educators should oblige us to do? After all, we do not have any qualms leaving the ivory tower and engaging in open battle the dragons of astrology or parapsychology. So why is it that we do not treat religion as we treat other forms of superstition, as a threat to human reason and welfare? I can offer three distinct, yet not mutually exclusive, explanations for this somewhat puzzling behavior.

1. Scientists are schizophrenic. Not in the usual pathological sense of the word, of course. This is what Provine refers to as checking your brain outside before entering church. I have met several rational scientists who simply shut down their higher cognitive functions when it comes to religion. They truly and honestly do not see any contradiction between studying evolution or the Big Bang while simultaneously believing in a supernatural being in charge of the whole business. The detailed, intimate acquaintance with a particular discipline fails to translate to the level of wide-ranging philosophical generalization. In other words, knowing how to apply the scientific method to solve specific problems does not necessarily make the application a way of life. I have no explanation for this pattern, but it certainly is of utmost interest to any psychologist attentive to the intricacies and contradictions of the human mind.

2. The "ivory tower" effect. Even scientists who are perfectly aware of the contradiction between a rationalist approach and the belief in God would rather keep it to themselves in order to avoid conflict. Scientists know very well that in modern times their ability to live the good intellectual life could be threatened if they embarked on a collision course with religious authorities. It is happening wherever fundamentalists have political power. Science's (but, astonishingly, not politics') image has already been tarnished by two world wars and a host of technological threats to human survival. Moreover, most people are frightened by novelty, and especially technological novelty, per se. The invention of the computer is being hailed as one of the greatest achievements of humankind, and at the same time blamed for all sorts of evil social consequences, from downsizing to the moral corruption of America's youth.[22] There has been much discussion on the extent to which scientists can claim that the result of their work is value-free, and the extent to which they are personally responsible for how their work will be applied. Instead of frankly entering such debate and attempting to educate the public and the politicians about the complexities of science, we avoid the conflict as much as possible. We have retreated high in the ivory tower, hoping that the whole thing will soon go away. Well, it won't. And the less we get involved, the more ultraconservatives will demolish the foundations of the ivory tower, till it will simply crumble down.

3. It's the money, stupid! The last explanation for the widespread equivocal attitude of scientists toward religion is connected to the second one, but it strikes much closer: it touches our laboratories, summer salaries, and graduate students. To put it candidly, science has always been a luxury activity at the mercy of wealthy or ignorant people. It is a sad commentary on the level reached by our entire civilization, but the fact remains that Galileo had to thank the Medici family and named the newly discovered satellites of Jupiter after them. Analogously, every one of our papers has to thank the National Science Foundation (NSF), the National Institutes of Health (NIH), or the Department of Energy (DOE) for the little we get in financial aid.

While these modern sources of funding for science are admittedly less volatile than an authoritative monarch or aristocrat, they are still far too unreliable for most scientists' peace of mind. In the United States, a steady movement on the part of conservative political forces is trying to undercut not just the easy target of government funding of the humanities, but also of the scientific enterprise, or at least of that part of science that does not have a direct application to human health or welfare. I hope that I do not have to convince my readers of the indirect benefits of basic science, or even of the "radical" idea that the pursuit of knowledge per se is one of humankind's noblest aspirations ("fatti non foste

---

22 Note that I am not saying that the widespread use of computers cannot or does not have such consequences. But there is a distinction between an invention (and its potential utility) and the actual uses such invention is put to by society.

per viver come bruti, ma per seguir virtute e canoscenza" says Odysseus in Dante's *Inferno* – you were not made to live like brutes, but to seek virtue and knowledge). But this sentiment does not encounter widespread approval on Capitol Hill these days. The U.S. House of Representatives and Senate are filled with superstitious people who not only believe in God, but who link the study of evolution to pure evil. And who wants to attract the attention of budget-minded bigots to her own source of livelihood?

So, what do we do about it?

The role of a skeptic cannot be limited to debunking. There has to be a positive, constructive part, lest we further the popular perception of skeptics as cynical individuals with nothing of value to contribute to humanity. In Descartes' words, the *pars destruens* of our arguments needs to be followed by an equally compelling *pars construens* (Descartes 1637). Unfortunately, as any demolition derby driver or politician well knows, to bring down is much easier than to build. Nevertheless, let me advance a few modest proposals on the topic of the relationship between science and religion (see also Chapter 6).

First, what is our goal? Belief in the irrational and supernatural is due mostly to ignorance (and to a few atavistic fears that might be much more difficult to eradicate). Therefore, our goal is simply to educate. Did I say "simply"? Quite obviously, education is an elusive goal, especially because it is not even clear what we mean by "education." The overwhelming majority of people in the world are, unfortunately, ignorant. By this I mean not necessarily that they do not hold college degrees (although most don't, at least outside the Western world and some pockets of the Eastern one), or that they are illiterate. I mean that they have a very poor understanding of the real world. Ironically, "real" world refers here not to the world of private corporations and stock markets (as opposed to the world of academia), but to the physical universe. Poll after poll of the American public reveals a very poor understanding of such fundamental scientific facts as evolution by natural selection or the expansion of the universe. Some Americans are still not entirely convinced that Armstrong actually went to the

Moon. How can we cry foul for people who believe in superstitions throughout their adult lives, if they do not comprehend even superficially the world they live in?

The fault, I suggest, is in part ours as scientists and educators. We do not accept as our mission to seek and *spread* the truth to the best of our abilities. We do not see that it is our duty as human beings to use our laboratories, classrooms, articles, and books to stimulate and guide people in the quest for a rational interpretation of the world in which we live. What is at stake here is not just the survival of one form of superstition or another, nor even the continuation of academic freedom or of science itself. It is the endurance of the human race in the face of environmental problems so complex that our best and possibly only hope for delaying extinction is the widespread application of science to our problems. Surely the survival of humankind cannot simply rely on good old-fashioned faith in superior beings who supposedly created this perfect place and will take care of their creatures in the best possible manner. Only when the majority of our fellow human beings will be as proficient in the understanding of the human world as the majority of scientists are today, will we really see qualitative changes in human behavior and welfare.

How do we pave the way toward such a rationalist society? To be frank, we may never get there. Nevertheless, scientists and educators have one simple step to make to start the process. Stop being on the defensive. Do not recoil whenever a student feels his personal beliefs are challenged because of a lecture you delivered on evolution. Do not avoid confrontation with school boards, trustees, journalists, and politicians. Do not fall into the trap of too much political correctness. Of course everybody has the right to believe in whatever they wish, but you have an equal right to teach the best of what you know to whomever wants to listen, just as a preacher has the right to stand at the corner of my Department handing out free Bibles to biology students. Never forget that religious fundamentalism doesn't play fair. It is literally out to get you. Its objective is nothing less than a frontal attack on science and rationalism. Finally, do not make the error of underestimating the current trend and dismiss it as a passing swing of the pendulum. By the time the pendulum swings back, the world might be a much worse place to live in than if we had stood the ground we have inherited from Copernicus, Galileo, and Darwin. As Thomas Huxley observed: "It is as respectable to be a modified monkey as modified dirt."

Chapter 6 - Personal gods, deism, and the limits of skepticism[23]

"The most common of all follies is to believe passionately in the palpably not true. It is the chief occupation of mankind." (H.L. Mencken)

The relationship between science and religion, and even the one between skepticism and religion, is warming up. At least, that is the feeling one gets from a cursory look at recent happenings, from the publication of books and articles in popular magazines about science "finding" God, to the frantic activities of the Templeton Foundation "for the furthering of religion." Even *Skeptical Inquirer*, which has traditionally steered clear of the science and religion topic, has devoted an entire issue (July-August 1999) to the subject by presenting an impressive spectrum of positions within the skeptic community.

The time is therefore ripe for a closer look at the whole discussion, which to me seems muddled by two basic sources of confusion: 1) we need to separate logical/philosophical arguments from those that are either pragmatic or concern freedom of speech. 2) We have to acknowledge that the possible positions on the science and religion question are many more than usually considered, and that a thorough understanding of the whole gamut is necessary to make some sort of progress. In this chapter, I offer an analysis of both these sources of confusion and present a classification scheme of the available positions on the matter. I will, of course, also present and advocate my own position, since I freely acknowledge that there is no such thing as objective reporting (Kitty 1998).

---

[23] This essay is in press in *Skeptic* magazine (2000).

Opening salvo: what the discussion is and is not about

Lest I be accused once again of being a "rabid atheist" (letter to *Skeptic*, vol. 6(4), p. 28) let me make my position clear: I am an atheist in the sense of someone who does not think there is any good reason to believe in a supernatural entity that created and somehow supervises the universe. I do not *know* that such an entity is not there, but until extraordinary evidence is provided to substantiate such an extraordinary claim, I relegate God to the same realm as Santa Claus. Rabid I am not, if by that one means an attitude of unreasonable adherence to a doctrine more accepted than carefully considered and of intolerance of other positions. My interest in religion has three aspects: first, it is part of my personal journey about finding

Fig. 6.1. Michael Shermer, founder of the Skeptic Society and publisher of *Skeptic*, has proposed three "models" for discussing the relationship between science and religion: I am here elaborating on his proposal to more comprehensively reflect the complexity of this relationship.

out how things really are; second, it is part of my interest as an educator and citizen in making as many people as possible think critically about anything, in the optimistic belief that a better society will result; third, it is a defensive action against other people's attempt to curtail my freedom of thought and speech.

This last point deserves further discussion because it lies at the root of at least one major misunderstanding in the science and religion debate, constituting one huge stumbling block that leads people, including skeptics, to react very emotionally whenever the subject is brought up for discussion. Let us briefly examine the three components of the science and religion debate and attempt to separate them as clearly as possible. I will then focus on the first component for the rest of the article:

1. The relationship between science and religion is a legitimate area of philosophical inquiry that must be informed by both religion (theology) and science.

2. Science and religion discussions, especially in the United States, carry practical consequences that do not affect the two components in equal manner.
3. Discussing science and religion has repercussions on the cherished value of freedom of speech for scientists, skeptics, and religionists.

As I said, point (1) is what we will be discussing in the rest of this essay. I think this is the only thing that really should be up for discussion, because it is the only one in which one can seriously engage in free inquiry and reach general conclusions (regardless of whether such conclusions will be shared by a majority).

The second point is a particularly murky one. It boils down to the fact that attacks on religion are considered politically incorrect and that scientists are especially aware of the fact that their funding depends almost entirely on public financing through various federal agencies such as the National Science Foundation (NSF) and the National Institutes of Health (NIH). Since federal funding is controlled by politicians, who in turn have a very unwise tendency to respond to every nuance of their constituency as gauged by the latest poll, it follows that no matter what your opinion as a scientist on matters of the spirit, it is wiser to stick to your job and avoid upsetting your prince and benefactor (see Chapters 2 and 5).

This is all the more so because of two other things that we all know about scientists: the overwhelming majority of them do not believe in a personal God (about 60% of general scientists and 93% of top scientists: Larson and Witham 1997; 1998 – see Chapter 5), and the reason they become scientists is to pursue questions for which science is a particularly good tool. Most of these questions are rather more mundane than the existence of God.

The result of this odd mix is that prominent scientists and educators do not believe in a personal God because of their understanding of science and of its implications, but come out in public with conciliatory statements to the effect that there is no possible contradiction between the two (Provine 1988).

The resolution to point (2) is that there is in fact a philosophical, if not scientific, contradiction between science and religion (see below), but it is not in scientists' interest to start an unholy war that they would lose hands down, given the religious

Fig. 6.2. A proposed conceptual framework of the universe of positions concerning the relationship between science and religion. The abscissa represents various degrees of contrast between science and religion, from the same worlds model of Shermer (no conflict at all), to the more neutral separate worlds to the definitively antagonistic conflicting worlds. The ordinate summarizes the variation present in the definitions of Gods used by people involved in the debate, from the personal God of most mainstream religions to a naturalistic God who acts only through physical laws he established, to the rather remote deist God who created the universe but did nothing afterwards. The different philosophical positions within this scheme are defined and discussed in the article; I apologize to individuals who might feel their position on the diagram has been misplaced; I assigned them on the basis of my interpretation of writings available to me. Also, the list of main characters in the debate should obviously be much longer, and not being included in the diagram does not mean that any particular author did not contribute substantially to the literature.

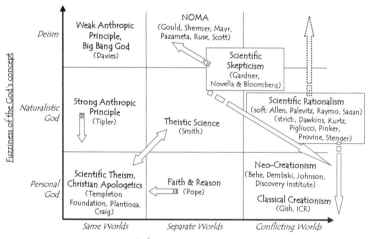

and political climate of the United States. Therefore, if asked, one could answer with the universally convenient "no comment" and live at peace with one's conscience.

Point (3) is rarely raised directly within the science and religion debate, but it clearly lurks behind some of the responses one gets when talking or writing about it. Let me make it as clear as possible: no self-respecting scientist or educator – religious or atheist – would want to limit the freedom of speech or expression of any party, including religionists or creationists. There is a fundamental, if rarely fully appreciated, distinction between openly criticizing a position, which is part of the very idea of free speech, and attempting to somehow coerce people into believing what you think is correct or limiting their ability to believe and practice what you think is not true. While religious fundamentalists often do not practice this distinction, most religious progressivists, agnostics, and atheists, follow it. It should therefore be clear that discussions about science and religion, or evolution and creationism, deal with free inquiry and education, and in no sense are meant to limit anybody's free speech. To put it into another fashion: asking to limit what is taught in a science classroom to what is pertinent to the subject matter is sound educational policy, not censorship. On the other hand, criticizing religion from either a philosophical or a humanist standpoint is an exercise in free speech valuable to our society, and it is not meant as a call to forcibly shut down churches and synagogues.

What's the problem? The many facets of science and religion

To continue our discussion of the legitimate philosophical, scientific, and religious aspects of the science and religion quagmire we need a frame of reference to guide such discussion. What I present here is an elaboration on a classification scheme proposed by Michael Shermer (1999). Shermer suggested that there are three worldviews, or "models," that people can adopt when thinking about science and religion. According to the *same worlds* model there is only one reality and science and religion are two different ways of looking at it. Eventually, both will converge on the same final answers, within the limited capabilities of human beings to actually pursue such fundamental questions. The *separate worlds* model represents a second possibility, in which science and religion are not only different kinds of human activities, but they pursue entirely separate goals. Asking about the similarities and differences between science and religion is the philosophical equivalent of comparing apples and oranges, so it shouldn't be done. Finally, the *conflicting worlds* model asserts that there is only one reality (as the same world scenario also acknowledges) but that science and religion collide head on when it comes to the shape that reality takes. Either one or the other is correct, but not both (or possibly neither, as Immanuel Kant might have argued).

Using Shermer's model as a starting point for thinking about science and religion, I realized that something was missing. One cannot reasonably talk about the conflict between science and religion unless one also specifies what one means by religion or God (usually there is less controversy on science is, though some philosophers and social scientists would surely disagree). So, what makes Shermer's classification incomplete is the very important fact that different people have different Gods. I am not referring to the relatively minor variations of the idea of God among the major monotheistic religions, but to the fact that God can be one of many radically different things (Pigliucci 1998; see also Chapter 5), and that unless we specify which God we are talking about, we will not make any further progress.

My tentative solution to the problem is therefore presented in Figure 6.2. Here the panoply of positions concerning the science and religion debate is arranged along two axes: on the abscissa we have the level of contrast between science and religion, which goes from none (same worlds model) to moderate (separate worlds) to high (conflicting worlds). On the ordinate is the "fuzziness" of the concept of God, which ranges from a very well defined personal God who intervenes in everyday human affairs to the more imprecise concept of a naturalistic God who acts only through the laws of physics, to the most esoteric position of deism characterized by an undefined God who created the universe but has not interfered with it ever since. Of course, all of these conceptions of God can take many forms. However, as we have discussed in Chapter 5, the common denominator to the belief in a personal God is the idea that she intervenes in individual lives, performs miracles, or otherwise shows direct concern for us mortals. A naturalistic God, on the other hand, is a bit more detached: if she intervenes at all it is through the tortuous ways of the natural laws that she herself designed for this universe. Finally, deism is broadly speaking the idea that God created the universe and then for all effective purposes retired to enjoy the fruits of such labor. This kind of God does not interfere, even indirectly, in human affairs, but simply answers the fundamental question of why there is something instead of nothing.

Big bangs, anthropic principles, and Christian apologetics

Figure 6.2 shows what personalities as diverse as physicists Paul Davies and Frank Tipler, conservative Christian apologist Alvin Plantinga, and science-religion crusader John Templeton have in common, as well as where they differ. Sir John Templeton is a British citizen native of Tennessee, and he has invested $800 million of his personal fortune into furthering a better understanding of religion through the scientific method. The Templeton Foundation has sponsored a panoply of activities resulting in articles, books, and conferences whose goal is to "discover spiritual information" (Holden 1999). According to Templeton, science has made incredible progress in discovering truths about the natural world. Ergo, its powerful methods should be useful to religion to augment our knowledge of God and all things spiritual. Templeton is putting his money where his mouth is, by funding several scientific projects (at the rate of hundreds of thousands of dollars each) as well as by giving out the Templeton Prize, which is currently heftier than the Nobel (the latest recipient is physicist Paul Davies).

Examples of the science-to-religion connection that Templeton envisions are illuminating. His foundation has given hard cash to Pietro Pietrini of the National Institute of Neurological Disorders and Stroke to study "imaging brain activity in forgiving people" ($125,000); Lee Dugatkin of the University of Louisville has been awarded $62,757 for research on "evolutionary and Judaic approaches to forgiving behavior." While Herbert Benson of Harvard is aided in answering the question "Does intercessory prayer help sick people?" and Frans de Waal of Emory University is investigating "forgiveness" among primates, also with grants from Templeton.

I think Templeton's efforts (but not necessarily those of all the researchers who are receiving his money) fall into what can be termed *scientific theism*, that is, the idea that one can scientifically investigate the mind of God. This particular position within the science and religion universe is actually a very old and revered one, having its roots in classical Christian Apologetics a la St. Thomas Aquinas and continuing today through the efforts of individuals like Plantinga and William Craig (see Chapter 10).

If, however, one believes in a more remote kind of God but wishes to retain the concept of science and religion uncovering the same truth, the choice is not limited to scientific theism. Two other positions are possible, depending on whether one subscribes to a naturalistic or to a deistic God. For lack of better terms I labeled them *Strong Anthropic Principle* and *Weak Anthropic Principle*, the latter also known as the "God of the Big Bang." Of course, throughout this discussion the actual position of individuals within my framework may be different from what I suggest here, either because the boundaries between categories are fuzzy rather than well delineated, or because I may have misunderstood particular individuals' positions based on their writings (in which case I of course apologize).

The Weak Anthropic Principle basically says that there is very little variation in the known constants and laws of physics that could be tolerated if the universe were to be a place friendly to life as we know it (Casti 1989). As is, this is a rather trivial observation, but if one wants to read philosophical implications into it, then it is a small leap of faith to claim that the universe was created *because* life had to exist. From here, there is another small logical gap to the Strong Anthropic Principle, which infers an intelligent designer with a purpose behind the whole shebang (Tipler 1995). Several physicists and cosmologists have played with different versions of the anthropic principle, including Frank Tipler (one of the original proponents of the principle) and Paul Davies, whose exact position on the matter is a bit more difficult to ascertain, but whose awkward combination of a connection with the Templeton Foundation and very careful speculative writings on cosmology (Davies 1993) puts him squarely in the upper left corner of my diagram.

The anthropic principle is difficult to counter on purely philosophical grounds (Ruse in press), other than it seems to be begging the question and somehow reverses the direction of causality (a general cause is inferred from the observation of a particular result of that cause). Furthermore, it is not useful as a scientific hypothesis, since all it says is that we are here because we are here because we are here. The principle has, however, been effectively attacked on positive scientific grounds by showing that in fact many more possible universes could support some sort of life, an attack that has weakened the "improbabilistic" argument on which the principle is based (Stenger 1996; Leikind 1997). A more fatal blow might come in the near future from superstring theory, the current working hypothesis for the reconciliation of the theories of relativity and of quantum mechanics, for which I will have to refer the reader to a more exhaustive and highly accessible treatment (Greene 1999).

While all these positions are compatible with Shermer's "same worlds" scenario, it is clear that a scientist feels more and more comfortable the closer one moves toward the upper end of the ordinate in my diagram, that is, the more fuzzy and distant the concept of God becomes (notice that one can adopt a Strong Anthropic Principle scenario and slip toward a personal God at the same time, as indicated by the arrow in the figure). This observation in and of itself, I think, points toward a fundamental degree of discomfort between science and religion.

Gould, the Pope, and Houston Smith

When we examine the portion of the graph in Figure 6.2 that falls in the area identified by Shermer as the domain of the "separate worlds" model, we deal with a range of characters that go from agnostic evolutionary biologist Stephen J. Gould (Harvard) and atheist Eugenie Scott (National Center for Science Education) to the pope himself, passing through the ambiguous position of the charismatic Houston Smith (the author of *The World's Religions*, Smith 1991). Let's see how this variation is again accounted for by the different concepts of God these positions reflect.

Several scientists, philosophers, and skeptics, including Gould, Shermer (1998), Scott, Ernst Mayr (1999), Z. Pazameta (1999), and Michael Ruse (in press) loosely fall into the position outlined by Gould as NOMA, or Non-Overlapping Magisteria (Gould 1997; 1999). As we have seen in Chapter 5, the idea is basically that science deals with facts and religion with morality;

the first focuses on what is, the latter on what ought to be. Citing what in philosophy is known as the "naturalistic fallacy" (Moore 1903), the principle that one cannot derive what ought to be from what is, Gould concludes that science and religion are forever separate. Another way to look at NOMA has been articulated by Scott (1999) when she makes the distinction between methodological and philosophical naturalism (see Chapter 2). According to Scott, science adopts naturalism as a convenient tool for conducting research, in a methodological sense. In order to deny the existence of God, however, one has to be a naturalist in the philosophical sense of the term, that is, one has to *conclude* that the physical world is all there is out there. Ergo, science cannot inform us as to the existence of God, because naturalism is not a scientific conclusion, but an assumption of the scientific method. If science does not have anything to say about God (and obviously, also according to Scott, religion is incapable of informing science about the natural world), then NOMA or a similar position logically follows. I have criticized Gould's (Pigliucci 1999 and Chapter 5) as well as Scott's (Chapter 2) positions already, therefore the reader is referred to those references for more details.

Moving down the God axis in Figure 6.2 we come to what I have termed "theistic science" (as opposed to scientific theism, which we have encountered above). It is not exactly clear how well Houston Smith actually fits into this category, but his position is the closest I could find to represent the land between NOMA and the pope (notice the diagonal arrow bridging theistic science and scientific theism, that could to some extent represent two sides of the same coin). Smith argues against scientism, an idea that can be defined in different ways. I would argue that scientism is the concept that science can and will resolve every question or problem in any realm if given enough time and resources. I do not think that even the most grant-hungry professional researchers readily subscribe to it, but I know of individuals who seem to. Smith, however, thinks of scientism (for example in a lecture delivered at Oak Ridge, Tennessee, in 1998) as the idea that the scientific method is the best way to investigate reality. According to Smith there are other ways, which include intuition and religious revelation. The important point is that these alternatives are not available within science, thereby excluding certain aspects of "reality" from scientific investigation. Smith was also – together with Alvin Plantinga, whom we have already encountered in the scientific theism corner – the one who asked the National Association of Biology Teachers (NABT) to change their definition of evolution by dropping philosophically (and politically) loaded words such as "impersonal" and "unguided" (referring to the process of natural selection: Palevitz and Lewis 1999 and Chapter 2).

While the area occupied by theistic science is in fact borderline and intermixed with different degrees of scientific theism and NOMA (and I do not know to which specific mix Smith would most gladly subscribe), the general idea is that according to theistic science it is perfectly sensible to say that there is a God as well as a physical universe out there. The distinctive point of theistic science is that the God behind the universe works in very subtle ways and entirely through natural laws, so that it is impossible or at least very difficult to infer his presence (unlike the case of the Anthropic Principle discussed above, where an intelligent designer is the only possible conclusion). As the reader can see, then, the center of the diagram in Figure 6.2 is a rather gray area from which one can easily move to almost any other position in the diagram by introducing one or more caveats. If applied to evolution in particular, theistic science translates into theistic evolution. This is the idea that evolutionary theory is by and large correct (therefore science is on solid ground), but it includes the added twist that evolution is the (rather inefficient and clumsy, I would add) way God works. This is what Barry Lynn (Americans United for the Separation of Church and State) may have meant when he concluded the 1997 PBS "Firing Line" debate for the evolution side by suggesting that the Word (God) in the beginning may simply have been "Evolve!"

The pope's position, which we have encountered in Chapter 5, assumes the personal God of Catholics but it includes an element of fuzziness as well, and it is accompanied by an arrow pointing left in Figure 6.2 because one could think of it as a variation of the same worlds model that does not go quite as far as scientific theism a la Templeton. In a letter written to the Pontifical Academy of Sciences (John Paul II 1997), the pope declared that Christians should not reject the findings of modern science, and evolutionary theory in particular. This is because, in his words, "Truth cannot contradict Truth" (which is why this position could be construed as leaning toward the left side of the diagram). However, as we have seen in Chapter 5, he drew a line at the origin of the human soul, which of course had to be injected directly by God. This creates a rather abrupt discontinuity because it introduces an arbitrary dualism within the process of human evolution, a stratagem with which science does not sit very well, as Dawkins pointed out (Dawkins 1999). John Paul II more recently published *"Fides et Ratio"* (available on the Internet at http://www.cin.org/jp2/fides.html), a scholarly contribution arguing for the fact that science and faith can be used to uncover parallel realities for which each is best equipped, pretty much what Gould states are the foundations of NOMA. It is because of this position and the implied dualism that I situated the pope toward the center of the diagram.

Within the separate (or almost separate) worlds, therefore, one can go from essentially no conflict between science and religion if a deistic God is considered, to a position that is logically possible but increasingly inconsistent with both Ockham's razor and Hume's dictum. Depending on how much importance one accords to the philosophical foundations of science, this area of the Science-Religion space can be more or less comfortably inhabited by moderate scientists or moderate religionists.

The many faces of creationism

The lower right corner of Figure 6.2 is inhabited by two positions whose exponents have a lot in common but who despise each other almost as much as they are opposed to everything else that populates the science and religion conceptual space. I am referring to "classical" creationism as embodied, for example, by Duane Gish (1995, see Chapter 11) and his fellow "scientists" at the Institute for Creation Research (http://www.icr.org/), and to the "neo-creationism" movement represented among others by Michael Behe (1996), William Dembski (1998), Phillip Johnson (1997) and other associates of the "Discovery Institute" (http://www.discovery.org).

No matter what kind of creationist you are, you are very likely to believe in a personal God and in a fundamental conflict between science and religion[24] (or at least, so it seems from the array of publications within both the classical and neo-creationist camps). The main difference between Gish's group and Johnson's ensemble is that the latter is more sophisticated philosophically and makes a slicker use of scientific terminology and pseudo-scientific concepts. They are also much more politically savvy, though they do not enjoy the grassroots support of classical creationists because they ironically tend to be seen by most people as "too intellectual." Essentially, most neo-creationists (among whom there is quite a bit of variation, by the way) do not believe in a young earth, accept micro-evolution (though recently so do some classical creationists – a sign of progress?), don't believe in the literal truth of the Bible, and don't even call themselves creationists: the preferred term for their version of things is "intelligent design" (some even go so far as to avoid stating just who this intelligent designer might be).

While debunking classical creationism is nowadays not too trying of an intellectual exercise (for introductions see: Trott 1994; McIver 1996; Shermer 1997; and Chapter 11), neo-creationists are quite something else. Behe's book on "irreducible complexity" makes the point that the molecular machinery of living organisms is so complex and necessitates all of its parts working in synchrony that it must have been designed. A good rebuttal has to span from David Hume's devastating critique of the generalized version of the argument from design (Hume 1779) to modern findings on the evolution of specific biochemical pathways (Shanks and Joplin 1999). Dembski's reasoning that intelligent design can be inferred by excluding all other alternative hypotheses on probabilistic grounds entirely misses the more parsimonious explanation of unintelligent design (i.e., natural selection) to account for biological history and diversity (Pigliucci 2000). Finally, Johnson's main thrust that science is really a philosophical enterprise with no better claim to reality than religion can be dealt with by using

---

[24] Of course, from a creationist point of view, this is a conflict between "poor" science, such as evolution, and religion. If the academic establishment were to adopt creation science or intelligent design theory, this group would shift to the opposite site of the diagram, together with scientific theism. For good reasons why this should not happen consult any defense of evolutionary biology (for example: NAS 1998; Wise 1998).

Provine's argument about philosophical naturalism discussed in Chapter 2.

The twin souls of skepticism

Last, but by no means least, let me consider the two main versions of modern skepticism, which have produced a lively debate within the skeptical community (e.g., Dawkins 1999; Kurtz 1999; Novella and Bloomberg 1999; Pazameta 1999; Scott 1999) and which represent the forefront of rational thinking about science and religion. I am referring to what in Figure 6.2 are labeled "scientific skepticism" and "scientific rationalism," positions associated with people such as Martin Gardner, Carl Sagan, Will Provine, and Richard Dawkins (the fact that my name falls in one of those fields merely reflects the influence that these people have had on my own thinking; see also: Allen 1999; Palevitz 1999; Pinker 1999; Raymo 1999).

First, notice that both skeptical positions are rather unusual, in that they span more than one quadrant, diagonally in the case of scientific skepticism, vertically for scientific rationalism. Scientific skepticism is the position that skepticism is possible only in regard to questions and claims that can be investigated empirically (i.e., scientifically). For example, Novella and Bloomberg (1999) state that "Claims that are not testable are simply outside the realm of science". However, scientific skepticism immediately embarks on a slippery slope that the same authors acknowledge in their article. They admit that "Testable religious claims, such as those of creationists, faith healers, and miracle men are amenable to scientific skepticism," so that religion is not *entirely* out of the scope of skeptical inquiry. Furthermore, they acknowledge that there is no distinction in principle between religion and any other kind of nonsense believed by all sorts of people: "There is no distinction between believing in leprechauns, alien abductions, ESP, reincarnation, or the existence of God – each equally lacks objective evidence. From this perspective, separating out the latter two beliefs and labeling them as religion – thereby exempting them from critical analysis – is intellectually dishonest." That is, scientific skepticism converges toward scientific rationalism (see below) when one considers personal gods that intervene in everyday life, but moves toward a NOMA-like position if God is defined in a distant and incomprehensible fashion.

One of the most convincing arguments adduced by scientific skeptics to keep religion out of skeptical inquiry is that a believer can always come up with unfalsifiable ad hoc explanations of any inconsistency in a religious belief. While this is certainly true, is this not an equally valid critique of, say, skeptical inquiry into paranormal phenomena? After all, how many times have we heard the "true believers" (Raymo 1998) saying that the reason a medium failed a controlled test is because of the negative vibrations produced by the skeptic? Nicholas Humphrey (1996) in his excellent *Leaps of Faith* even reports that paranormalists have come up with a negative theory of ESP that "predicts" that the frequency of genuine paranormal phenomena is inversely proportional to attempts at empirically investigating them! It surely sounds to me very much like a religious believer attempting at all costs and in the face of evidence and logic to save her cherished myth.

As much as one might question scientific skepticism on the basis of more or less subtle philosophical points, there is of course another, more practical side to this position, that also makes for a convergence toward NOMA. As Novella and Bloomberg honestly admit, it is a matter of resources: "This single issue, which is not central to our purpose {as skeptics}, could potentially drain our resources, monopolize our public image, and alienate many potential skeptics" (Novella and Bloomberg 1999). This is, unfortunately, very true. It is also true that the skeptic community cannot and should not require any article of faith (such as unbelief in God) from any of its members. However, we must require an agreement to the principle that there are no sacred cows. Anything and everything must be the subject of free inquiry and skeptical investigation. To allow otherwise, for practical or any other kind of reasons, is an intellectual travesty. On the other hand, what can and should be admitted is that God and religion truly do represent only one facet of the universe of interest to skeptics, and that skeptical analyses of the God question may or may not be fruitful. Therefore, let us proceed with caution, but proceed nevertheless.

Of course, I left the best for last This is the position of scientific rationalism. Within this framework, one concludes for the non-existence of any God, not because of certain knowledge, but because of a sliding scale of methods. At one extreme, we can confidently rebut the personal Gods of creationists on firm empirical grounds: scientific evidence is sufficient to conclude beyond reasonable doubt that there never was a worldwide flood and that the evolutionary sequence of the Cosmos does not follow either of the two versions of Genesis (Ledo 1997; Chapter 5). The more we move toward a deistic and fuzzily defined God, however, the more scientific rationalism reaches into its toolbox and shifts from empirical science to logical philosophy *informed* by science. Ultimately, the most convincing arguments against a deistic God are Hume's dictum and Ockham's razor. These are philosophical arguments, but they also constitute the bedrock of all of science,[25] and cannot therefore be dismissed as non-scientific. The reason we trust in these two principles is *because* their application in the empirical sciences has led to such spectacular successes throughout the last three centuries.

Admittedly, the scientific rationalist is on less firm ground the more she moves vertically up in Figure 6.2, but that is not a fatal blow, because no reasonable skeptic asserts her positions as definitive truths. All we are saying is "show us." The main reason I prefer scientific rationalism to scientific skepticism (which is more akin to the philosophical position known as empiricism and espoused by many English philosophers between the 17th and 19th centuries) comes down to a matter of which trade-offs one is more willing to accept. Scientific skepticism trades off the breadth of its inquiry (which is limited) for the power of its methods (which, being based on empirical science, are the most powerful devised by humankind so far). Scientific rationalism, on the other hand,

---

[25] Incidentally, let me clear up a common misunderstanding of Ockham's razor. It does not say that the simplest hypothesis is always the true one; rather, it merely states that when constructing theories to explain an array of observations, one is best served by keeping the number of theoretical constructs to the necessary minimum.

retains as much of the power of science as possible, but uses other instruments – such as philosophy and logic – to expand the scope of its inquiry. As a scientist I have been trained within scientific skepticism; as a somewhat rational human being, I yearn for the wide horizons of scientific rationalism.

Chapter 7 - Is religion good for you?

"If you wish to strive for peace of soul and pleasure, then believe; if you wish to be a devotee of truth, then inquire." (Friedrich Nietzche)

"Use your mentality, wake up to reality." (Cole Porter)

I have argued in Chapter 5 that religion is neither more nor less than one of many forms of superstition. Furthermore, although the unshakeable atheistic position is not defensible on scientific or rational grounds, one can safely conclude against Pascal's wager and consider the probability of the existence of God as minuscule and therefore irrelevant (Chapter 4).

Yet, as much as the rational person should not seriously entertain the possibility of the existence of God, a very interesting and closely related question deserves the attention of even the staunchest secular humanist. What if religion, *in spite of being not true*, is actually good for (some) people? This pragmatic approach to the question has been brought forth by an unlikely source. A religious fundamentalist with whom I have been in contact because of my involvement with "Darwin Day" at the University of Tennessee (http://fp.bio.utk.edu/darwin) has sent me an article published in the *Backgrounder*, a publication of the Heritage Foundation, one of the most powerful conservative think tanks in the United States.

The idea is not, of course, a new one – for example, Benjamin Franklin, George Washington, and others among America's Founding Fathers argued for the social wisdom or even necessity of promoting religious belief for the ordinary citizen. As Edwin Gaustad has noted, "Though himself surely a freethinker, Franklin cautioned other freethinkers to be careful about dismissing institutional religion too lightly or too quickly: 'Think how great a proportion of Mankind,' he warned in 1757, 'consists of weak and ignorant Men and Women, and of inexperienc'd Youth of both Sexes, who have need of the Motives of Religion to restrain them from Vice, to support their Virtue, and retain them in the Practice of it till it becomes *habitual*, which is the great Point for its Security'" (Gaustad 1987). And Washington biographer Barry Schwartz wrote about the U.S.'s early leaders, "Following a tradition transmitted from Cicero, through Machiavelli, to their own contemporaries like Paine and Jefferson, the less pious men of the time [late 18th century America] saw in religion a necessary and assured support of civil society. Although guided in their own conduct by secular traditions, they felt that only religion could unite the masses and induce their submission to custom and law" (Schwartz 1987).

In the following, I will be using an article by P.F. Fagan (1996) not because he presents novel (or even particularly authoritative) arguments, but simply because his line of reasoning is so widespread among conservative religious Americans of the late 20th and early 21st century. Fagan simply serves the purpose of providing a consistent and comprehensive presentation of a doctrine that has undergone many transformations throughout the history of humanity – and therefore a more firm and current starting point for a discussion on religion and society. Perhaps most importantly, the Heritage Foundation article (and their policy in general) is characteristic of modern religious conservatives' approach of presenting pseudo-scientific arguments backed by apparently incontrovertible statistics to make their case. Essentially, this case is that religion matters because it has a positive impact on social stability. Assuming for the moment that social stability actually is a good thing (at least in some countries and for some period of time) is there any evidence to support this interesting claim? And if so, should a rational person accept religion as a sort of unavoidable evil that somehow benefits society, or is there an alternative?

The evidence on the social effects of religion

Fagan's article is an amusing mix of rhetoric, a not very subtly trumpeted political agenda, a dearth of references to the long traditions that try to make or counter his same case, and not much in the way of supporting evidence. Nevertheless, some of the basic assertions still hold true. For example, Fagan presents a diagram that illustrates quite clearly two interesting facts: first, between 1979 and 1982 people who never attended church had a lower income than people who attended on a weekly basis. Second, regardless of income level, broken families were less likely to attend church than intact families.

The author's conclusions from these data are that church attendance keeps families together, and that if you go to church you'll make more money. That may very well be true. However, Fagan doesn't even consider some of the logical alternatives. For example, it may be that if you find yourself in a broken family, you will have a much lower income due to the fact that your spouse is not there to support you. This, in turn, might put so much pressure and demand on your time and efforts, that you might not consider attending church a high priority in that phase of your life. This alternative explanation completely reverses Fagan's implied chain of causality while leaving the facts unaltered. I am not suggesting that my explanation is better, but simply that the data do not provide us with a way to discard one possibility in favor of the other. There is a profound difference between correlational evidence and an understanding of causality.

Another piece of "hard" evidence presented by the Heritage Foundation's pamphlet concerns the relationship between suicide rate and church attendance. When comparing male and female white and black populations in the U.S., it turns out that the more one attends church, the less likely that person is to commit suicide. Interestingly, the suicide rate is highest for white males, followed by black males, then white females, and finally black females. Fagan's conclusion, obviously, is that if you like to keep your skin longer, you better show up on Sunday mornings. Again, however, all we have is a correlation, that by its nature can be the outcome of many different causal pathways. For example, it is very plausible to argue that if you are depressed enough to think about taking your own life, church attendance is not going to rank high on your priority—a conclusion that would again reverse the causal link.

That a high level of stress in life and less time available may be the true factors underpinning this relationship is consistent with the other observation that Fagan leaves unexplained: the gender gap. Regardless of race, males are more prone to suicide and less to going to church than females. Could it be that this is because in our still not egalitarian society males spend much more time than females outside the house and are under more intense stress on the job? Once more, I am not claiming that this is indeed the case (the data presented by the Heritage Foundation are insufficient to decide one way or the other); I am simply suggesting that a little bit of mental elasticity will show that there are plenty of other explanations, and that therefore more research, not a moral pronouncement, is necessary.

What else is religion good for?

Fagan goes on to say that religion also has the following (less clearly substantiated) benefits on society and individuals. It decreases alcoholism and drug abuse; it causes fewer out of wedlock births; it leads to a lowering of the divorce rate; it increases childbirth; it reduces cohabitation; it increases obedience to authority; and it encourages "conventional" morality. Furthermore, husbands are more "stable" (probably meaning that they don't go around having sex with other people) and wives have more satisfying orgasms if they attend church regularly (as funny as the latter statement may sound).

Notice that there are four groups of assertions here that I will analyze in turn. A first group comprises alleged effects of religion that we all would like to see no matter what caused them. It is indubitable that less drug abuse (though not necessarily *use*) or decreased alcoholism are good for individuals and for society at large. Again, however, we are faced with the perennial problem of causality. Even if there is a significant negative correlation between drug use and church attendance, this does by no means imply that going to church is the *cause* of reduced drug use. It is equally (or more?) reasonable to suggest, for example, that if your life is in such a state of disrepair that you don't think there is anything better to do than take drugs, chances are you also think that it is pointless to go to church. Therefore, both decreased church attendance and increased drug use may be the outcome of the same underlying cause, and not lead from one to the other. Of course, the truth may lie somewhere in between. We simply do not know at this point, a situation that – again – justifies caution, not grand statements of any sort.

A second group of effects are to say the least morally neutral (unless you happen to be advocating a very partisan and remarkably conservative viewpoint, such as the Heritage Foundation's). For example, out of wedlock births are not intrinsically good or bad. They are just part of life. What makes them a problem in modern American society is the widespread condemnation and social ostracism of the practice. Single mothers (or fathers) find themselves in the position of having to deal with artificial hurdles such as lack of economic or social assistance, which makes their already logistically precarious position often desperate. But the church doesn't have anything positive to contribute to this situation, since it is mostly *because* of widespread religion-inspired bigotry that out of wedlock children are so much worse off than their in-wedlock counterparts.

To this second group also belong lowered divorce and cohabitation rates. If you want to cohabit with somebody before (or instead of) getting married, that is your business, and nobody can sustain a reasonable argument that such practice is bad for everybody. As for divorce, it is quite clear that a lower divorce rate imposed by religious superstition also brings a higher frequency of spousal (mostly women's) abuse, both physical and mental. And the effects of a violent (or even simply unhappy) family environment on children's development are well known. As for conventional morality, this is also a vague and questionable benefit. Conventions (and morality) change through history as a reflection of human needs and understanding of the world and of other humans. It seems to me that one can easily make an argument that "conventional" morality is as much detrimental as it may be desirable, and that the choice of which morality to follow in the case of actions affecting consenting adults should be left to individuals.[26]

---

[26] Notice that even Christian morality has evolved, like any other set of social rules. As much as Christian theologians cry foul when one points out the relativity of moral judgments (see Chapter 10), not many modern Christians would stone to death their children because of disobedience, as the Bible says they should. *Prov. 23:13-14* reads: "Withhold not correction from the child: for if thou beatest him with the rod, he shall not die. Thou shalt beat him with the rod, and shalt deliver his soul from hell." According to Mosaic law, parents were to stone children to death or run them through with a sword if they were stubborn or espoused a "false doctrine" of some sort (Green 1999). Has God

The third group of alleged "positive" effects of religion actually comprises outcomes that no rational human being would really want to see occur. Increased child birth rate is probably the most stunning one. In a rare show of sympathy with the current Catholic doctrine promulgated by pope John Paul II, the Heritage Foundation would like the world to grow even faster than it already is. Forget about overpopulation, famine, environmental pollution, and war. What we really need are more children. One cannot avoid be reminded of the immortal *Monty Python*'s song in *The Meaning of Life*:

> Every sperm is sacred,
> every sperm is great,
> if a sperm is wasted,
> god gets quite irate.

As for obedience to authority, I hardly see how that is a virtue that we want to spread farther than it already has. In the name of authority for authority's sake human beings have repeatedly massacred each other since the beginning of time, and I really don't see why anyone would want to encourage such a blind-faith approach to life's complex situations. On the other hand, if attendance to church will be found to increase the ability to think rationally and to make decisions based on evidence, then I will send a few bucks to the Heritage Foundation right away. But I doubt that my savings are likely to be threatened any time soon by this promise.

The final group of "consequences" of church attendance is made up of things that are simply incredible or at least hard to prove one way or the other. Nothing that I learned in catechism prepared me for the assertion that church ladies have better orgasms than the rest of the world (but then again, I attended a Catholic course). The problem with these sorts of statements is that they are based on self-evaluation, and every psychology major knows that self-reported levels of satisfaction are always suspect. It is also very possible that a woman with "worldly experience" may be satisfied some of the times but not all of the times. That is a

---

changed his mind about what is right during the last few thousand years, or are modern Christians more charitable than their own God?

reasonable outcome of most experiences in life. On the other hand, a woman with no available paragons, may very well be satisfied with what she has simply because she doesn't know any alternative.

As for marital "stability," it may or may not be a good thing, since it also varies with different societies and species, and therefore depending on the genetic background and environment one is considering. Regardless, this is again a problem of self-reporting. Obviously, to say one thing is advantageous (you come across as an honest, god-fearing man) and to say the opposite

Fig. 7.1. The difference between the simple observation of a correlation between two variables (left) and the actual chain of steps that leads to a sound acceptance or rejection of such correlation as being the reflection of a causal connection between the two variables (right). A correlation is simply a mathematical or graphical relationship (broken line) between any two variables characterized by a slope that is a direct estimate of the correlation coefficient (the intercept, where the broken line meets the Y-axis, becomes relevant in a related statistical analysis known as regression). A correlation is usually computed between two variables because of some initial observations or a specific hypothesis one wishes to test (such as the healing effect of prayer). However, a good scientific investigation would not stop at these first steps but proceed to: a) formulate as precise an hypothesis as possible on how the actual causal mechanism might work; which leads to b) the design of further experiment or observations in order to test the proposed causal mechanism; c) finally, the hypothesized causal connection between the two variables is either rejected or provisionally accepted as true, depending on the outcome of the previous step.

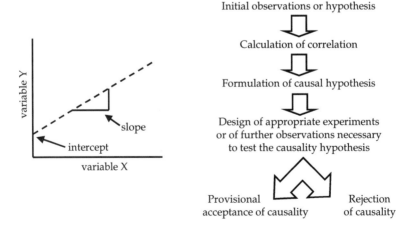

(even if true) may lead you into uncharted territory, or straight into trouble. In other words, both for orgasms and for marital stability (and even more so for vaguer claims to higher "happiness") there is no baseline and no independent objective measurement. One may still suggest, however, that even "perceived" happiness (that is, inconsistent with factual evidence) may be better than other – perhaps more realistic – attitudes because it will improve the individual's sense of self-esteem and belonging. I will return later to why this is not as good as it sounds.

Given that of the several "advantages" to religion and church attendance mentioned by Fagan, many are either neutral or deleterious to both society and individuals, one is tempted to forgo a bit of drug and alcohol abuse for the sake of reduced world population and increased self-determination. But even if you were hoping for a brave new world of people who blindly follow authority and spend their time making babies, there are more and larger problems with the scenario presented by the Heritage Foundation and uncritically adopted by so many conservative Christians.

A side-trip into the healing effects of prayer

Before we proceed to discuss more wide-ranging problems with the benefits of religion using Fagan's article as our reference point, I have to comment on an inconspicuous observation on his part that, if true, would entirely demolish whatever arguments I am going to propose in this chapter. The reference is to the alleged healing effects of third-party prayers. Fagan himself must be aware that this is a delicate and potentially exploding (or imploding) matter, because he carefully prefaces his explanation of the experiment as "one of the most *unusual* ... in medical history" (my emphasis).

The facts are these. Dr. Robert B. Byrd, a cardiologist at the University of California-San Francisco, has performed a double blind study in which he compared the aftermath of cardiac surgery in a control group of patients with those of patients for whom someone else was praying (unbeknownst to them). The double blind protocol, in which neither the patients nor the doctors knew who was in the treatment and who was the control, is one of the safest and most accurate approaches to experimental science. The results, published in the *Southern Medical Journal* in 1988 were, if taken at face value, astounding. The patients prayed for had significantly (in a statistical sense) fewer complications than the control group. Is this the first experimental proof available of the existence of the supernatural? Given the implications, you would expect that people rushed to do what scientists always do when they smell Nobel Prize: to repeat the experiment.

A careful search of the literature and inquiries with editors of medical journals revealed only two other studies along the same lines as Byrd's, both with negative results (Witmer and Zimmerman 1991). Furthermore, a critical reading of Byrd's original paper by Witmer and Zimmerman found a few inconsistencies and causes for doubt.

First, many of the complications listed by Byrd were actually multiple symptoms of the same biological problem, but they were counted as independent occurrences. Therefore, even if just one patient had experienced the problem, her contribution to the statistical results would be multiplied by however many symptoms were described. Given the typically small sample size of this kind of study, this may be enough to invalidate the whole enterprise since one hit is counted as multiple ones (a problem known in statistics as lack of independence in the data).

Second, apparently the double blind protocol was not followed too scrupulously, because the people who prayed were regularly updated on the status of "their" patients. This implies an unbroken chain of knowledge of who was in the control group and who in the treatment between the patients and the praying group. Once this kind of information is out, the door is open for the possibility of a placebo effect (see below).

Third, even if we can find a *statistically significant* effect of prayer, what does that tell us about God? That he works by small increments, putting energy into a task that is proportional to the amount of prayer that is done? Alternatively, one could think that God's power is actually very limited, so that he can only increase the chances of survival of a patient by a little bit, but not much. Either way, I am quite confident this is not the kind of God Fagan and the Heritage Foundation were thinking about.

There is one final fundamental flaw with pray-at-a-distance experiments. How do we control for the background "noise"? Presumably, both subjects and controls had relatives, and these relatives might have been religious (and even belong to different religions). How do we know that *they* were not praying, thereby interfering with the outcome of the experiment? And what about people throughout the world who pray for *everybody*, presumably including both the control and the experimental group in Byrd's experiment? Much more stringent scientific protocols would have to be devised before we can accept *prima facie* evidence of the effects of intercessory prayer.

A more recent review of the entire available literature on the religion-medicine connection by Sloan et al. (1999) published in the prestigious medical journal *Lancet* should dampen Fagan's and associates' enthusiasm even more. Sloan and colleagues found that sophisticated multivariate statistical techniques have been used in published papers on the healing effect of religion, but that the authors did not provide the necessary details about the statistics so obtained, as normally required in peer-reviewed journals. Sloan et al. also encountered studies in which the subjects were not chosen randomly, violating another fundamental tenet of scientific analysis. They reported that many studies do not adequately control for additional variables that may affect the outcome, and that when this control is carried out the results become not significant (in a statistical sense). They concluded their analyses with a very sober warning: "suggestions that religious activity will promote health, that illness is the result of insufficient faith, are unwarranted."

These cautionary statements notwithstanding, the belief in the healing prayer phenomenon is hard to kill. A few weeks after Sloan et al.'s paper, another study along the same lines of Byrd's was published by the *Archives of Internal Medicine* (Harris et al. 1999). The study claimed to have found a significant *overall* (i.e., cumulating several different indicators) difference between the medical course of people prayed for vs. non-prayed for. Yet, when one examines the paper closely, it turns out that *none* of the 35 medical indicators used was actually statistically different between the two groups. This puts the existence of an overall effect in question, and under the best-case scenario it reduces it to a little more than a blip on the statistical screen. Yet, hope, like faith, springs eternal.[27]

What is the control group?

Let us go back to the main argument, exemplified by Fagan, that religion is good for society regardless of its potential supernatural connection. As we have seen in the case of Byrd's experiment, any scientific survey requires a "control group," that is a group of individuals or subjects or observations that provide the logical contrast with the "treatment group." So, for example, if you are interested in the potentially beneficial effects of a new drug to cure cancer you will not simply report the number of patients who took the drug and had a positive outcome of the disease. That way you have not established that it is better to take the drug, because "better" implies the question "better than what?" A more proper way to go about it is to establish two groups of patients, one to which you administer the drug, the other that does not get it. If the group that took the drug experiences a significantly (in a statistical sense) higher rate of recovery, this is positive evidence that the drug is indeed beneficial.

It may superficially appear that the Heritage Foundation's report does meet this basic criterion of scientific analysis. After all, the document is comparing people who attend church regularly to people who don't (or who attend less frequently). Shouldn't that be enough? Actually, no. The art of devising the correct control in any study is a very sophisticated one (Figure 7.2). For example, let us consider again our anti-cancer drug. The simple control of patients who did not receive the drug is not sufficient. It may be that the very act of taking something (regardless of what it is) may have improved the health of the treated patients. How is that possible? Through the power of self-suggestion, an effect known as a "placebo" (Beyerstein 1997; Brown 1998). Therefore, the proper way to conduct an experiment to distinguish between improvements due to the drug and those due to the placebo effect is to have *two* controls. On the one hand we need patients who are

---

[27] For a more comprehensive critique of both Byrd's and Harris et al.'s studies, see Tessman and Tessman (2000).

not treated at all. On the other hand, we need patients who think they are being treated (e.g., they receive a pill, or an injection), but they are not (the pill is made of pure sugar, or the injection contains only water).

Analogously, the Heritage Foundation's report is missing a crucial control: people who don't go to church but espouse a positive alternative, such as active atheists, or secular humanists. If we just compare the attitudes and behaviors of people who are fervent believers with those who are disenchanted with religion but have not found an alternative, we are automatically biasing the outcome. What we are doing is to compare happy (for whatever reason) people with people who are going through a crisis. Is it such a surprise, then, that we find that church attendance has a "positive" effect?

On the other hand, let us consider as a second control group people who have made a positive decision of being non-religious. These are individuals who may be as happy, outgoing, and satisfied (sexually or otherwise) as much as the most fervent Christians. Furthermore, they may not be alcoholics or drug abusers, and may even experience marital "stability" (although my experience is that they will probably still not blindly follow authority, and that they would be scared by anything labeled as "conventional morality"). Unfortunately for our discussion, this group of people has hardly been probed by sociologists and psychologists (Madigan 1993), so we are left with an inconclusive study at best.

What is so bad about religion?

Even if one cannot make a good case in favor of the alleged positive social effects of religion, does this institution actually harm society? If not, then a reasonable person should just let people fall for whatever superstition they wish to believe in and not be too concerned about the consequences. But the social case against religion is indeed compelling. Of course, no one can blame all the evils of society on one kind of practice or behavior. Equally true is the fact that many (indeed most) religious people are not directly harmful to other individuals. In fact, religious charities can be credited with numerous actions that clearly have benefited humankind. So, what is the problem?

I argue here that intrinsic to the belief in a supernatural power and its worship are a series of inevitable negative consequences that impact individuals and society. You can think of religion as a very powerful medicine with too many side effects. The best thing that can be said about it is that it should be taken with caution, and only in cases in which nothing else has worked.

Some of these side effects of religion have been briefly summarized by Haught (1993), who wrote a book documenting them in more detail (Haught 1990). Religious riots and "holy wars" have been with us since the beginning of recorded history, and they do not seem to go away in our enlightened century. Conflicts between religious groups inhabiting the same geographical areas are everyday news (e.g., Catholics and Protestants in Ireland, Serbs and Muslims in the former Yugoslavia, or Palestinians and Jews in Israel). Cult leaders who bring their followers to mass suicides, or

Fig. 7.2. The necessity of double controls to exclude the possibility of a placebo effect. The rat on the left is being treated with a drug (e.g., to lower his cholesterol). An obvious control is not to inject the rat at all (middle). However, any difference between control and treatment could be due either to the drug or to the shock of receiving an injection. To rule out the latter possibility, we need a second control (right) in which a rat is being injected with water – if the drug has an effect beyond the placebo, one would expect the rat on the left to behave differently from both controls. The magnitude of the placebo effect can be estimated by comparing the two controls (if there is no difference, there is no placebo effect).

| Treatment (drug in syringe) | Control 1 (no drug or syringe) | Control 2 (no drug in the syringe, checks for placebo effect) |

at least sexually abuse and rob them are certainly well known to the American public. The generally abject condition of women wherever fundamentalist religion (especially, but not limited to, the Islamic flavor) takes hold are well recognized. Christian extremists in the United States have bombed medical facilities and killed doctors because of dissenting beliefs. Religious zealots have assassinated great political figures: among them, Egyptian President Sadat, Indian Premier Indira Gandhi, and Israeli Prime Minister Rabin.

And these are just crimes that have been on the front pages of 20th century newspapers. The fact that the so-called Holy Inquisition burned an estimated 200,000 women, that 20 million people were killed in the Taiping Rebellion in China, that Anabaptists were exterminated by both Catholics and Protestants, or that the Crusades caused thousands of victims are just a few of the examples that come to mind. How can we doubt that there is at least *something* wrong with religion? More generally, there is something wrong with *any* ideology, religious or not in nature, which is blindly followed by a mass of people. Religion simply happens to account for the overwhelming majority of ideologies that humans have adopted through history, although other examples during the 20th century include national socialism in Germany and communism in the former Soviet Union. Things are quite different for humanism and science. As Bertrand Russell once put it, "Persecution is used in Theology, not in Arithmetic."

Religion as Prozac for the masses?

Throughout Fagan's article and other similar writings, religion seems to be presented as a sort of supernatural equivalent of Prozac. The argument is roughly that regardless of the truth of religion (that is very sagely rarely expressly advocated), if it does good, it should be supported; of course, Karl Marx had the same idea in mind (albeit with a different take) when he said that religions are the opium of the masses. Should we buy into this utilitarian argument? Are the Heritage Foundation and the modern American Christian Right proposing a non-chemical alternative to mass use of Prozac? Something that can make people happy and content, regardless of the objective reality upon which such feelings may rest?[28] There are two main arguments against the religion-as-Prozac approach.

First, religion, like Prozac, can have undesirable side effects. We have already seen that increased church attendance is not correlated only with positive life styles, such as decreased alcoholism or drug abuse. It seems to bring along definitely negative attributes as well, increased childbirth and blind obedience to authority being the most striking ones. Of course, from a conservative point of view these are not negative side effects, and they only reinforce the main argument. But a large portion of Americans do not seem to think that way, and in fact unconditional obedience to authority is one of the most un-American attributes one can think of. What ever happened to intellectual freedom, freedom of speech, and all those individual liberties that justly figure prominently in the U.S. Constitution and Bill of Rights?

Second, a side effect of religious affiliation seems to be social stagnation. By not doubting authority, one is led not to question the social status quo. While embracing "conventional morality" one is restrained from exploring alternative, possibly better, moral systems. These attitudes would maintain our society in a static limbo, forever stuck in its current status. It can be argued that not even a much better and fairer society than our own should be static, because conditions change and societies and human beings need to adapt to the new conditions. But we are a far cry from any universally desirable societal state (assuming that such a thing is anything more than a naïve utopia)! So, any force that stifles progress and change should be seen as having a negative social effect, not to be encouraged.

Of course, I am not advocating change for the sake of change. Basic theorems of mathematical evolutionary biology tell us that change in the presence of constant conditions can only lead to trouble (usually extinction) (Fisher 1930). But modern biology

---

[28] Notice that I am not for a moment suggesting that Prozac or other similar medicines are intrinsically bad. They are of tremendous help for *sick* people who suffer from depression or other mental illnesses. What I am saying is that no sane society would apply Prozac to anybody just so that that person would feel "content" about her life.

also provides clear evidence for the so-called "Red Queen" model (van Valen 1973). In Lewis Carrol's *Through the Looking Glass*, the character of the Red Queen is forced to constantly run just to keep her place. Similarly, according to paleontologist Leigh van Valen, species of biological organisms need to keep evolving because the environment in which they live is constantly "deteriorating." Environmental deterioration (i.e., change away from the conditions to which a species is adapted) is often caused by the very existence of that species because of the way it changes its own environment. Humans are certainly a prime example of a species that dramatically alters its own environment, and that therefore has to find a way to adapt to the new conditions that it continually generates.

The same Red Queen principle may well apply to societies. The pre-Colombian societies of northern, central and south America had been essentially stable for long periods of time before they were wiped out by the rapidly changing (after the Renaissance) western society. It does not matter a bit if the American natives were a "better" society because more harmonious with nature: they were exterminated just the same.[29]

I am also not necessarily advocating the kind of change that would make a liberal glow and a conservative tremble. The real world is much too complicated for that simplistic dichotomy. For example, I personally think that sexual freedom is good and that people should experiment whatever and with whomever they want (of course, given reciprocal consent). Nevertheless, the spread and social cost (not just monetary, but in body counts) of fatal diseases such as AIDS has to force a rational mind to reconsider the kind of change in conduct that was a result of the sexual revolution of the 1960s. Not to do so on a matter of principle would be foolish and self-destructive.

All in all, Haught's (1993) conclusion that religion is something akin to Dr. Jekyll and Mr. Hyde seems fair to me. Now, the question is: is there a way of retaining the inestimable services of Jekyll, while pushing Hyde back into the obscure recesses of ignorance and superstition from where he came?

---

[29] Incidentally, there is by now quite a bit of evidence that the moral values and relationship with nature of many "primitive" societies was not at all what our cultural myths portray them to have been (Shermer 1997b).

The real need: a model of reality and positive ways to interact with it

One of the revealing tidbits emerging from the Fagan article is that church attendance may be more efficacious as a social force than religious feelings per se. According to Fagan's own words: "overall church attendance was more strongly related to less drug use than was intensity of religious feeling." Therefore, religion works because it provides people with a community, a sense of belonging, and a way to access moral and practical support from others. This is entirely independent of the supposed Truth of religion or of the existence of God.

Again according to Fagan: "religious beliefs help the individual acquire central organizing principles for life." That is *truly* what human beings need. We need to make sense of life, to feel that it is not a chaotic, random, and most of all uncontrollable series of things that just "happen," despite the fact that it looks that way to the naïve observer. And that is exactly the source of religion's immense power: it is the easy answer to existential questions. If something doesn't make sense or hurts, do not worry yourself too much: there is a higher purpose that, although you currently do not understand, will be clear to you eventually. You will be compensated many times over for the suffering and injustice you are experiencing in this life. There is a universal father who truly loves you and looks after you (though at times he may seem a bit distracted). Who could resist the attraction of such a comforting scenario?

It is not enough to point out its patent absurdity, its contrast with all we know about reality, its internal contradictions. The alternative is too scary for too many people. Science and rationalism, however, can go no further. They cannot provide us with a substitute for a cushy idea of God. They can only guide us through our search to find out what *really* is going on, as opposed to what we wish were happening. According to Schumaker (*Free Inquiry* – Summer 1998), human beings will never be happy with just that, because we have a need for "transcendence." In his words: "We are creatures who do not like an exclusive diet of literal reality."

Perhaps, but perhaps not. I submit that the real fundamental human need is not transcendence, is not fantasy, and does not derive from a "god module" in the brain (see *Skeptical Inquirer* – July/August 1998). The answer, however, is indeed to be found in the brain. Simply put, we need explanations about the world in which we live.

Neurobiologists have long studied the effects of the so-called "split brain." This is a phenomenon in which the *corpus callosum*, the mass of fibers and neurons that connects the left and right hemispheres of our brain, is somehow severed (usually because of preventive surgery to control epilepsy). Once the operation is done, the two parts of the brain work mostly independently of each other, opening the way for scientists to understand which specific tasks each one normally performs.

One of the most mind-blowing (no pun intended) experiments on the split brain sheds a new light on our quest for answers and even on the power of religion. The experiment deals with the mechanism originating false memories. In a specific version of the experiment (Gazzaniga 1998), the left brain (which controls the right eye) is presented with the image of a bird's foot. It is then asked to pick (with the right hand that it controls) among a series of images the one that can be logically associated with the bird's foot. Predictably, it picks the picture of a chicken. The right brain is simultaneously shown (through the left eye) the image of a house and a car under the snow, complete with snowman. It (through the left hand) logically enough picks a shovel. Then the experimenter asks the left brain (the only one capable of articulating vocal responses – the right one is better at drawing) why did he pick the shovel. The left brain could not answer the question, because it literally didn't know what the right brain was doing, given the interruption of the *corpus callosum*. Here is where things become interesting. The left brain *made up a story*. It said that it picked up the shovel in order to clean the chicken's den! Please keep in mind that that was *not* the reason the shovel was chosen, but in the absence of an alternative explanation, the left brain *had* to come up with a plausible scenario, and rapidly made one up from nothing.

This, I think, is how belief in religion works. I am not suggesting that religious people have a severed *corpus callosum*, of course. I am merely pointing out that these experiments demonstrate an innate and fundamental need for the brain to come up with explanations about the world. And if these explanations are missing, as was the case for most of the history of the human species before the recent progress of science, we just invent them.

Where did this compelling necessity to explain the world come from? It is a consequence of evolution, of course. It turns out that this marked asymmetry of functions between the two hemispheres of the brain (called lateralization) is peculiar to humans and possibly to our very close relatives, the chimpanzees. Scientists have thought for a long time that lateralization was an add-on, something that evolved to increase the efficiency of the brain. Recent evidence seems to suggest that, on the contrary, the phenomenon is due to loss of some functions from either

Fig. 7.3. The way the brain works. The two hemispheres are in charge of different aspects of our way of interpreting the world. The left hemisphere controls our general worldview and rationalizes every bit of information within such a view. Dissonant facts are either ignored or twisted to fit. The right hemisphere, on the other hand, feeds discordant data to the left, in a continuous feedback controlled by the corpus callosum, the substance that joins the two hemispheres. In a sense, the right brain is providing "seeds of doubt" to the left one. When enough dissonant information has been fed by the right brain, the left brain occasionally alters its worldview, and we experience a "sudden" change of mind. Our innate necessity to hold on to a coherent worldview, regardless of how flawed it actually is, probably explains why so many people believe in supernatural entities and powers of which there is no evidence.

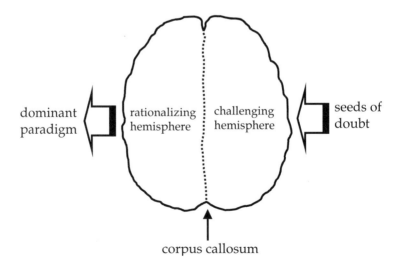

dominant paradigm — rationalizing hemisphere : challenging hemisphere — seeds of doubt

corpus callosum

hemisphere (Gazzaniga 1998). This loss is probably due to the fact that the human (and perhaps other primates') brain has acquired so many functions while being physically constrained in size, that the only way to make room for a new one was to eliminate something else from either hemisphere. Another way to put this is that the two parts of the brain started out (evolutionarily speaking) being exact copies of one another, with all their functions duplicated. Now, if you have a machine that cannot grow much more in size, but each part of which has a double, one way to add new functions is to forgo some of the redundancy and recycle the now freed parts to take over the new functions. That is very likely why the human brain is asymmetric and also why, incidentally, we can understand much more about our own internal information processor than about most other animals' (that tend not to be so asymmetrical).

Now, if the need for religion is not a need for irrationalism and transcendence, but rather a basic need for a model of the world that makes sense, what is the alternative to widespread religion as an engine of social betterment? We need both science (to provide the real answers to questions concerning the world and its meaning), and a positive humanist movement. This latter component is what goes beyond Schumaker's "just the facts are not enough" problem. And religious authorities have understood this (perhaps subconsciously) ages ago.

If you think about it, who has ever heard of a religion practiced by individuals in total isolation? How many people would join a cult that does not provide for a physical (or even virtual) location to meet, exchange ideas and feelings, and generally foster human contact? Even if a religion were true, and it could provide all the answers one wanted, it would fail miserably without Sunday morning congregations and summer picnics. Because human beings do need not only answers (that can be provided by both science and religion), they also need a sense of community and belonging (that so far has mostly been provided by religion).

The reason for this second necessity is, again, evolutionary. Humans are social animals. As such, we have an innate impulse toward companionship and social interactions. It is a biological need. Research on the genetic basis of depression shows that children who are abused or neglected react by turning on physiological anti-stress mechanisms that alter the biochemistry of the brain. If the stress due to social deprivation is prolonged, the brain chemistry becomes permanently altered, and the individual is likely to suffer severe bouts of depression as an adult (see *Scientific American* – July1998).

With all these pieces of the puzzle coming together, it seems clear that the rationalist and humanist movement cannot limit itself to debunking and explaining. It has to provide a social network, a connection that people can use as an alternative to the mindless recitation of prayers on Sunday mornings. Some of the leading exponents of the secular humanist movement in the United States are starting to understand this point, and to do something about it. Of course, how exactly are we going to construct a functional and widespread secular alternative to churches is very much an open question, especially considering that we have a late start by several millennia. The solution will depend on tackling huge logistical problems and gathering large financial resources. And it will especially depend on experimentation throughout communities with what people need and what humanism can offer. But it is a type of experiment that we are strongly advised to foster immediately, because religion is really *not* good for us.

Part III - Creation tales

Perhaps one of the most peculiarly American and most pernicious attacks on science is the threat posed by the many forms of creationism. It is astounding that at the verge of the 21ˢᵗ century, in a society dominated by computers, world economy, and the Internet, still tens of millions of people in one of the most industrialized countries in the world refuse to accept that organisms—including humans—evolve from simpler forms. There are of course very complex cultural and psychological reasons for this regretful situation, ranging from the singular religious and political history of the United States to the threat that so many people feel at admitting that they are not special in the cosmic scheme of things. Nevertheless, one cannot cease to be amazed by the astounding capability of the human mind to ignore the evidence and to continue living in self-constructed fairy tales.

There are many kinds of creationists and the spectrum of opinions they hold about science in general and evolution in particular is wide indeed. It is therefore not easy to address "creationism" in general, as it is impossible to refute the existence of "God" unless one is more precise about what kind of creationism or gods one is talking about. Nevertheless, I think that all beliefs in gods and creationism are essentially wrong, although to a greater or lesser extent, in proportion to how much scientific evidence such positions are willing to include in their creed.

The first of the following two essays deals with the relationship between academic freedom and the teaching of evolution by revisiting one of the most infamous instances in American academic and legal annals: the decision by Judge McGeehan that the noted philosopher and later Nobel Prize Bertrand Russell was "unfit" to teach at City College in New York City. The case offers much to think about in terms not only of what academic freedom is and what its limits are, but also about the very concept of democracy as a balance between the rule of the majority and a tyranny over the minority. Ironically, modern creationists invoke the very same principle of academic freedom when they are barred from teaching their clearly religious doctrines in American public schools, in contradiction with the separation of state and church sanctioned by the First Amendment. They confuse freedom with license, of course. Academic freedom does not mean that anybody can teach anything, regardless of the validity of such teachings. But who establishes such validity? The experts, of course, which in this case are biologists, not creationists. Which brings us to another phobia of the American public, the distrust toward experts of any kind, especially if scientific. It is this pervasive anti-intellectualism that I believe is at the roots of so much trouble between science and religion in the U.S. today.

The second essay is actually a composite of arguments against two books published recently, both advocating the "impossibility" of evolution on mathematical grounds. William Dembski and Fred Hoyle, the authors of the books, could not be further apart on philosophical grounds, and yet they are both convinced of the falsity of the Darwinian theory. Their confidence in such a conclusion is matched only by the size respectively of their own ideological agendas or egos and by their misunderstanding of what evolution is all about. I hope to have made clear in the following pages why their arguments are completely unfounded and, consequently, why Darwinian evolution remains the best—albeit imperfect—explanation of the diversification of life on earth.

Chapter 8 - Academic freedom, creationism, and the meaning of democracy[30]

"Aristotle could have avoided the mistake of thinking that women have fewer teeth than men, by the simple device of asking Mrs. Aristotle to keep her mouth open while he counted." (Bertrand Russell, Unpopular Essays)

This essay was inspired by the reading of "Freedom and the Colleges," by Bertrand Russell, originally written in 1940, and published as part of the collection *Why I am not a Christian* (1957). Russell wrote his piece immediately after American judge McGeehan found him unfit to teach as a professor at City College in New York City, on the grounds of his philosophical and political ideas. It was one of the most public and shameful chapters of academic and judicial history in the United States, and one that is essential to bear in mind more than half a century later.

Something that has plagued America ever since the infamous Scopes trial (Larson 1997) is the debate over what should or should not be taught in the country's schools and especially over who is to make that decision. The evolution-creation controversy is a case in point, and I shall support a view that is unpopular among both religious fundamentalists and evolutionary scientists. But it may turn out to be the healthiest for the American children and therefore the public at large.

Russell opens his essay with a superb definition of "academic freedom":

"The essence of academic freedom is that teachers should be chosen for their expertness in the subject they are to teach and that the judges of this expertness should be other experts. Whether a man is a good mathematician, or physicist, or

---

[30]My friendly nemesis, creationist Phillip Johnson, told me he loved this essay, which made me suspicious that I had not made myself clear enough. Upon re-reading it, however, I still don't see why he should rejoice at its publication. At any rate, here it is.

chemist, can only be judged by other mathematicians, or physicists, or chemists."

This is exactly what exponents of religious agendas do *not* want. From Jennings Bryan at the Scopes trial (1996) to the more recent campaign by Phillip Johnson (1997), the "experts" are painted as a tyrannical elite bent toward undermining the morality of American youth. These self-styled saviors of innocence never explain, of course, exactly why teachers and college professors should conspire to warp the minds of their pupils, but never mind such details of logical consistency.

What fundamentalists and educators mean by democracy is apparently the major stumbling block in the dispute. Following Russell,

"There are two possible views as to the proper functioning of democracy. According to one view, the opinions of the majority should prevail absolutely in all fields. According to the other view, wherever a common decision is not necessary, different opinions should be represented, as nearly as possible, in proportion to their numerical frequency."

The problem, it seems to me, is that educators tend to subscribe to the second view, while religious and – to some extent – political leaders much prefer the first one. In America, this tyranny of the majority is especially evident in the way public schools are run. This appears to be a direct result of the idea that the United States is not made up of citizens, but only of taxpayers. To put it as Russell did:

"Taxpayers think that since they pay the salaries of university teachers they have a right to decide what these men shall teach. This principle, if logically carried out, would mean that all the advantages of superior education enjoyed by university professors are to be nullified, and that their teaching is to be the same as it would be if they had no special competence."

In other words, are we going to teach the best of what we currently know about the world (however provisional such knowledge may be), or shall we decide if the earth is flat or round by majority consensus? Reality has a rather nasty habit of not conforming to our wishes, no matter how majoritarian our views happen to be. Consequently, education is *not* a democratic process by any means, however distasteful this may sound to the American public.

Do any negative consequences result from curtailing or entirely abolishing academic freedom? While Russell offers the case of the economic collapse of Spain after the expulsion of Moors and Jews, and was prophetically hinting at a similar fate for Nazi Germany, I would like to suggest a third, more recent example. It is popular among American conservatives to ascribe the fall of the Soviet Union to the valiant foreign policy of Ronald Reagan. Needless to say, that is simply preposterous, politically motivated, wishful thinking. The USSR in 1989 simply hit a hard wall, which it slowly raised during the course of decades, by adopting absurd economic, political, educational and scientific policies. Reagan just happened to be there when the system collapsed. One of the best-studied instances of the causes of the Soviet collapse is the rise of Lysenkoism during the 1950s, which basically destroyed Russian genetics and set back the entire agricultural machine of that nation by decades. Lysenko was the embodiment of what happens when bigots take hold of academia. His theories of genetics and plant breeding were based not on the best science available, but on political demagogy and ideology, not different in substance from the religious ideology currently permeating most of American politics and promoted by the Christian Right movement.

Fig. 8.1. Bertrand Russell (1872-1970), British philosopher, mathematician, and Nobel laureate. A staunch supporter of freethought and academic freedom, and a harsh critic of organized religion.

As Russell pointed out, part of the problem is the thrill that ignorant bigots get out of dictating what smarter and more educated people than they are can teach or say. He speculates that if the Roman soldier who killed Archimedes were forced to take geometry in school, he must have felt a particular pleasure at repaying the man responsible for his sufferings over triangles and their hypotenuses. We should remember that there usually are very good reasons to trust the "experts." I am certainly not advocating a frame of mind that relinquishes any and all criticism of the official authorities, in whatever guise they may come. But I would hardly appeal to majority opinions upon entering an operation room in a hospital, or while trusting my life to the hands of an airplane pilot. Why should teachers be deprived of a similar level of respect?

Given all of the above, it is hard to disagree with the endless streak of court decisions in favor of teaching evolution and against teaching creationism in the public schools. (Larson {1997} notes that the Scopes trial was the only case in which evolutionists actually lost in court). So far, I trust my biologist colleagues will have found only reasons to rejoice from reading these few lines. The following is why they shouldn't.

Phillip Johnson is a leading creationist (Gardner 1997); Will Provine (http://fp.bio.utk.edu/darwin – to see his address to "Darwin Day 1998"), is a historian of science and evolutionary biologist (see Chapter 2). They actually agree on more than would be expected on the basis of their philosophical and scientific positions (and they both disagree with the majority of creationists and evolutionists, respectively). Provine, in particular, suggests that teachers should encourage open discussions of the creation-evolution controversy in the classroom, contrary to the mainstream position of most educators (embodied by the National Center for Science Education's {NCSE} policy statements: http://www.natcenscied.org/).

The outcry that usually follows Provine's suggestion (which I completely support), is based on five points:

1. We should not teach views we know to be incorrect.
2. The students are not capable of carrying out an informed discussion on the subject.
3. There is not enough time during the academic year.
4. If this is a valid approach for evolution, why not teach flat vs. round earth, or the geocentric vs. the Copernican theory?
5. The teachers are not well equipped to handle a discussion on evolutionary theory.

Of these, point one completely misunderstands Provine's line of reasoning. He does not say that teachers should *teach* both creationism and evolutionism. Of course we know better, therefore we teach evolution. However, the students should be allowed to debate their opinions on the matter. Why? First, because guided discussion (the so-called "Socratic method") is probably one of the best ways to teach critical thinking, as opposed to just imbuing kids with notions they'll forget as soon as the term is over. Second, because about 50% of the American population believes in some form of creationism and only about 10% of Americans think that a god doesn't have anything to do with evolution! These are staggering statistics that must be faced with something more honest and constructive than silencing a large portion of the class under penalty of failing the course.

The second point, that the students don't have the ability of carrying out such discussions, is not only an insult to the intelligence of young people, but it also dramatically underestimates the wealth of information on the subject available in libraries or on the World Wide Web. The teacher could easily *guide* the pupils to clear and informative web sites *on both sides* of the issue, making the teaching of evolution a fun and interactive part of the curriculum.

The idea that there isn't enough time to do this is more a reflection of misguided priorities than anything else. As a teacher myself, I am much happier when my students get their critical sense sharpened and their understanding of evolution improved by the end of the semester, rather than go through every single nuance of the curriculum and come up with a bunch of empty factoids at the end.

Why not advocate doing this for other obsolete theories as well (I wish to remind the reader that creationism is indeed obsolete *from an academic standpoint*)? Simply because there are not many flat-earthers or Ptolemaic supporters out there! What students need to learn about are the best theories available on the nature of the universe, as well as the most controversial ones, where the word "controversy" cannot be narrowly limited to the academic sort, but must include the social variety as well.

The last point, that the teachers may not be sufficiently prepared and will not themselves have a solid enough background in evolutionary biology is probably very true (of course, with individual exceptions). But it seems to me that this is an excellent argument for retraining teachers, not for continuing to have them regurgitate what they have force-fed their own brains just a few minutes before entering the classroom!

To conclude again with the words that Russell wrote in a different context sixty years ago:

> "Opinions should be formed by untrammeled debate, not by allowing only one side to be heard. ... All questions {must be} open to discussion and all opinions as open to a greater or less measure of doubt. ... What is curious about this position {of not allowing discussions} is the belief that if impartial investigation were permitted it would lead men to the wrong conclusion, and that ignorance is, therefore, the only safeguard against error. ... Uniformity in the opinions expressed by teachers is not only not to be sought but, if possible, to be avoided, since diversity of opinion among preceptors is essential to any sound education. ... As soon as a censorship is imposed upon the opinions which teachers may avow, education ceases to serve {its} purpose and tends to produce, instead of a nation of men, a herd of fanatical bigots."

Interestingly, both creationists and evolutionists have paid lip service to this argument, only to proceed to stifle a sane and productive discussion in American schools, for religious or ideological reasons respectively. It would be good for both parties to remember that the very concept of academic freedom was invented (chiefly by John Locke) as a reaction against 130 years of religious wars in pre-17th century Europe. Furthermore, the principle was originally applied to defend *the church* against undue interference on the part of the state. The First Amendment does, indeed, cut both ways.

Chapter 9 - Chance, necessity, and the improbability of evolution[31]

"To a superficial observer, so wonderful a regularity may be admired as the effect of either chance or design; but a skillful algebraist immediately concludes it to be the work of necessity." (David Hume)

Every now and then somebody allegedly "demonstrates" the impossibility of evolution. This despite the fact that evolution has been so thoroughly documented empirically and so finely dissected from a theoretical standpoint that its basic correctness is beyond reasonable doubt. These "demonstrations" are usually by lone gunners, either eager to further a preconceived ideology (usually religious) despite all available evidence, or characterized by an amusing combination of a huge ego and poor scholarship. In this chapter I will discuss two such cases that have come out in the recent literature: a book published by a respected university press and another written by a well-known scientist. It is a good exercise in the sociology of science and pseudoscience as well as in critical thinking to examine the arguments produced by these two authors, together with their motivations and potential impact on the general public. As we shall see, in both cases the departure point is represented by legitimate scientific questions and the approach is seemingly rigorous. Yet, both products do not constitute good science while providing endless ammunition for irrationality and propaganda.

---

[31] The first half of this Chapter was originally published as a book review in *BioScience* 50:79-81, 2000. The second part is currently in press, also as a book review, in *Skeptic* magazine.

Chance, necessity, and the war against science

More than 200 years after Hume's (1779) devastating critique of the argument from design, somebody else is trying to mathematically demonstrate the impossibility of natural explanations for the order of the universe, and of biological evolution in particular. To be sure, William A. Dembski's *The Design Inference* (Dembski 1998) explicitly talks about evolution in only one section spanning a mere seven pages, and quoting only one evolutionist, Richard Dawkins. However, the book has been hailed (e.g., in the endorsements assembled at http://www.discovery.org/w3/ discovery.org/fellows/design.html) as a revolutionary contribution to design theory (the latest incarnation of "creation science"). Furthermore, it is soon to be followed by a more explicit attack by Dembski on evolution, *Uncommon Descent*, which "seeks to reestablish the legitimacy and fruitfulness of design within biology"(http://www.leaderu.com/offices/dembski/menus/bios ketch.html).

What is the "design inference," and why should evolutionists and scientists at large care about the concept? The answer to the first question: a mix of trivial probability theory and nonsensical inferences. The answer to the second one: this book is part of a large, well-planned movement whose objective, I contend, is nothing less than the destruction of modern science and its substitution with a religious system of belief. Let me briefly explain both claims. The basic tenet of Dembski's book is that there are three possible explanations for any observed set of events: regularity, chance, and design. Regularity describes such phenomena as the rising and setting of the sun. Chance is most simply exemplified by the outcomes of tossing a fair coin. Design can be found – according to Dembski – in biological evolution, cryptography, plagiarism, and the suspicious doings of one Democratic election commissioner in New Jersey named Nicholas Caputo (more on him later). Dembski then proposes what he calls an "explanatory filter" to determine which explanation correctly accounts for any particular phenomenon. The filter works by successive exclusion: if something is not a "regular" natural phenomenon, it may be chance or design. If it is not the former, it must be the latter. This kind of reasoning is, of course, quite trivial, and it was worked out in probability theory well before the appearance of this book. As Dembski himself acknowledges, the statistician Andrei Kolmogorov had all the pieces of the puzzle in place by 1965. But never mind that. If Dembski had simply defined "design" as what in biology is known as "necessity" (Monod 1971), his book would have reduced to another case of somebody reinventing the wheel. Instead, he goes much further, asserting that *"in practice, to infer design is not simply to eliminate regularity and chance, but to detect the activity of an intelligent agent"* (p. 62). This claim is what turns his opus from triviality to nonsense.

Although Dembski cloaks his logic with obscure pseudo-mathematical jargon and symbolism, the essence of his argument is easy to understand. It is best exemplified by his own treatment of the above-mentioned New Jersey election commissioner. Nicholas Caputo, nicknamed "the man with the golden arm," was charged with electoral fraud because in 41 elections he oversaw, 40 had seen the Democrats at the top of the ballot and only one had the Republicans placed first. The probability of this occurring by chance in the random drawings that Caputo claimed to have conducted is less than one in 50 billion. Regardless of the odds, however, the New Jersey Supreme Court did not convict Caputo because, after all, even very unlikely events can occur by chance. In the absence of additional evidence, the Court simply ordered Caputo to change the way in which the drawings were conducted to avoid "further loss of public confidence in the integrity of the electoral process." Who says that jurists have no sense of humor? Dembski – as would anyone else with a bit of common sense and an elementary understanding of probability theory – concludes that the Court indeed had enough evidence to convict. Why? Because additional information available at the time – that is, that there is an advantage in being first on a ballot and that Caputo was a Democrat – clearly pointed to design, not chance. In other words, chance can be discarded as a reasonable alternative if two conditions hold: the probability of an event is very small, and the information available about that event allows someone to specify a particular pattern in advance. To put it even more simply, the following sequences from flipping a coin, TTHTTHTHHT and HHHHHHHHHH, have exactly the same probability of occurrence. However, your suspicion that the first one is genuinely random, whereas I created the second one by simply typing the letters on a keyboard, would indeed be correct.

An important component of Dembski's argument is what he calls "probabilistic resources." Because the design inference is established on two pillars – the occurrence of a specifiable ("detachable," in the author's jargon) pattern and a small probability of occurrence – Dembski is faced with the problem of how small such a probability actually has to be before chance can be ruled out. Instead of relying on the commonly understood limitation of statistical theory, which recognizes that any probability level is arbitrary and, therefore, that answers in science are only tentative and always subject to revision, Dembski wants more, much more. He submits that there is an absolute probability level that can be used as a universal yardstick for inferring design: $1/2 \times 10^{-150}$. How did he get there? By estimating that there are 10^{80} particles in the universe, that no transition between physical states is possible at a rate faster than 10^{-45} seconds (the well-known Planck time: Greene 1999), and that the universe is not likely to exist for a total

Figure 9.1 - William Dembski, for him, Intelligent Design in the universe is a reality.

of more than 10^{25} years (which is a figure not many cosmologists would bet their pension on). $10^{80} \times 10^{45} \times 10^{25}$ is indeed 10^{150}. The $1/2$ multiplier in front of the probability expression is to insure that our chances of reaching the correct conclusion are better than one in two (a rather arbitrary number in and of itself, of course; why not be content with one in three, or one in ten?). The basic idea here is powerful: if Dembski can demonstrate that the probability of a molecule of DNA forming in the primordial soup (see Chapter 12) approaches what he calls this "universal small probability" then life did not evolve by chance.

Too bad he missed the solution to this riddle, which has been proposed several times during the last few centuries, most prominently (and in various fashions) by Hume (1779), Darwin (1859), and Jacques Monod (1971). According to these thinkers, if a given phenomenon occurs with low probability and also conforms to a pre-specified pattern, then there are *two* possible conclusions: intelligent design (this concept is synonymous with human intervention if one does not consider the possible works of a god) or necessity, which can be caused by a nonrandom, deterministic force such as natural selection. Caputo's doing was the result of (fraudulent) human design; biological evolution is the result of random phenomena (mutation or recombination, among other processes) and deterministic phenomena (natural selection). It is disheartening to see how many people don't seem to be able to understand or accept this simple and beautiful conclusion.

More than disheartening is the background into which Dembski's book falls. In fact, I find it rather maddening. I will list a few pieces of additional information and then let the reader decide if I am justified in inferring a conspiracy behind this book. Dembski's book is endorsed on the back cover by two people from the same universities where he graduated, a rather unorthodox procedure for an academic author. The inside cover comes with a bold hail by David Berlinski, who represented the creationist side in a nationally televised PBS debate on evolution versus creation. And Dembski's list of acknowledgments reads like a "Who's Who" of the neocreationist movement, including Michael Behe, Phillip Johnson, and Alvin Plantinga. According to the book, Dembski is "a Fellow of the Discovery Institute's Center for the Renewal of Science and Culture" (CRSC). A bit scarce as an academic reference, no? The reason may be that the Discovery Institute (http://www.discovery.org/crsc/index.html) is a conservative public policy think tank with the declared intent of promoting the intelligent design theory as "a scientific research program" that "has implications for culture, politics, and the humanities, just as materialist science has such implications." A document called "The Wedge," which has been associated with the CRSC, has recently been circulated on the Internet (http://humanist.net/skeptical/wedge.html). The Wedge amounts to a detailed plan for insinuating intelligent design and other creationist ideas in the public as well as the academic arenas, with the ultimate goal of overthrowing the current scientific establishment and instituting a theistic science. Dembski's book is part of one of the steps of the Wedge strategy.

Unfortunately, Cambridge University Press has offered a respectable platform for Dembski to mount his attack on "materialist science" – which, of course, includes evolution. Scientists should be careful not to dismiss this book as just another craze originating in the intellectual backwaters of America.

Neocreationism should be a call to arms for the science community. The battle is already raging, and scientists and educators are still not sure if they should even bother paying attention. Just to reinforce the point, soon after the publication of Dembski's book, mathematical physicist Fred Hoyle has provided yet another piece of ammunition to creationists, and yet another unfounded mathematical demonstration that Darwin was wrong.

Impossible evolution: Darwin vs. Fred Hoyle

Sir Fred Hoyle, a British cosmologist, does not believe that evolution can occur, and has written a book about it (Hoyle 1999). Hoyle is no creationist, and has had a distinguished and rather peculiar scientific career. He is perhaps most famous in academic circles for proposing the theory of the stationary universe, thus triggering a large research effort that culminated with the rejection of his theory and the building up of a large amount of theoretical and empirical evidence in favor of its rival conception, the Big Bang (Hawking 1993). Later on, Hoyle went on record with his inseparable colleague, Chandra Wickramasinghe, to propose even more esoteric hypotheses for the origin of life on earth, regarded by professional biochemists and biologists as Pindaric flights of fancy rather than serious scientific theories (see Chapter 12).

However, Hoyle is not a naïve creationist with no scientific background, so if he claims that he has a mathematical demonstration of the fact that evolution cannot occur, an honest skeptic has to give him a hearing, read his book, and figure out if and where Hoyle is wrong. That is exactly what I did, and my conclusion is that – as for the case of Dembski described above – the claim has been made a bit too hastily and without the necessary biological foundations. The major difference between Hoyle and Dembski is that while the latter has a clear religious agenda that guides (and blinds) his effort, Hoyle is in the business of doing real science – albeit the wrong kind of science.

In *Mathematics and Evolution* Hoyle seeks to put evolutionary theory on solid mathematical foundations or to disprove it in the attempt. This approach is laudable, given that mathematics has been the official language of the "hard" sciences since Galileo and Newton. However, there are two points that Hoyle neglects right at the start of his book: first, some objects of study – such as biological organisms or geophysical cycles – are much too complex for the mathematics that humans have devised so far. That is why biology, geology, and to an even larger extent psychology have always been less amenable than physics and chemistry to rigorous mathematical treatment. Instead, the so-called "soft" sciences are the realm of statistical treatments and probabilistic statements. While this state of affairs may be a regrettable one from the point of view of a mathematical physicist such as Hoyle, it is the simple and undeniable reality. Second, and perhaps most surprisingly, Hoyle seems to be only vaguely aware that a limited – yet vast and sophisticated – mathematical theory of evolution already exists. Its foundations were laid down by people such as Sir Ronald Fisher, Sewall Wright, J.B.S. Haldane, Mooto Kimura and countless others who have published on the topic since the 1920s (Hartl and Clark 1989). While Hoyle does mention a few of these scientists here and there (the book comes with *no* references at all!), he dismisses them as a bunch of incompetents and delusional dilettantes, without ever giving the reader a detailed justification of such a radical position (notice that all these were professional mathematical biologists).

The core of Hoyle's argument is that natural selection is sufficient to explain what is usually termed "microevolution," i.e. variation within species and small, gradual changes of species over time. However, according to the British astronomer, Darwinians made the mistake of rashly extrapolating their findings to macroevolution – the origin of new body plans and of major transitions in the history of life – something that is alleged in the book to be pure nonsense. In this, Hoyle comes close to the position that most creationists have entrenched themselves in, although again both the motivations and the arguments of the latter are dramatically different and infinitely less sophisticated (see Ham 1998, for example). Instead, Hoyle suggests that the real explanation for major evolutionary changes is to be found in what he calls "genetic storms," hypothetical periodic events during which the earth is suddenly flooded with genetic material from outer space carried by meteors. Let's examine the two components of Hoyle's argument – the inadequacy of natural selection and the necessity for imported genetic material – to see where he does have a good point and where he completely misses the mark.

On p. 20 of *Mathematics of Evolution*, Hoyle claims that natural selection can at best keep a species from sliding down into the abyss of extinction, but cannot play any significant role in improving that species' adaptation to the environment, let alone create novel organismic features: *"The best that can be done is to hold the position, which is basically what bacteria have done for almost 4000 million years."* This is, of course, the old conceptual misunderstanding of selection as a force that can weed out but cannot build, which countless authors ever since Darwin have attempted to dispel. Biologists, contrary to Hoyle, think that bacteria have remained bacteria simply because they are very well adapted to their environment, and their particular niche in that environment has not changed for billions of years, thereby not necessitating any further improvement. As my professor of biophysics, the late Mario Ageno, once put it, "the ideal of a bacterium is not to become a man, but to become two bacteria."

Of course, Hoyle's statement does not come just out of thin air, but is based on some good mathematical reasoning (at least, as far as I could tell). However, like all mathematics when applied to real life problems, his is as good as the assumptions on which it is based – and these assumptions reveal little knowledge of biology on Hoyle's part. The whole premise of Hoyle's "demonstration" of the ineffectiveness of natural selection is that there are a lot more mutations with markedly negative, or even lethal, effects than there are with any positive effect (the same reasoning, based on a similar misconception, that creationists such as Duane Gish have always adopted: Gish 1995, also see Chapter 11). This, coupled with another fundamental assumption of Hoyle, that living organisms are so complex and finely tuned that *any* change in their machinery is overwhelmingly more likely to cause damage than benefit, must lead to the conclusion that evolution by natural selection cannot possibly work.

There are two problems with this reasoning. First, biologists have known now for decades that most mutations are neither positive nor negative, but neutral or quasi-neutral (Kimura 1983). This leaves much more room for natural selection to maneuver than in the tight scenario adopted by Hoyle. The reason for such a surprising amount of neutrality of mutational effects is related to the second problem embedded in Hoyle's argument: organisms are *not* designed according to stringent engineering principles where every part has to work exactly in a particular manner and interact with precision with all other parts. Rather, living beings are put together in a rather loose way, with a lot of redundancy and sub-optimal design, exactly as one would expect if they were the result of a natural process instead of an intelligent designer. Modern molecular developmental biology, entirely ignored in Hoyle's book, has clearly demonstrated that genetic redundancy and sub-optimality are a universal characteristic of life on earth (Pickett and Meeks-Wagner 1995; Schlichting and Pigliucci 1998).

Curiously, the bulk of Hoyle's book is actually about the advantages of sexual reproduction over the asexual alternative in terms of genetic variation, which partly explains why sexual organisms got to become so much more complex than bacteria. While Hoyle makes a huge deal of this to show that bacterial evolution is much more limited than its counterpart in more complex organisms were sex is the norm, his arguments would not raise any biologist's objection, and are hardly a challenge to the theory of evolution. It is certainly true that the ability to recombine existing genetic material has opened a whole new venue to evolution by natural selection compared to what is possible when all the genetic variation in a population must come from mutations alone. But that is not enough, according to Hoyle. He thinks that to explain the major transitions in evolution one needs something more – an additional source of genetic variation not considered by biologists so far. And he thinks he has the answer. This "external incidence" is described for example on p. 108 of *Mathematics of Evolution*:

"External incidence appears to come in storms of rather short duration, the most recent very large storm being the one that occurred 65 million years ago ... Species seems to vary considerably in their sensitivity to genetic storms."

In other words, salvation comes from outer space. Somehow, genetic material compatible with life on earth is imported aboard meteorites that periodically destroy life forms such as the dinosaurs and simultaneously infuse new life into the terrestrial biosphere; if such "theory" sounds rather like science fiction, that is because Hoyle is also a renowned sci-fi writer, though in this case he is very serious.

There are two considerations that must be made in reaction to Hoyle's idea of genetic storms: first, the idea is almost certainly wrong; second, its roots are to be found in a genuine problem with which evolutionists have been struggling for most of the 20th century. Let me start by acknowledging the problem and discussing how it is in the process of being solved by means completely different from Hoyle's fanciful proposal.

One of the classical assumptions of the so-called neo-Darwinian theory of evolution that emerged during the 1930s and 40s from a synthesis of Darwin's work and the new field of genetics (Mayr and Provine 1980) is that evolution occurs very slowly over long periods of time. Furthermore, evolutionary change has commonly been thought of as the result of alterations in the frequencies of many different genes, each with a very small effect on the phenotype, i.e., on the way organisms look and behave. It was clear already at the time, however, that there must be more than that to evolution by natural selection. For example, noted geneticist Richard Goldschmidt (1940) published a severe critique of the neo-Darwinian model, concluding that something else was necessary to account for macroevolutionary changes. He proposed that a "genetic revolution" would have to occur from time to time to produce entirely new types of organisms, which he called "hopeful monsters." Does that sound familiar? Except for the fact that Goldschmidt's genetic revolutions were to be caused by major internal reshuffling of an organism's chromosomes, the idea is identical to Hoyle's genetic storms.

The evolutionary community rejected the hopeful monsters as rather hopeless on two grounds: 1) there was no known mechanism by which the postulated revolutions were actually possible. This turned out to be eventually confirmed by the explosion of the field of molecular biology and the elucidation of how the genetic material changes over time. 2) Even if a genetic revolution could occur, the result would be disastrous because a major alteration of the molecular machinery of an organism would be fatal – again something that has been born out by countless instances of experimental evidence. (Notice that Hoyle wants it both ways: he claims that even most minor changes in the genes are bound to be fatal or highly detrimental, but then turns around and invokes entire "storms" affecting the whole of the genetic complement.)

But the neo-Darwinians did not enjoy a lasting victory, being challenged again first in the early 1970s by paleontologists Niles Eldredge and Stephen Jay Gould (Eldredge and Gould 1972; Gould and Eldredge 1993) and then by a sleuth of developmental geneticists (Brakefield et al. 1996; Raff 1996) and evolutionary ecologists (West-Eberhard 1989; Schlichting and Pigliucci 1998). The currently emerging consensus is that reality lies somewhere in the middle between the strict neo-Darwinian paradigm and Goldschmidt's monsters: while most everyday evolution occurs because of incremental changes in the frequencies of genes with small effects, some major changes do occur from time to time and trigger what we have referred to as macroevolution. This second category of change, however, is not caused by any new genetic mechanism, nor does it imply the dramatic effects postulated by Goldschmidt (or, sixty years later, by Hoyle). What happens instead is that standard mutations occur in regions of the genome (the ensemble of all genes) that *regulate* the functioning of a cascade of other genes. In this way, one small change actually has multiple, far-reaching, yet coordinated effects because of the way genes interact with each other throughout the development of an organism – a sort of a domino effect with consequences that may or may not be negative. This mixed model of evolution is still very much in the process of being shaped and probed experimentally, and it will probably take decades to fine tune, but it is based on a very solid foundation of both theoretical and empirical evidence.

Another genetic mechanism that has recently been shown to be more common than previously thought is lateral (or "horizontal") gene transfer, that is the shuttling of some genes from one species to another (Doolittle 2000). This phenomenon has been known in bacteria for quite some time, and it has now been demonstrated to occur even between multicellular organisms. Furthermore, there is good, albeit preliminary, evidence that some such gene transfers have in fact played a role similar to Hoyle's genetic storms, on a much smaller scale. Ironically, Hoyle has put the finger on the right problem, but his complete ignorance of the biological literature has led him to propose outlandish theories good for a mediocre episode of *Star Trek*. The point is that both the evolution of gene regulation and horizontal gene transfer still represent the mechanistic basis of good old evolution by natural selection, that Hoyle allegedly "demonstrated" to be impossible.

Hoyle's genetic storms, on the other hand, are truly impossible – or at least unlikely beyond reasonable doubt. This is for a variety of reasons: first, contrary to what Hoyle suggests (without empirical evidence) it is very difficult to imagine how the genetic material embedded in meteorites would reach the earth in a sufficiently unaltered state as to be useful to terrestrial organisms. Cosmic radiation and the temperatures generated by the entry of meteorites in our atmosphere would severely damage the delicate structure of DNA that we now know so well from biochemistry. It is true that meteorites have been found to harbor organic material such as amino acids, but this is in no condition to be used by a metabolically active organism (and – incidentally – has been demonstrated to be of an entirely different chemical origin). Second, it is astronomically unlikely that genetic material wandering at random from the rest of the universe would repeatedly happen to be compatible with its equivalent evolved in almost complete isolation on this planet for tens or hundreds of millions of years at a time. Third, of course Hoyle never explains – nor could he – where these genetic storms are coming from. Where and how did DNA originate in the cosmos? There is not a shred of evidence that it ever did, nor do we know of any mechanism that would make it possible. While the absence of evidence is certainly not evidence of absence, the burden of proof rests on Hoyle, given that he has set out to accomplish nothing less than the overturning of one of the major contributions to science and human thought on record, Darwin's theory of descent with modification.

Challenges to established science are not only possible, but a crucial component of the scientific endeavor (Kuhn 1970). They are usually received with skepticism, sometimes even with acrimony, not only because people feel threatened whenever the accepted paradigm is challenged, but more importantly because scientists have to be conservative to minimize the likelihood that any crackpot theory can take over their field simply because it's new and sounds reasonable: a certain degree of resistance to new ideas is actually healthy (Snelson 1992). Nevertheless, I did take Hoyle's (and Dembski's, for that matter) book seriously enough to actually get to the end of it, which is probably more than a lot of other scientists will be inclined to do or find the time for. His attempt is not a serious challenge to Darwinism; it is rather the simplistic outcome of an ego large enough to consider himself far ahead of thousands of others despite the fact that he has no training in the specific field and has obviously not bothered reading much about it. To overthrow a paradigm is much harder work than Fred Hoyle has been willing to put in with his casual approach to biology, and his only lasting accomplishment will be to provide apparent justification to hordes of creationists who, ironically enough, he despises as much as any evolutionist. Not much of a legacy for one of the most brilliant minds of 20th century cosmology.

Part IV - Tales of the personal

The next two essays are based on personal encounters I had with William Lane Craig and Duane Gish, respectively a Christian apologist and a young-earth creationist. The encounters were also very public, since they were debates that I engaged in against these two defenders of the irrational. Debates are a funny business, and some of my colleagues and even fellow skeptics criticized me for engaging in such exercises. Let me summarize their arguments as well as my responses as to why debating may be a good thing, if appropriately done.

The main argument against debating is that it offers the other side an unnecessary platform and official recognition by juxtaposing in the public eye the image of a creationist and of a (more or less) respectable scientist. That may be true, but I contend that the alternative is worse. First, most scientists never get a chance to talk to the general public while creationists always do, which means that we are the ones gaining a platform. Second, if prepared scientists or philosophers don't debate, some unprepared ones will, which means that the creationist in question will have a field day making fun of their poor opponent, reinforcing the idea that scientists are a funny bunch with no common sense.

Another alleged argument against debates is that the scientist is unlikely to "win." This is a gross misconception of what debates are for. Nobody wins a debate, simply because there is no objective way to score points, and more importantly because it wouldn't matter who scored what even if we could keep track of the outcome. From a scientist's viewpoint, debating is yet another tool to reach an audience and make a few good points in a reasonable manner. Nobody should expect to convince anybody on the spot. Such naïve expectation is an incarnation of the rationalistic fallacy—the idea that all you need to do to convince people is to make a reasonable argument. What one really aims at during a debate is to stimulate the little gray cells to think critically, to instill seeds of doubt, to make people think that maybe they should read a bit more about the topic in the future. The immediate results are absolutely intangible, but the long-term ones can be very significant. I know this because I know of people who were religionists or creationists and have changed their mind through repeated exposure to new ideas in a variety of contexts, until they eventually developed enough doubts to continue the quest on their own.

A related, and perhaps the most important reason to debate, is to confuse people's minds. I mean this seriously. Too often people hold on to absurd ideas simply because they are never challenged. To go to a debate where your trust in a young earth or in the existence of God is challenged perhaps for the first time can spur people to ask more questions, do more readings, and hopefully learning more about themselves and the world in the process.

A third challenge to the idea of debating is the charge that "science doesn't work that way," since scientific controversies are never settled by public acclaim in a three-hour event. That, of course, is perfectly true, but—again—irrelevant to the question at hand. Debates against theists or creationists are not scientific debates at all; they are educational opportunities. All one has to do is to unequivocally state that such is the case at the beginning of the debate, to make clear to the public that the forthcoming exercise is one in science education (and a bit of rhetoric), not in scientific research.

There are other reasons to engage in debates, but one of them came in clear focus to me in the afterward of a debate with creationist Duane Gish at Mississippi State University. Several students from the local Biology department approached me to thank me for having stood up in defense of their career choice. They are normally the object of scorn and ridicule among their peers because of their professional preference, and it was invigorating for them to see someone finally taking a prominent creationist to task. This component of "energizing the troops" is the main reason why creationists themselves engage in debates, and it can work both ways.

Debating in defense of reason has a long and venerable tradition, from ancient Greece to the modern engagements of the Oxford debating society. I think it is something that should continue, if properly done, as the quintessential form of public engagement of scientists and philosophers who would otherwise spend too much time inside the ivory tower—a dangerous position considering that funding for the tower itself comes from the general public.

Chapter 10 - The white knight of Christianity: an evening with William Lane Craig[32]

"He spends his life explaining from his pulpit that the glory of Christianity consists in the fact that though it is not true it has been found necessary to invent it." (Saki {H.H. Munro}, The Unbearable Bassington)

It was a nice, crisp evening of early March 1998 when I walked into the University of Tennessee Alumni Gymnasium to face my first debate in defense of reason and against irrational positions. My opponent was none other than William Lane Craig, perhaps one of the most famous and articulate Christian apologists active today. It was going to be tough, but I figured that if I wanted to sharpen my arguments and oratorical ability, the best of the best would certainly do. Of course, there was also the possibility that I would be humiliated, but my ego relegated that thought to a corner well within the least accessible recesses of my conscious mind.

I had been recruited for the debate by the campus "Issues Committee," a neutral organization that had been contacted by Craig during one of his debating tours. The publicity was handled fairly enough, though I had to insist that they would label me as a "non-theist" instead of the simpler but more generally offensive term "atheist." I still have the sneaky suspicion that it wasn't by chance that Craig's photo in the posters was on a white background while mine was on a black one, but sometimes I am paranoid. The topic of discussion: nothing less than "Does God exist?" As soon as I walked into the auditorium it was clear that many people cared about the question: the place was packed with what official estimates put at 1200 plus people. This was going to be interesting.

What I would like to present in this chapter is a discussion of Craig's and my arguments more or less as they were laid out at

---

[32] The full text of this debate can be found at http://fp.bio.utk.edu/skeptic.

the time. This of course means that if I had to do it again I would probably present some of them in a different fashion, drop others as not appropriate for the format or the audience, and raise new objections I have come across or thought about in the meantime. I am less sure that this would be the case for Craig, since his presentation in Tennessee was identical, word for word except for the interjection of my name, to the one available at his web site, which has still not changed last time I checked (http://campus.leaderu.com/offices/billcraig/menus/index.html) But perhaps I am wrong, and anyway he is a professional debater, I am not. Also, I of course have here the double advantage of hindsight and of being able to present my own case without fear of immediate rebuttal. Then again, this is my book, and I am entitled to some home advantages.

It seems to me a valuable exercise to present not only the arguments themselves – which hopefully have a more general appeal than the specific debate at which they were presented – but the dynamics of the debate itself, as an insight into the rhetorical component of the dialogue. After all, intellectual confrontations of this type are always based in part on the actual arguments and in part on the personalities involved. And how could it be otherwise? Even the most rigorous intellectual inquiry is still a human activity, with all the strengths and pitfalls that this implies.[33]

Opening salvo: the alleged existence of God

After a short introduction, Craig went straight to the core of the problem, suggesting five lines of evidence for the existence of God:

---

[33] As I noted in the introduction to this section, some of my scientist colleagues disapprove of my debating activities on the ground that in such fora rhetorical skills are more important than arguments and logic. While I do agree that scientific debates in the published literature are *less* subjected to this problem, my colleagues would be well advised to keep in mind how large the role of individual personalities can be in science. See for example Rothman (1989) and Collins and Pinch (1998).

o   "Number one, *the origin of the universe.* Have you ever asked yourself where the universe came from, why anything at all exists instead of just nothing? ...

o   Number two, *the complex order in the universe.* During the last thirty years scientists have discovered that the existence of intelligent life depends upon a delicate and complex balance of initial conditions simply given in the Big Bang itself ...

o   Number three, *objective moral values in the world.* If God does not exist then objective moral values do not exist ...

o   Number four, the historical facts concerning the life, *death and resurrection of Jesus* ...

o   Finally number five, *the immediate experience of God.* This isn't really an argument for God's existence. Rather, it's the claim that you can know that God exists apart from arguments simply by immediately experiencing him."

Let's start with the first argument, why does something exist instead of nothing? Of course, this fundamental philosophical question resonates deeply with just about everybody. It is also the kind of question that science is ill-equipped to answer, since science deals mostly with questions of the "how," not the "why" type. Nevertheless, it seems to me that even philosophical discussions of why questions cannot afford to ignore whatever science can tell us about the fundamental nature of the universe. Craig, however, did just that and started out with an unreasonable straw man. (Unlike the kind that I defended as useful to discussions in Chapter 3.) He claimed that: *"Typically atheists have said that the universe is just eternal and uncaused, but surely that's unreasonable; just think about it for a minute. If the universe is eternal and never had a beginning then that means the number of past events in the history of the universe is infinite. But mathematicians recognize that the existence of an actually infinite number of things leads to self contradiction."* First of all, "atheists" don't have a uniform position about the origin of the universe. Second, a truly infinite universe without a beginning has been ruled out by cosmology for more than 30 years. Notice that Craig has immediately attempted to enlist the help of scientists and to blend it with common sense to show that the position that God does not exist is not only illogical, but in fact unscientific. Also keep in mind that my stance at the debate was not that God does not exist, but only that I don't see any reasonable motive to believe in its existence. There is a fundamental philosophical difference between the two.

Craig then went on further substantiating his point by adding that the current theory of the Big Bang holds that the universe was "created" at one point – just like Christian doctrine tells us. But he points out that if that is the case, then the universe must have started literally from nothing, as noted astronomer (and opponent of the Big Bang theory) Fred Hoyle maintains. Craig here does put his finger on an interesting conundrum of modern cosmology. If we use the equations of the general theory of relativity to play the movie of the history of the universe backwards in time we do get to an ever shrinking and increasingly hotter universe, up to the point in which the equations tell us that all started with an infinitely small and infinitely hot universe known as the "singularity." This truly is a kind of infinity that creates problems (for physicists, not mathematicians). As Brian Greene wonderfully explains in his *The Elegant Universe* (1999) the singularity problem arises because when relativity is pushed to such small scales it actually invades the territory of quantum mechanics, and the two theories – while very accurate in their respective macro- and microscopic realms of application – actually do not mesh with each other very well. That is why physicists ever since Einstein have been looking for a way to merge the two into a larger and more unified theory capable of describing the behavior of matter at any scale. Such a solution has been tentatively found in what is known as superstrings theory. This is certainly not the place to get into details about the latest advances of high-energy physics; suffice it to say that – unbeknownst to me at the time of the debate – the physics community has tentatively agreed that superstring theory is a way to reconcile quantum mechanics and general relativity. As far as the particular problem we are concerned with here goes, superstring cosmology predicts that the origin of the universe was determined by the instability of a finite object characterized by a

Figure 10.1. William Lane Craig, the white knight of Christianity whose positions are discussed in this chapter.

finite amount of energy. As Greene puts it in his book: "in the beginning there was a Planck-sized nugget."[34]

The second argument presented by Craig for believing in God – in fact for believing in the Christian God – is the very well known argument from design (see Chapter 9). This is by no means a novel proposition, as it was suggested by William Paley with his analogy of the watch that has to have a watchmaker (Paley 1831). Here is how Paley himself put it:

> "In crossing a heath, suppose I pitched my foot against a stone and were asked how the stone came to be there, I might possibly answer that for anything I knew to the contrary it had lain there forever; nor would it, perhaps, be very easy to show the absurdity of this answer. But suppose I had found a watch upon the ground, and it should be inquired how the watch happened to be in that place, I should hardly think of the answer which I had before given, that for anything I knew the watch might have always been there."

Of course, still one of the best responses to date against that argument was put forth by David Hume even before Paley himself (see Table 10.1 and Hume 1779, you can find the complete works of Hume available for free on the Internet at http://www.utm.edu /research/hume/hume.html). One of the characters in his dialogues concerning this topic, Philo, says:

> "If the universe bears a greater likeness to animal bodies and to vegetables than to the works of human art, it is more probable that its cause resembles the cause of the former than that of the latter, and its origin ought rather to be ascribed to generation or vegetation than to reason or design. The world plainly resembles more an animal or a vegetable than it does a watch or knitting-loom. Its cause, therefore, it is more probable, resembles the cause of the former. The cause of the former is generation or vegetation.

---

[34] Planck size is the size below which a quantum mechanic description of matter is necessary because relativity breaks down. This threshold corresponds to 10^{-35} meters – pretty small, but not quite zero.

Table 10.1 - Hume's arguments pro and against intelligent design.

Argument:

- Premise: the universe resembles the production or effects of human intelligence
- Premise: similar effects proceed from similar causes
- Because of (1) and (2), the universe must be the production or effect of some intelligent being
- Additional premise: but the universe is much more complex than any production of human intelligence
- Therefore, from (2) and (4), the production of the universe required an intelligence much greater than the human variety
- Conclusion: there is a designer of the universe whose intelligence far surpasses ours.

Objections:

- The analogy between the universe and human artifacts is unconvincing
- Intelligence is only one of the active causes in the world
- Even if intelligence is everywhere operative now, it does not follow that we can ascribe to it the origins of the universe
- The origin of the universe is a single unique case and so analogies are pointless
- The analogy between human and divine mind is clearly anthropomorphic. Nature resembles a mindless organism rather than a purposeful and intelligent one
- The fruit of anthropomorphic thinking is a finite God. In the absence of an independent argument for the designer's perfection, the design argument does not yield a being who is infinite in perfection (like the Christian God) or indefectible, eternal, necessary, incorporeal, etc.

The anthropic principle reflects a valid question about the nature of the universe: where do the constants of physics come from? So far, no theory has been able to answer that question satisfactorily, although the progress of high-energy physics during the 20th century has occurred precisely along the lines of gradually reducing the number of elementary parameters and conceptually unifying the forces governing the universe. Again, this is exactly the promise (as yet only partially realized) of superstrings theory, the best attempt so far at what some physicists call (a bit immodestly) a "theory of everything." Of course, neither superstrings nor anything else will provide a truly universal theory, but the hope is that they will explain why it is that we have a universe characterized by certain forces and elementary particles, and if indeed a different universe is physically possible.[35] Notice the difference here between science and religion. Craig says that he *knows* the answer, and the answer is that God did it. Yet, of course, such an answer is not only unsubstantiated – since we don't know and cannot know if a god with the necessary prerequisites exists – but it is no answer at all. It only shifts the question to where did this God come from and how. Science, on the other hand, admits that the question is a tough one and gives it its best shot, which depends on a complex interaction of solid theoretical arguments and verifiable empirical evidence, all of which is always taken as provisional until (and unless) we know better.

The anthropic principle has also been attacked on its own merits, most effectively by Stenger (1996; 1999) who actually produced calculations showing that a surprisingly high number of possible alternative universes would be compatible with life as we know it. I think that an even more radical objection to the calculations that Craig so casually dished out to his public is that they are absolutely impossible to carry out in principle. The fundamental assumption underlying all such calculations is that any other value of all the fundamental constants of our universe is possible and equally likely. That being the case, the values of those constants typical of our universe would be only one in an infinite ocean of other values. If our particular universe originated by chance and could have been any other universe with any other combination of values, our existence would indeed be miraculous (in fact, its probability would be infinitely small, a much smaller number than the one allegedly provided by Davies). But an elementary principle of statistics and probability theory is that one has to know something about the population of values from which a given sample has been obtained. That is the only way to

---

[35] Mathematically, several other universes are indeed possible. In fact, there are an infinite number of them.

determine what is the probability of a particular value to occur in the sample. Unfortunately, we don't know of any other universe and therefore our sample size is one (see one of Hume's objections in Table 10.1). For all we know, it is conceivable that the measurable values of the physical constants are the *only* possible values and that therefore the probability of existence of our universe had to be 100%. We simply do not have the relevant information, one way or the other. Statistical theory than tells us that our best bet with a sample size of one is to follow what is known as the "principle of mediocrity" (see Chapter 13) and conclude that the only values we have are also the best estimates for the average of the population of universes. Accordingly, the probability of existence of our universe when compared to a random sample of alternative universes is very high.

Craig's third argument is that there cannot be objective moral judgment without God. Since objective morality *obviously* exists, we must have God. As he puts it: *"On the atheistic view there's nothing really wrong with your raping someone. Thus without God there is no absolute right and wrong which imposes itself on your conscience. But the problem is that objective values do exist and deep down we all know it; there is no more reason to deny the objective reality of moral values than the objective reality of the physical world."* This is an entirely different approach from the ones discussed so far. We are now leaving the realm of empirical evidence to enter into moral philosophy and ethics. I don't know where Craig gets the idea that morality is universal. Comparative anthropology (the study of different human cultures) and primatology (the study of different species of non-human primates) clearly point to a different conclusion. It is quite clear that humans at large are not exactly what we would consider a moral animal (Miele 1996), and that what is moral or not changed with time and place throughout human history. This includes what Craig would consider "absolutes," such as murder and rape. Murder and rape, of course, are also quite normal in the animal kingdom, and in particularly among our closest relatives, the chimps (de Waal 1996). This observation does not translate into a license for humans to do the same because our biology, psychology, and societal structures are different. It only implies that there is no universal standard followed by any species, including ours. Of course one could argue that other primates and most human societies simply don't

Table 10.2 – Some atrocities in the Bible.

Verse	Atrocity
Genesis 34:13-29	The Israelites kill Hamor, his son, and all the men of their village, taking as plunder their wealth, cattle, wives and children.
Exodus 21:20-21	With the Lord's approval, a slave may be beaten to death with no punishment for the perpetrator as long as the slave doesn't die too quickly.
Leviticus 26:29	As a punishment, the Lord will cause people to eat the flesh of their own sons and daughters and fathers and friends.
Numbers 21:35	With the Lord's approval, the Israelites slay Og "... and his sons and all his people, until there was not one survivor left ...."
Deuteronomy 20:13-14	"When the Lord delivers it into your hand, put to the sword all the males .... As for the women, the children, the livestock and everything else in the city, you may take these as plunder for yourselves."
Joshua 8:22-25	With the Lord's approval, Joshua utterly smites the people of Ai, killing 12,000 men and women, so that there were none who escaped.
1 Samuel 15:3, 7-8	"This is what the Lord says: Now go and smite Amalek, and utterly destroy all that they have; do not spare them, but kill both man and woman, infant and suckling, ox and sheep, camel and ass ....' And Saul ... utterly destroyed all the people with the edge of the sword."
2 Kings 2:23-24	Forty-two children are mauled and killed, presumably according to the will of God, for having jeered at a man of God.
Psalms 137:9	Happy will be the man who dashes your little ones against the stones.
Isaiah 14:21-22	"Prepare slaughter for his children for the iniquity of their fathers."

recognize the only true and universal morality, the one offered by Christianity. But one has to explain a couple of things: first, how come all these other species and societies are apparently doing very well by following their own brand of ethical rules? Second, Christianity does not fare much better either: Table 10.2 reports a very partial list of all sorts of atrocities condoned or encouraged by the Christian God, to which I am sure not even Craig would readily subscribe. And they accuse evolution of implying an immoral universe!

What does science have to say about morality? So far not much, other than informing us of the degree of variability in people's and species' behaviors. However, the suggestion has been put forth that we could derive semi-rational moral rules by the application of what is known as "optimization theory" in biology (Wilson 1998). Once we agree on one or more quantities to be maximized (e.g., individual freedom, ownership of property, financial status, etc.) it may be possible to determine the combination of behaviors that would tend to maximize such quantities – of course, always considering the fact that human beings are far from being rational agents. Overall, it seems to me more logical to conclude that morality is an invention of humanity (and other primates) to construct a livable society. This invention works to some extent but has to retain some flexibility because the circumstances under which we live change continuously.

With the fourth argument Craig entirely leaves the realm of rational discourse and enters the territory of pure faith. He claims that the resurrection of Jesus is an historical fact: *"New Testament critics have reached something of a consensus that the historical Jesus came on the scene with an unprecedented sense of divine authority, the authority to stand and speak in God's place."* Of course, so did David Koresh, the mentally deranged nutcase who caused the death of men, women, and children at the Branch Davidian compound in Waco, Texas on 19 April 1993 (his "sense" was not unprecedented, but no less real). Craig then adds: *"there are actually three established facts, recognized by the majority of New Testament historians today, which I believe are best explained by the resurrection of Jesus."* This facts are:

o   An empty tomb was found after Jesus' crucifixion.
o   Different people saw him appearing after his death.
o   The disciples suddenly came to believe in the resurrection.

It is hard to believe that an intelligent person such as Craig would actually believe in a miracle just because the followers of a sect wrote down, several decades after the alleged "facts," that it happened! So much for logical rigor. If we were to apply the same standards to other fields of inquiry, there is more reason to believe in psychic predictions and alien abductions or, for that matter, that Koresh himself was in fact a divinely inspired prophet (after all, he had a lot more witnesses on record, including TV cameras). Needless to say, there is very little proof even that Jesus ever existed – though this is quite possible – let alone of his divinity and resurrection. There are therefore several objections to this particular line of reasoning: first, there simply is no good reason to think that the whole story (empty tomb, resurrection, etc.) is true (it is based on few and biased testimonies). Second, one could easily explain the fact that people *thought* they saw Jesus alive if they already believed in the resurrection (much in the same way some modern beliefs, such as UFOs and ESP, make the gullible person more likely to *experience* occurrences springing from such beliefs). Third, Craig really needs to first show the existence of God to make the resurrection plausible (since this is a supernatural phenomenon); therefore, he cannot use the resurrection itself as proof for the existence of God.

The last argument is the shakiest of them all: the direct experience of God. As Craig himself readily acknowledges: *"This isn't really an argument for God's existence. Rather it's the claim that you can know that God exists apart from arguments simply by immediately experiencing him."* Of course, there are plenty of things that we think we experience and that are only in our minds. The world is full of people – whom Craig would not consider worth listening to – trying to convince other people that they experienced all sorts of supernatural or unusual occurrences, from sex aboard alien spaceships to chatting with divinities that Craig does not recognize. A book from Indian neuroscientist V.S. Ramachandra (1998) discusses the neurological basis of hallucinations, both of an auditory and visual nature. It turns out that people affected by minor seizures at the temporal lobes are not only particularly prone to these hallucinations, but usually ascribe to them a cosmic or religious meaning. It is tempting to speculate that perhaps the world's history has been disproportionately affected by a few people with particularly strong seizures who came to consider themselves prophets or gods (of course, the question still remains of why so many other people followed them: see Shermer 1999). To paraphrase a famous American psychiatrist: if you talk to God you are a believer; if God talks back, you are a schizophrenic.

Round two: sliding into sophistry

After my presentation, mostly along the lines of the objections I discussed so far, Craig was allowed the first rebuttal. It is interesting to see which arguments he focused on and which, if any, new ones he brought into the arena for discussion. He started by attacking my claim that the best objection to the argument from design is that the universe is actually pretty badly designed. Craig mentioned several alleged weaknesses of the argument from bad design, starting with the fact that it *"assumes a static theory of creation, that God created each individual creature which never changes."* All right then, if the universe started in a state of perfection (but how do we know that?) God is still culpable of having designed a universe that would assume such a sorry state as the one we observe today, with evil being widespread not only as a human phenomenon, but imbued in all sorts of natural catastrophes and diseases. Second, Craig states: *"the objection presumes to know what God wouldn't do if he were to design something, that we know that God would create the eye in a certain way if he existed or he would create the digestive system in this way if he existed, and I personally think that's simply presumptuous."* Of course, saying that we could have designed a better eye than God does sound a bit presumptuous on the face of it. But it is in fact pretty easy to demonstrate that the human eye *is* less than perfectly designed from an engineering perspective, as long as we make the reasonable assumption that the purpose of the eye is to collect visual information in the best possible way. Here Craig is either underestimating human science or overestimating God's powers. Also, consider the most profound implication of his objection: if it is not possible to discuss the nature of creation, then the entire topic of the existence or not of God is taken out of the realm of rational discourse and plunged back into pure faith. That being the case, Christian apologetics – Craig's line of work and source of living – should cease to exist: it would be by definition impossible to talk about God and what he does – we must simply accept him or not. Hardly a *reason* to believe! Craig's third objection to my argument from imperfection is related to the second one: *"perfection is a relative term after all."* No, it isn't. Maybe in fashion and aesthetics, but not in the realm of optimization and engineering. To argue that a world with cancer and earthquakes is in any sense "perfect" is quite simply absurd.

The white knight of Christianity then proceeded to use evolution itself as an additional proof of the existence of God. Citing the dubious source of Barrow and Tipler (the physicists, not biologists, who proposed the anthropic principle discussed above), he said that the odds of the evolution of the human genome by random chance are 4 to the negative 360 to the 110,000 power (whatever that number actually means). Obviously, it is easier to believe in miracles. Not quite. Notice again the use of "science" and of impressive-sounding numbers to bolster his case, numbers that make no more sense than the one cited above concerning the probability of existence of the universe. Like several physicists who don't understand biology (fortunately, not many overall), Barrow and Tipler assume that evolution is a random process (see Chapter 9 for a similar mistake made by William Dembski and by Fred Hoyle). Evolution is *not* random by any stretch of the imagination. As I will explain in more detail commenting on my debate with creationist Duane Gish (Chapter 11), the raw material of evolution, variation among organisms, is provided by random phenomena such as mutations. But mutations are sorted in a very deterministic fashion by natural selection, and because of this only the individuals with the highest number and quality of offspring will survive each generation. It is this combination of a random and a deterministic phenomenon that makes evolution by natural selection such an effective explanatory principle for the diversity of life on Earth.

Craig then shifted gear and addressed my objection based on the God-of-the-gaps argument. The idea is that the more we know about the natural world, the less we need to invoke God as an explanatory principle to understand the world. If carried to its logical (albeit tentative) limit, we would conclude that there actually is no God and that we invented him to explain things that our ignorance and intellectual limitation precludes us from understanding, at least temporarily. Craig's response was very surprising: *"even if it were true that God doesn't often intervene in the universe in miraculous ways, that's not incompatible with Christianity. After all miracles by their nature are relatively rare and I don't think that God would frequently go around intervening in the universe in miraculous ways."* The God-of-the-gaps argument does not have anything to do with how frequently God resorts to miracles, and to respond in the way Craig did implies either that he did not understand the argument (hard to believe, given his familiarity with the atheistic literature) or that he somehow deemed it necessary to duck the question while providing some sort of a superficially reasonable answer. If the latter is the case, we are once again leaving the realm of rational discourse, this time to enter into pure sophistry.

When I said that the best reason to go with science is that it works, Craig's answer was that that does not prove that the philosophical position of naturalism (see Chapter 2) is also correct: *"the hypothesis that there is a creator God who has designed the universe to operate according to certain natural laws, could also work so the fact that the scientific theories work is in no sense a proof of naturalism."* This is a convoluted way of saying that the laws of nature may work simply because God decided that that should be the case. True enough, but remember that Craig is trying to defend not just the position that a generalized kind of God exists, but that the Christian God who created the universe out of his personal handiwork, stopped the sun dead in the sky, and poured a lot of water on unsuspecting earthlings to drown them all actually exists. Science definitely dismisses *that* kind of God (Chapter 5).

Perhaps one of the most crucial and interesting moments of the evening came when Craig finally tackled the problem of evil, which had popped up here and there during the debate, and that probably is the single most damaging argument against an all-powerful and all-good God. The first objection to the problem of evil apparently is that there is no logical contradiction between the existence of God and the existence of evil itself. Why? Because *"God has morally sufficient reasons to permit evil."* Of course, we are in no position to inquire as to what these reasons may be, and it doesn't seem to bother Craig that the human mind cannot possibly conceive of the destruction and suffering of the world as morally good in any sense. This, of course, is once again a cop-out: by closing to rational discussion the most important objection to the existence of the Christian God, Craig is forfeiting logic and implicitly admitting that he has no idea of how to answer the objection. Now, I have heard Christians making the argument that God relates to us as we do to our pets: our dog simply cannot understand why he is being punished by his owner; he does not know that it is for his own benefit that the owner does not want him to go play in the street and run after cars. While superficially convincing, this analogy breaks down once we consider that God is allowing countless human beings to *die* in order to fulfill his plans. Now, death is a terminal condition as far as we know. There is no way to treasure the experience and do better the next time around, and what would the "moral lesson" of an earthquake be, anyway?[36] In fact, if we really have to deduce God's character from his work with nature – a fundamental premise of apologetics ever since Thomas Aquinas – what we learn is that if he exists we should gang up to fight against him as hard as we can, because no self-respecting human being would want to worship such a monstrous creature for all eternity. Undaunted, Craig went further and tried to use my argument that morality is relative to turn it around and prove the existence of the Almighty: "*My argument would go like this: if God does not exist, objective moral values do not exist, Dr. Pigliucci agrees; number two, evil exists; three, therefore objective values exist, some things are really evil; four, therefore God exists.*" I almost threw my hands up in despair after listening to this example of allegedly tight logical reasoning. Who ever said that evil is an objective value? AIDS is bad for humans, but it surely is good for the HIV virus. As for earthquakes, they just happen, the earth does not have any intention – evil or otherwise – concerning human or any other beings. It is only our truly presumptuous habit of considering ourselves the pinnacle and center of attention of the whole universe that leads us into this kind of nonsensical arguments.

Craig then dismissed objections based on the literal interpretation of the Bible (e.g., Noah's flood, which he suggested – actually contradicting the Bible – was only a local event) as not sufficient to falsify the Christian God. Well, it depends on what kind of Christian one is. There are literally millions of people, several hundreds of whom were present in the audience, who subscribe to fundamentalist interpretations of the holy scriptures and who support the creationist movement (Chapter 11). They

---

[36] The possible existence of an afterlife does not solve the problem either, since it is supposed to be eternal. That way, you made one mistake and, zap, you are condemned to eternal punishment, a rather disproportionate reaction from our supposedly benign "owner."

would wholeheartedly disagree with Craig's cavalier dismissal of their most cherished beliefs. In fact, right in front of the podium where Craig was standing, a large sign affirmed the very fact that the speaker was denying: the flood was real, universal, and directly caused by God. But let us concede that the Bible does not need to be interpreted literally. In fact, it couldn't, since it is the result of the work of many human writers over many centuries, all pretty much ignorant of the nature of the universe as understood by modern science. As creationists and fundamentalists clearly realize, Craig and more liberal Christians put themselves on a logical slippery slope. If not all the Bible is true, then how do we pick and chose? If we cannot trust its factual statements, why should we trust its moral teachings? Good questions, it seems to me.

The debate then turned again to philosophical matters, an approach that evidently Craig considered his best and most secure weapon. He claimed that his arguments for the existence of God are deductive, so that if the premises are true, the conclusion has to be true. Which indeed is correct, assuming one has not made a logical error in the chain of reasoning nor has started with a false premise. In particular, by saying that the universe could not have created itself, Craig opened himself to the question I asked above: where did God come from? He confidently stated that he could easily answer this objection: *"there cannot be an infinite regress of causes, therefore there must be a first cause which never came into being; whatever begins to exist has to have a cause, but a being which exists timelessly, spacelessly and necessarily is uncaused."* For one thing, we don't know if everything has to have a cause. Some aspect of quantum mechanics would tend to suggest that small quantum fluctuations such as those hypothesized to be responsible for the beginning of the universe actually do not have to have a cause, at least in the sense we are used to consider. Regardless, the true giant leap is to say that the ultimate cause – God – *had* to be timeless, spaceless and uncaused. Why? How? Craig is introducing a dangerous duality here: he is saying that everything *else* has to have a cause, but not God. But that statement is completely arbitrary. We could just as easily (in fact more easily because we are not calling into existence something of which we know nothing about) say that the universe itself was uncaused in the sense that

Craig intends. He has most definitely not answered the question of where God came from.

An almost comic moment came toward the end of the first rebuttal, when Craig once again tackled the problem of relative morality. Referring to my statement that relative morality does not mean "anything goes," because a stable society could simply not exist if random acts of violence were allowed to occur unchecked, he said: "*That is not at all true. Look at Nazi Germany. In his book Morality after Auschwitz, Peter Hass asks how an entire society could have existed in which the mass extermination of Jews and Gypsies went on for a decade with hardly a protest being offered.*" But the Nazi society was *not* stable, and it only lasted for a couple of decades! Q.E.D.

Finale: Is the absence of evidence also evidence of absence?

Of course not. Yet, Craig started his final rebuttal in the debate with precisely this time-honored defense of absurdity. Obviously the absence of evidence cannot and will never be evidence of absence, no matter if we are talking about God, Santa Claus, flying saucers or unicorns. In this context, I am often reminded of an old Tarzan movie in which the good ape-man dismissed the existence of germs because he couldn't see them. If modern society would adopt the same attitude we would be in dire straits indeed. Furthermore, a lot of modern science is founded on invisible things of which there is no evidence to our senses and that somewhat contradict our common sense; consider quarks and DNA as examples.

The point is that science and rational thought can only address positive statements for which one can examine either the empirical evidence or the logical arguments allegedly supporting such statements. In that case, since there is no empirical evidence of the existence of God and the logical arguments definitely point toward either his non-existence or the fact that he certainly is not the kind of God Craig is thinking about, my provisional rejection of God's existence seems perfectly rational and consistent with the absence of evidence (Chapter 5). As Hume pointed out, the burden of proof is on those who make extraordinary claims.

Craig, however, is a bit more subtle than that, claiming that *"we have no positive evidence of the early inflationary era in the history of the universe and yet if you look at many cosmologists, they believe that such an inflationary era actually existed."* This is absolutely true, but there are two important caveats. First, the inflationary theory of the early expansion of the universe is not an ad hoc hypothesis concocted by scientists to explain away the evidence, as Craig makes it to be. Rather, it is one of the possible (albeit not the only) solutions of Einstein's equations of general relativity, a rigorous mathematical theory that has withstood countless empirical challenges.[37] Second, inflationary theories have the potential to make specific predictions that can be tested by further astronomical observations or high-energy physics experiments. Inflation is cutting edge speculative science, but it is not arbitrary. God, on the other hand, is an entirely arbitrary solution to the problem of existence.

Next, Craig either presented an argument that he did not understand, or was being intentionally deceitful. I will give him the benefit of the doubt and settle for the first hypothesis. He said: *"Aaron Tipler in that same book reported that there's a consensus among evolutionary biologists today that life of comparable information processing ability to* Homo sapiens *is so improbable that it's unlikely to evolve anywhere else in the visible universe."* Notice again that he is citing a physicist on matters of biological evolution. I keep pointing this out not just as a matter of professional pride (I am an evolutionary biologist), but because it is simply not a sensible thing to do. This would be equivalent to quoting evolutionists Stephen Gould or Richard Dawkins on the latest state of superstring theory in physics. While both are very smart and with an indubitable science background, they are not physicists, and whatever they know of superstrings comes from reading popular accounts of the theory, not from a deep understanding of the physics and

---

[37] In essence, inflation is a time period immediately after the Big Bang when the universe expanded at an accelerated rate. This is different from the standard cosmological model, in which the universe steadily decelerated after the Big Bang. If inflation is correct, it would explain why the background temperature of the universe is so uniform – since different parts of the universe would have been close enough to each other before the inflation episode to exchange heat and therefore homogenize the distribution of temperatures in the universe.

mathematics behind it. Nevertheless, Craig's statement is most disconcerting simply because it is false. The conclusion he (or rather, Tipler) says evolutionists have reached is neither universal nor implies what he thinks it implies. Gould has been the main proponent of such an idea, mostly in popular books as *Full House* (1996). The point is that contingency plays a fundamental role in biological evolution, at least as important as natural selection. There is no widespread agreement that this idea is correct, although I think it is, at least in some sense. More importantly, what Gould and any sensible biologist is saying is that the *specific* species *Homo sapiens* would not evolve again if the tape of the history of life on earth were played again from the same beginnings. This is not to say – as Craig needs to imply for his argument to be effective – that evolution was highly unlikely to produce *any* sentient being characterized by consciousness, a concept of self, and the ability for technological and cultural evolution. For all we know, this more broadly defined outcome was highly likely given the increasing complexity of life on our planet and the advantages that high intelligence, social life and technology afford whatever species can master them (Damasio 1999).

Craig slipped dangerously close to the line separating honest from dishonest rhetoric when he summarized my own positions: *"He dropped his regression argument, dropped his naturalistic works argument, dropped his problem of evil argument, dropped his Noah's Ark argument."* I absolutely did no such thing, I merely further explained what these arguments were based on and under what circumstances they provide a challenge to the idea of the Christian God. But by then the debate was coming to a close, and as a good salesman, Craig had to make his final pitch to the audience, regardless of what actual arguments had been presented up to that point.

More rhetoric came a minute afterwards: *"What about our objective morality? Here Dr. Pigliucci is clearly in a deep existential dilemma: he confirms that morality is not objective, it is the invention of human beings, but he cannot bring himself to say therefore anything goes."* I am in no such dilemma. My point is simply that we need moral rules, otherwise society as we know it (and like it) could not exist. But I also realize that such rules are not given and eternal, they need to be invented and fine tuned by humans, and they need to remain flexible enough to adapt to new conditions. Not having an arbitrary, ready-made, and inflexible position does not by any means translate into not having any position at all. It is another convenient and unjustified straw man (in the bas sense of the term – see Chapter 3) that many Christian apologists keep shooting at despite the obvious empirical evidence that the overwhelming majority of atheists and non-believers do not go around raping and killing. Then again, as a good friend of mine – Ed Buckner – once remarked to me, if an irrational belief in an all-powerful and vengeful God is all that keeps *you* from killing and raping, by all means, go ahead and believe.

The resurrection of Jesus was then brought back into the discussion, because that is the only link Craig can make between a generic God and the Christian flavor: *"isn't it arbitrary to believe in a miracle in this case, if you don't believe in miracles in many other cases? Not at all. You would believe in a miracle, I think, when number one no naturalistic explanation of the facts is available that plausibly explains the facts, and number two when there is a super natural explanation suggested in the religious historical context in which the event occurred."* Notice that here the level of logical discourse is getting dangerously low. Of course if we had incontrovertible *facts* that could not be explained by any natural occurrence and would easily be explained by a supernatural one, we would have to be fools not to consider the alternative. The problem is much more fundamental: there is no incontrovertible "fact" here. As I remarked above, we only have the testimony of a few believers who had a clear interest in perpetuating the myth and who only bothered to write down the alleged facts decades after the events. Furthermore, even these witnesses do not agree on essential details of the events, including the number of angels or people present at the discovery of the empty tomb and the actual sequence of events. Incontrovertible indeed. Such a testimony would be thrown out of court immediately by today's legal, let alone scientific, standards.

In the final statement, Craig brought up an interesting point: *"Frankly I can't imagine where he {Pigliucci} got that idea; Christians believe God is perfect but not that the world is perfect. Look at Genesis, as God saw that the creation was good and I think it certainly is good, but the idea that it is a perfectly functioning machine is no part of Christian theology."* Well, how interesting. First, my Catholic priest clearly seemed to have that idea of perfection in mind when he was teaching catechism to my class back in Rome – but Craig probably subscribes to a different sect where the world is only good, not perfect. Even so, this is a tremendous admission: it amounts to say that either God *cannot* make a perfect world, in which case he is a fallible God; or that God does not *want* to make a perfect world, in which case he is directly responsible for evil.[38] Either way, Christianity loses quite a bit of its appeal.

Yet another important concession, already alluded to above, came a second later: *"he {Pigliucci} argued that naturalism is tested every day and it works; I would say that it only tests that there are natural laws, but that's consistent with the idea that there is a creator who has made the universe that functions normally according to natural laws."* As I pointed out above, of course it is possible to imagine a God who works only through natural laws. Indeed, that is the deistic position embraced by thinkers of the caliber of Voltaire (1949) and Thomas Jefferson. But the emerging picture is once again very different from the micro-managing God of the Old Testament. And this points to one major problem with the theistic argument: the definition and attributes of God keep shifting according to the convenience of the moment. If Craig had to defend a typical version of the Christian God he would have had to drop most of his arguments. Instead, he tried to convince the audience that one cannot rule out *every* kind of God (which is indeed true: Chapter 5), and then attempted to imply that the only game in town is the Christian one. Slick, but not exactly rational.

Craig even went so far as to justify the vast cosmos just so that human life could emerge as if that were the only way an omnipotent God could have done it: *"These stellar spaces are necessary in order for the stars to cook up the heavy elements which are necessary for the existence of life on earth, and in order to be that old the universe would have to expand for 15 billion years, so the size of the universe is related to the age of the stars which is related to the furnaces necessary to make the elements requisite for intelligent life."* This statement would have been considered blasphemous by my priest back in Rome, because it clearly poses very strict limits to what

---

[38] Once again, notice that I am not talking about the imperfections of humans – allegedly determined by free will – but of the imperfections of the universe at large (diseases, natural catastrophes, widespread suffering across species, etc.).

God can do and how he can do it. I think this is at least as pretentious of Craig as it was of me to criticize God for the evil of the world.

The last appeal was, predictably, the least rational of them all. Referring to his personal conversion to Christianity, Craig said: "*I discovered in the person of Jesus a figure that just arrested and captivated me. His words had the ringing truth about them, and after a period of about six months of the most intense soul searching, to make a long story short, I just gave my life to God and I experienced a sort of inner rebirth, God became an immediate living reality in my life, a reality that has never left me.*" That the figure of Jesus is arresting and captivating is obvious, but that does not prove his divinity any more than Ronald Reagan's charisma proves his. The rest of the sentence is describing a genuine and interesting psychological phenomenon, but again, there is no reason to believe it is anything more than personal delusion.

All in all I enjoyed the experience of debating William Craig, and I learned much by preparing for the debate, and later on while writing this Chapter. My own intellectual journey has definitely been enriched by it, and perhaps also that of some of the 1200 people in attendance, regardless of their convictions at the time. Of course, I did not move Craig's position by an inch, and he did little that could alter my own. But that is not necessarily a demonstration of intellectual rigidity on the part of either of us. After all, we have both been thinking for quite some time about all of the above, and we feel we have pretty good reasons to stand by our current positions. As for me, I may change my mind, but that would require quite a bit more than William Craig was able to offer during that stimulating evening at the University of Tennessee.

Chapter 11 - Creationism's numero uno: surviving Duane Gish

"Imagine spending four billion years stocking the oceans with seafood, filling the ground with fossil fuels, and drilling the bees in honey production – only to produce a race of bed-wetters!" (Barbara Ehrenreich, The Worst Years of Our Lives)

Duane Gish, biochemist and preacher, is by far the most famous and interesting character on the creationist scene, and well worth spending an evening with (Shermer 1997). I did it four times and may again. Gish has a degree in biochemistry from Berkeley, although he has not practiced science in decades. Most importantly, he is one of the most prolific writers (Gish 1995) and debaters of the so-called Institute for Creation Research (ICR), undoubtedly the preeminent creationist organization devoted to the "scientific" backing of a literal interpretation of the Bible. Before delving into the delights of my encounters with Gish, let me make clear that the ICR is a ministry, not a scientific institute. To convince yourself, just check out their web page (at http://www.icr.org/) and you will find the following statement:

> "The Institute for Creation Research Graduate School has a unique statement of faith for its faculty and students, incorporating most of the basic Christian doctrines in a creationist framework ... a firm commitment to creationism and to full Biblical inerrancy and authority."

I don't know of any scientific institution that requires anything like this from its faculty, and I couldn't think of a better demonstration of the fact that Gish is wrong on a crucial point: religion is not science (contrary to what the term "creation science" implies) and science is most definitely not a religion (as Gish and colleagues stubbornly maintain). This said, let us look at the details of Gish's arguments as he expressed them to me and another thousand

people on a hot and humid evening on 17 September 1998 at
Mississippi State University.[39]

Being slick is half the trick

The debate at Mississippi State started with my
presentation, in which after a few words of introduction I went
straight to the point. Not so for my opponent, a consummate
debater who has developed the art of working a crowd. His first
few sentences were:

> "Certainly, it is good to be here in Starkville at this great
> Mississippi State University. You know, it is bad enough
> when you come onto the campus and you do not preach
> what is accepted as politically correct. It is even worse
> when you come onto the campus and you preach, or say or
> explain that and they just lost a football game. So I am
> delighted that you won the game against the University of
> Memphis. I had the pleasure of shaking hands with Matt
> Ryan, your quarterback. When I looked at him, I wondered
> who it was that said, all men were created equal."

To this day I have never met Matt Ryan, nor do I wish to shake his
hands since I am not a football fan and it wouldn't help by CV a
bit. But the public loved it, and an already favorable crowd was
now even more ready to buy whatever Gish would tell them. The
item that followed was even better delivered than the first one.
Gish had actually read an article I published in *BioScience* (Pigliucci
1998b) and quoted from my writing. The article was a review of
Larson's excellent book on the history of the Scopes trial (Larson
1997). In it I made the remark that now as in 1925 the creationist-
evolution controversy comes down – among other things – to
academic freedom and to the fact that the majority does not have
the right to impose its opinion on matters of personal choice and
education. What do you know? With one stroke of rhetorical
genius Duane Gish had managed to transform the creationist

---

[39] The full transcript of the debate is available at
http://fp.bio.utk.edu/skeptic.

movement from oppressor to oppressed, arguing that today it is the *atheist majority* that unfairly precludes the righteous voice of Christianity from being expressed! Never mind, of course, that the U.S. has a well-known clause in the First Amendment to its Constitution barring the mixing of state and church, including the imposition of any atheistic philosophy. Never mind also that Christians are perfectly free to express themselves in all of the plethora of outlets made possible by modern society and technology. And most especially, never mind that the very concept of an atheist majority persecuting Christians is a ludicrous figment of Gish's imagination. He went on with the same theme by adding:

> "I believe in academic freedom; good science and good education requires that the scientific evidence for both the creation and evolution should be taught freely in our schools, devoid of reference to any religious literature including the Bible and the Humanist Manifesto. Dr. Pigliucci did not agree with that. He said that we must teach what we think is best science. Who is we? It is the evolutionists, of course. Certainly not democratic, and it certainly violates good education, good science and our academic and religious freedoms."

Now, regardless of the fact that no scientist I know has ever talked about the Humanist Manifesto in front of her class (in fact, most scientists don't even know what the Humanist Manifesto is to begin with), Gish does have a good point about education and democracy. Education is not, and I would argue should not be, democratic (see Chapter 8). Of course it is evolutionists who teach biology. Who else? Physics is taught by physicists who subscribe to Einstein's theory of relativity, not by proponents of the flat earth. This is not because of ideological reasons, but simply because Darwinism and relativity are – so far as we know

Figure 11.1. Duane Gish, creationist par excellence.

– the best explanations of what happens in nature. Should a serious challenge to either arise, scientists will take it up and the worst theory will eventually fall by the way side.[40]

Gish then went on to attempt to score on another ground that I had already tried to undercut: he claimed that the issue in front of the public that night was to decide if evolution or creation is a better theory to explain "origins." But origins of what? According to Gish, the arena of discussion included nothing less than the origin of life and the origin of the universe. This is a strange definition of evolution, since Darwinism actually only deals with the variety of life on earth, and it therefore assumes that both life and the earth were here to begin with. Admittedly, both the origin of the universe and the origin of life are crucial fields of scientific endeavor, but they belong to cosmology and biochemistry respectively, not to evolutionary biology. To apply a theory to something it was not designed to explain is a cheap rhetorical trick to convince the audience that it doesn't work. Putting evolution and ultimate origins of matter (living or not) in the same sentence is the scientific equivalent of mixing apples and oranges and it is not justified on logical grounds.

Gish then proceeded by asking his audience to consider what is science and what is not. Here again he came up with a definition that would baffle both scientists and philosophers of science. He claimed that science deals only with things that can be observed occurring today. If something happened in the past, science cannot tell us anything about it because *"There were no human witnesses of the origin of the Universe. There were no human witnesses to the origin of life. There were no human witnesses of the origin of a single living thing. These events happened in the unobservable past. They are not occurring in the present."* Following that logic, we

---

[40] Notice that I am not subscribing here to a naïve view of science as a perfect and spotless march toward truth. Being a practicing scientist, I realize that human passions and fallibility do enter into the equation. Cutting edge science is a much more messy business than most people realize – including most scientists themselves (Collins and Pinch 1998). As physicist Max Planck put it, new theories eventually become accepted because the old people die and the new generation grows accustomed to the new ideas. Yet, the process is not arbitrary, and ideas are not accepted simply because they are new. Most of them are rejected and condemned to a perpetual limbo in the sea of abandoned theories.

cannot know anything that happened when nobody was looking, and therefore our legal system should be thrown away because very few crimes are witnessed by anybody. Furthermore, perfectly respectable sciences such as geology and cosmology, which deal mostly with what happened in the past, should also be relegated to history or philosophy classes. This is a fundamental misunderstanding of the nature of science.

Science is not limited to phenomena that are repeatable today in the laboratory. It is much more complex and fascinating than that. Evolution, like geology and cosmology, is partly an historical science. Some of its observations concern events that occurred in the past, and some of its methods deal with how best to reconstruct such past events. This does not mean, as Gish implies, that hypotheses about historical events are untestable. For example, if the Big Bang really happened, one would expect to find a background thermal radiation permeating the universe, which is exactly what astronomers found. This does not *prove* the Big Bang, but it is an impressive piece of corroborative evidence. When a scientific theory accumulates many such instances of corroboration, it is tentatively accepted as correct, and retains this status until a better theory comes along that explains the same facts and more. This is the true nature of science, always in flux and always striving for a better understanding of the natural world. Furthermore, of course evolution *does* happen today, right under our very nose. The appearance of insects resistant to insecticides, or of new types of viruses such as the HIV variety, are examples of evolution in the making and can even be dissected and replicated under controlled laboratory conditions. To deny this is to put huge blinders on your eyes while claiming that you can see far better than anybody else. In other words, denying that evolution is occurring today is like saying that mountains are not currently forming simply because nobody has ever observed a mountain appear out of nothing. We can see and measure the slow movement of the continental plates, which is what causes mountains to form. Similarly, we can see and measure microevolutionary changes, the stuff of which large-scale evolution is made.

Gish's next move was to paint me, however subtly, as the devil. Seizing on the fact that I wrote for *Skeptic* magazine, he branded me a skeptic (which is true), and therefore an atheist

Figure 11.2. The developmental biology and ecology of butterflies Is a very active field of evolutionary research, and we understand a lot more about it than Duane Gish would want his audiences to believe. These butterflies of the species *Bicyclus anynana* have evolved two seasonal forms: the dull-colored ones with small "eyespots" (left) live during a season of low activity – the insect mostly stays still and tries to avoid predators by being inconspicuous. The bright-colored form with large eyespots lives during a much more active breeding and foraging season; the eyespot catches and diverts the attention of possible predators from the vital organs of the insect. The laboratory of Paul Brakefield in the Netherlands (who kindly provided the pictures) has made fantastic advances toward an understanding of the developmental mechanisms and evolution of these butterflies.

(which doesn't necessarily follow, see Chapter 6, but is indeed true in my particular case). The consequence of my positions, he alleged, is that I *have* to accept evolution because I don't have any alternative (i.e., any god) available. While this reasoning is fairly common among Christian apologists, it simply goes against the facts. I did not become an evolutionist because I was a skeptic; I became a skeptic because I am an evolutionist. Like most people in this world, I was born in a more or less religious family, who brought me up within their religious tradition (Catholicism in that case). It was only my later exposure to science that opened my mind to the fact that there are much better ways than scriptures and revelation to find things out. Of course, the other reason Gish's argument is untenable is because there are several examples of people who are religious, even Christian, and at the same time are evolutionists. It is the particular brand of intransigent Christianity upheld by Gish that doesn't square with science.

One of my arguments against creationism is that even if evolutionary theory as we understand it today will turn out to be wrong, this does not by any means automatically imply a victory for creationism. The history of science is littered with discarded theories, and in no case have we needed to turn to the supernatural as an alternative explanation. But Gish doesn't see it that way. For him it's yes or no, black or white, one or zero. Any crack in the evolutionary edifice is a brick for God. He is correct only in the most abstract sense: it must be true that a given phenomenon is either natural or supernatural. But there are many different possible natural explanations for any given phenomenon, so the fact that one doesn't work does not necessarily lead to discarding them all. Creationism has to do the hard work of accumulating positive evidence in its favor; there are no shortcuts in the quest for truth.

Gish then spent quite a bit of his time providing what he considers a decisive example of the failure of neo-Darwinism. He introduced this segment of his presentation by invoking what is known as "naïve falsificationism" (though he didn't use this term). Falsificationism is the idea, proposed by Karl Popper, that if a theory fails a test against empirical evidence even once, such theory should be discarded (Popper 1968). This is naïve because both science and the real world are much more complex than it is assumed by most philosophers of science. It is true that failure to predict or explain a *crucial* piece of data is a serious problem for a theory. But it is also true that there may be alternative explanations for why such failure occurred. Perhaps the theory needs to be modified slightly, while still retaining the core of its ideas (Lakatos 1974). Or maybe the experimental results were in fact incorrect. It is only the accumulation of several unexplained and apparently unexplainable pieces of evidence that causes a crisis for a theory. And even then, a better alternative has to be proposed (and usually is) before the complete abandonment of the previous paradigm (Kuhn 1970). Nevertheless, Duane Gish sat out to destroy Darwin with one stroke, and chose metamorphosis in insects to do so.

Gish presented in detail the process by which the chrysalis of the monarch butterfly transforms itself into the adult, emerging from its protective case in a matter of a few minutes. So far so good. Gish's astonishing claim was that since the process takes a few minutes, it could not have been shaped by natural selection over a long period of time as neo-Darwinism claims, Q.E.D.! I had already called Gish's attention to the absurdity of this statement in a previous debate, but he tried the trick again with a new audience. Superficially, his reasoning sounds good enough. That is, until you realize that it is based on two pieces of misinformation and a non sequitur. First of all, the "process" of transformation of the chrysalis into the adult does not take a few minutes, it takes a variable number of weeks, depending on the species. It is only the *emergence* of the butterfly from its case that takes a few minutes. This would be like claiming that human gestation is only a few hours long because that's what it takes to get the baby out of the womb. Second, contrary to what was implied by Gish, modern science knows a lot more about the development of organisms and its evolution. For example, papers are published at a high rate precisely on how butterflies develop and how evolution by natural selection has shaped their ability to do so (e.g., Brakefield et al. 1996; Nijhout 1996). Third, and most importantly, the tempo of evolutionary change of a structure or function does not have anything to do with the tempo of developmental change of the same structure of function. To make a technological parallel, Gish's line of reasoning would lead you to conclude that since it takes only a few minutes to get to the top of the Empire State Building, then the skyscraper could not possibly have been built over a period of years. One simply does not follow from the other because in one case we are considering a finished structure (the current development of the butterfly, or the completed ESB), while in the other we are dealing with the process that led to the formation of that structure (evolution for the butterflies, planning and engineering for the ESB).

Let me add just as an aside note that whenever I give technological examples within an evolution-creation debate, the creationist usually jumps up and says something along the lines of "but that (e.g., the Empire State Building) was built by humans, who are capable of intelligent design." Such an objection is so obtuse it would be hardly worth rebutting, except for the fact that it is so universal. The point of my ESB example was to show why one cannot infer too much about the process that led to the formation of something from the way that something works today, and I chose a technological example because this is familiar to people. Responding that conscious engineers built the ESB and implying that an intelligent designer built the butterflies too is to shift the question entirely. Now we are talking about *how* that structure came about and how well it fits with its purported function. That is *not* what we were discussing initially, and I would not have chosen that specific example if the question were different. To shift the target in the middle of a discussion is purely and simply a sophistic device and it is either the reflection of poor comprehension of the subject or of downright intellectual dishonesty.

Gish then started a rapid fire of anti-evolution attacks, beginning with the infamous drawings of different embryos of vertebrates originally published by Ernst Haeckel at the turn of the century. These drawings represent embryos of vertebrates at different times during their development, showing that animals as diverse as chickens and humans start with embryos that look very much alike and then slowly diverge until the adult animal is formed. This is of course what you would expect according to evolution because all vertebrates have a remote common ancestor from which the animals living today are derived: shared stages of development are a reflection of shared ancestry. However, Haeckel wanted to go much further and suggested a specific hypothesis known as recapitulation. He proposed that each "higher" animal (say, humans) actually recapitulates throughout its development the evolutionary stages of "lower" animals (e.g., fishes). That would explain, for example, why human embryos go through a phase in which they develop gill slits. The theory of recapitulation is by and large rejected by modern biologists as a general explanation of the evolution of development, though there are some compelling examples of it in specific instances. The point Gish seized upon is the recent discovery that Haeckel fudged his drawings a little bit, in a way that the details are in better agreement with his expectations (Richardson et al. 1998). Unfortunately the mistake has been discovered only recently, and most (though not all) introductory biology textbooks still publish the original drawings. While this is certainly a regrettable occurrence that will be corrected as time passes and authors and publishers become more aware of it, it is by no means a blow to the theory of evolution, as Gish would want his audience to believe. The embryos in question are still very similar at the beginning of their development, and they do diverge gradually – Haeckel *fudged* his drawings (perhaps unconsciously), he did not made them up out of thin air. Consequently, the only theory that is no longer compatible with the reality of embryology is Haeckel's recapitulation, not Darwin's modification by descent.

Gish then acknowledged my observation that all organisms are made of the same components, in particular nucleic acids (DNA and RNA) and proteins. My point was that this essential similarity is the hallmark of an historical process: we are made of the same things as other animals and plants because we came from the same ancestral forms. The creationist response is that we are made of the same things because, in Gish's words *"It had to be that way; it could not have been any other way. We live in the same world, we eat the same food, we drink the same water and we breathe the same air."* As in the case of my debate with Craig (Chapter 11) this is a rather blasphemous restriction on the power of God: is Gish implying that God had to bow to the laws of physics and biology that he himself made? Furthermore, the statement is factually incorrect: we *do not* all share the same food and breathe the same air. That is one of the amazing things about biodiversity: organisms have been able to use a restricted number of tools such as nucleic acids and proteins to adapt to an incredible variety of environmental conditions. Lastly, there is absolutely no reason to think that life *has* to use the same materials that it happened to use on earth. The existence of other life forms using different building blocks is perfectly conceivable and does not violate any known law of physics or chemistry. The fact that all life on earth shares the same fundamental constituents is an indication of common descent, not of universal constraints.

Gish did raise a good point during the debate, but of course made it to be a crucial hurdle for evolutionary theory instead of an interesting problem that biologists are working on. He said that the evolution of new structures, such as the neck of a giraffe, is an impossible puzzle because it also requires the simultaneous change of several other structures and functions, such as the capacity of the heart to pump the blood higher up, or the ability of the skeleton to support and balance an animal with an elongated neck. This is a well-known problem in evolutionary biology, and evolutionists have proposed two explanations: mosaic evolution and phenotypic plasticity. First, let me make clear that Gish's presentation of the problem is, as usual, a caricature. The way he put it to the debate's audience is that according to evolutionary theory giraffes (for example) acquired an elongated neck all at once, so that clearly their skeleton, lungs, heart, etc. would not be adequate for the new task. What instead happened was a more or less gradual elongation of the neck, which at any point in time would have required only a slight difference in the skeleton, lungs, and heart. The idea underlying mosaic evolution (Futuyma 1998) is that once one change has happened, for example the neck of the giraffe has elongated a little bit because of a favorable mutation, the rest of the body is still adequate for the functions it has to carry out. At a later time, a mutation is selected that changes, say, the heart rate to make a better fit with the longer neck. Then another mutation can be selected that modifies the lungs appropriately, and so on. This means that not all the changes have to happen simultaneously, a situation that is genetically very unlikely simply because mutations, beneficial or not, are rare. The alternative hypothesis, known as evolution by phenotypic plasticity, is that most of the changes can indeed occur simultaneously, but they are not initially determined genetically (West-Eberhard 1989; Schlichting and Pigliucci 1998). This is rather complicated, but in essence all organisms are known to be able to respond to environmental modifications by altering their phenotype (i.e., their external appearance or their physiology) rather than their genotype (i.e., the ensemble of their genes). These alterations are somewhat reversible (hence the term plasticity), depending on the environmental conditions. However, if the environment is permanently modified, the changes can become apparently fixed. Mutations may then occur that actually do fix the new phenotype by no longer allowing a reversal to the original condition. The character in question is then said to have been "genetically assimilated" (Waddington 1961).[41] The advantage of phenotypic plasticity and genetic assimilation is that the first modifications of the phenotype do not require any genetic change at all. The latter occurs later and it becomes fixed (the new character is "assimilated") only if it is advantageous for the individual. The important point for this discussion is that phenotypic plasticity allows a simple mechanism by which several characters can change simultaneously in an apparently coordinated fashion without requiring multiple mutations to occur simultaneously or at the onset.

Just to prove that this is not a hypothetical situation made up by evolutionists to get themselves out of trouble, let me briefly summarize the example of the famous bipedal goat described by Slijper (1942). The goat in question was born with a detrimental mutation that produced highly reduced forelimbs. To the astonishment of researchers, the goat rapidly developed the ability to walk on two legs, albeit clumsily. Furthermore, this ability was accompanied by a whole array of changes in the structure of the bones and muscles that were modified to facilitate the bipedal posture. All these changes were not the direct result of the original mutation, but simply of phenotypic plasticity of the developing skeletal and muscular system that molded themselves to the new task. A change in the environment (in this case forced by a mutation) had translated into a completely different morphology and behavior for the animal. If the goat were allowed to breed and produced some progeny, this too would have probably shown

---

[41] Please notice that genetic assimilation, a still controversial topic of investigation in evolutionary biology, is by no means to be confused with Lamarckism, the idea that an organism can respond to changes in the environment and that this response becomes inherited by its progeny. The difference is that phenotypic plasticity does not alter the genetic make up of an individual and that for genetic assimilation to work (i.e., for the initially plastic phenotype to become fixed) new mutations have eventually to occur. The process is therefore Darwinian in nature, in that it still depends on mutation and natural selection.

phenotypic plasticity of a similar sort.[42] With time, mutations in the descendants of the original goat might have been selected that fine-tuned the plastic response, until potentially the entire line of descent would have been made of bipedal animals. That is most likely what happened during our own evolution as hominid originating from non-bipedal primates. More importantly, had Slijper's goat been found in the fossil record, scientists would have been amazed at the complete lack of intermediate forms linking normal quadrupedal goats to the bipedal variety! We do not currently know how many "missing links" are actually due to evolution by phenotypic plasticity and genetic assimilation.

Speaking of the fossil record, Gish did not waste any time declaring evolution *"dead in the water"* because very few fossils have been found before the so-called Cambrian explosion. The Cambrian explosion is a relatively brief geological period (5-15 million years) that occurred about 550 million years ago. A variety of life forms appears in the fossil record in correspondence with the beginning of the Cambrian period, including essentially all major groups of animals known today (and a few extinct ever since). The problem is that few direct ancestors of these same forms are known from pre-Cambrian rocks. If evolution is true, asks Gish, why not? Where did the Cambrian animals come from? As usual, the point represents a valid scientific question, but the presentation is naïve and the conclusion (that God did the trick directly) is a non sequitur. First, we actually know quite a bit more about the origin of the modern taxa of animals than Gish implies, with most of this knowledge originating from modern studies in molecular biology (Raff et al. 1994) rather than paleontology.[43] Second, paleontology does in fact have something to say about the evolution of pre-Cambrian and early Cambrian animals, and what little we know so far poses no threat to the theory of evolution in

---

[42] Incidentally, breeding of even severely handicapped animals is known to occur in nature, for example among chimpanzees (de Waal 1996). Even though such animals are at a disadvantage, that does not mean they will have necessarily no progeny at all, which in turn implies that they may play a role on the Darwinian stage.

[43] Briefly, comparisons of the DNA of different groups of animals living today reveals varying degrees of similarity, which is best explained by the fact that some of these groups are more closely related to certain others. See also Lynch 1999.

Figure 11.3. A cranium of *Homo sapiens* (our species, on the right) compared to that of one of our ancestors, *Homo habilis* (on the left). What would an intermediate form look like?

Homo habilis ? Homo sapiens

that pre-Cambrian animals do show a relationship, albeit remote, to their Cambrian counterparts (Morris 1998). Third, the fact that we know very little of pre-Cambrian life is simply because there are very few pre-Cambrian fossils; that in itself is not surprising for two reasons. On the one hand, we are talking about rocks formed more than 600 million years ago, many of which have been destroyed by subsequent geological events; on the other hand, most of the pre-Cambrian animals were soft-bodied (i.e., they did not have a hard skeleton) and were made of substances that do not readily fossilize. I realize that to the general public these may sound like a bunch of excuses, but if you study a bit of geology and geochemistry you will realize that this is science, not sophistry.

This business of the intermediate fossil forms or lack thereof requires more discussion. One of the problems is that creationists have been given a formidable weapon by some old-fashioned evolutionists who have taken Darwin a bit too literally. One of the tenets of Darwinian evolution is that the process occurs slowly, little by little. Gish therefore rightly asked where are the millions of intermediate forms that one would expect if biological change always occurred over millions of years. The fact is, it does not seem that evolution is that slow after all. Most of modern research in paleontology as well as in molecular developmental biology leads to the conclusion that evolution is episodic. To put it as Harvard evolutionist Stephen Gould once did, evolution seems to be much like baseball: nothing happens most of the time, then a crucial play is over before you can raise your eyes from the hot dog. This, however, does not mean that evolutionary change occurs instantaneously (as Gish also accused his opponents of suggesting, when it is convenient for his arguments): while the play may be rapid on a geological scale, it still requires tens or hundreds of thousands of years. The point is that tens of thousands of years are very little time compared to the normal life span of a species, usually measured in millions or tens of millions of years. That is why most of the fossil record shows the same forms for a long period of time and then new ones appearing with few (but not zero) intermediates.

The other problem with creationists' call for intermediate forms is that it very conveniently never ends. As Michael Shermer pointed out (1997), once evolutionists present an intermediate fossil filling a gap in the record, the creationist typically reacts by saying that the situation has gotten worse, since there are now *two* gaps, between each of the original forms and the new found one! This is illustrated in Figures 11.3 and 11.4: 11.3 shows the crania of modern humans and of one of our ancestors, *Homo abilis*. It is a legitimate question to ask what an intermediate link would look like. This happens to be known as *Homo erectus*, whose skull is shown in Fig. 11.4. While *H. erectus* clearly has the right characteristics for being intermediate between *H. abilis* and *H. sapiens*, creationists will either deny that it is a link (usually by saying that it was an unrelated animal, or one or the other of the two already known forms), or claim that evolution has not been proven because of the now additional missing links. This is of course a travesty of the way science works. We will never find all the intermediate forms between all of the species that ever existed. This is simply not the nature of the fossil record. But we do not need *all* of the information before reaching a reasonable conclusion. As in the detective work aimed at solving a crime, as long as the available information is sufficient to clearly point to one conclusion (or culprit), that is good enough to convince

Figure 11.4. A cranium of *Homo erectus* which represents the intermediate link between the two skulls depicted in Figure 11.3.

Homo erectus

the jury beyond reasonable doubt. Except for a jury of creationists, that is.

Gish then came to one of his favorite battle horses, despite having been rebutted on this point by virtually everybody who ever debated him: the second principle of thermodynamics. He said: "*If life evolved on this planet I expect that life evolved into everything living today including people. So we've gone from hydrogen (at the beginning of the universe) to people. Someone said that if that is true, we could say that hydrogen is an odorless, tasteless, invisible gas which when given enough time, becomes people.*" To which the audience, of course, laughed heartily. Well, hydrogen really is an odorless, tasteless, invisible gas that, given a large amount of time, the laws of physics, and a bit of luck, does indeed become people. The argument he was trying to make is that evolution runs against a fundamental law of physics known as the second principle of thermodynamics. Simply put, the principle says that in a closed physical system (i.e., a system that does not receive either matter or energy from outside) entropy (i.e., the degree of disorder in the system) will grow until it reaches a maximum, after which no other change in the system will occur (on average). According to this argument, since living organisms are physical systems characterized by low entropy, and since evolution has allegedly produced increasingly complex (and therefore lower-entropy) systems over the course of billions of years, there is an inherent contradiction between physics and biology. Given that physical laws are much better established than biological ones, evolution must be wrong.[44] The argument is not tenable. For one thing, no physicist actually seems to have a problem with biological evolution, only creationists do; this should sound a warning bell

---

[44] Physicists have actually used this argument in the past, only to be demonstrated wrong. At the time Darwin published his work, the leading physicists of the time, and particularly Lord Kelvin, thought that the earth could not be older than a few million years. This was because physicists assumed that the sun must be burning chemical fuel, like a candle; the alternative of nuclear fusion was still unknown to the science of the time. Darwin, however, strongly suggested that the earth (and therefore the sun) must have been much older, of the order of at least hundreds of millions of years, or there would not have been enough time for evolution to occur. Since evolution obviously did occur, physicists must have been missing something. They were.

that there is something wrong with Gish's reasoning. On the biological front, the matter was put to rest by Jacques Monod, who clearly explained why there is no contradiction between evolution and the second principle in his *Chance and Necessity* (Monod 1971). It all boils down to the clause in the second principle that specifies its applicability only to closed systems. The earth and its biosphere are *not* closed systems, as I and countless others repeatedly pointed out to Gish. There is a continuous flux of material from space and from the interior of the earth and, most importantly, of energy from the sun. The overall entropy of the sun-earth system is indeed increasing in part as a result of the evolution of life on our planet, in perfect agreement with the second principle.

Gish, however, recently raised the stakes about the second principle, by pushing the argument back to the origin of the universe. His point is that the universe itself cannot be considered an open system, because by definition there is nothing "out there." If that is true, doesn't the principle preclude the very origin of the universe by natural means? The point is very cleverly put, but it betrays a complete ignorance of modern physics and of the specific matter being discussed, thermodynamics. First, notice that this is obviously not an objection to evolutionary theory, since the theory does not have anything to do with cosmology and the origin of the universe. Second, the principle is a result of what is called statistical thermodynamics, i.e., it is a law that applies to systems with large quantities of component parts, such as gases or ecosystems. The universe at the beginning was made of a single entity known as a singularity. By definition such object could not exchange heat, energy or anything else with other such systems and entropy, for all effective purposes, simply did not *exist* before the Big Bang (and neither did space and time as we understand them today). Third, our best theories about the origin of the universe, tentative as they are, imply that it originated because of a quantum fluctuation in the original singularity and that this singularity was actually a nugget of Planck size (see Chapter 10). There is no contradiction with any known law of physics. It seems worth pointing out here that Gish's arguments *sound* scientific because they are based on a combination of common sense and scientific jargon. While his own understanding of science is very limited, unfortunately so is that of a large part of the general public, which is why he can be convincing and come across as defending at least as respectable a point as his opponent in a debate. Science, especially cutting edge research in physics, biology, or cosmology, is in fact counterintuitive and not a matter of simple common sense writ large. These are issues of which anybody planning to defend science in public should be cognizant. I am not suggesting that scientists should not lecture and debate about these issues; in fact I think this is one of our duties as active members of the community. But to engage creationists effectively one has to spend some time not only studying his own and other sciences (after all, I am no cosmologist, geologist, or physicist, but I have to discuss issues pertinent to all those disciplines), but also consider issues of effective communication to the public and even oratorical skills.[45] The consequences of not doing so may be disastrous.

Duane Gish can come very close to intentional deception during a debate. Toward the end of his discussion of the second principle he mentioned the famous experiments of Stanley Miller on simulating the original atmospheric conditions of the earth before the origin of life (Miller 1953; see also Chapter 12 and Figure 12.1). These experiments yielded the formation of organic molecules that include some of the basic constituents of life after a mixture of gases was exposed to a variety of energy sources, including simulated lightning. I do agree that Miller's experiments are much less important than it was once thought because we are now not at all certain that the conditions he used were indeed the ones prevalent on prebiotic earth. However, here is Gish's comment: *"What happens to you when you get hit by lightning? Do you become more complex, more highly ordered? No, you get obliterated."* That's a good quip, but – as a biochemist – Gish should know better. Lightning would have discharged energy in the atmosphere, and it is a *fact* that this can catalyze chemical reactions

---

[45] As an example of this, let me cite Gish again while introducing a quote from Isaac Asimov concerning the definition of the second principle of thermodynamics: *"I am going to allow an evolutionist to define that for us, Isaac Asimov. He actually became a creationist, I believe about five seconds after he died."* Regardless of the fact that such a statement is offensive and in poor taste, our culture is such that a creationist can get away with it (because it plays into the beliefs of the majority of the audience) while a much milder satirical remark on the part of an evolutionist or, worse, of an atheist, would be jeered at for being insensitive. Alas, such is the imbalance of the world in which we live.

that produce more complex molecules. This is an entirely different situation from a living being directly struck by lightning. In this case I am not willing to concede Gish the benefit of the doubt; he simply must have known better.

Gish then went into some detail on the origin of life problem and especially on Fred Hoyle's calculations about the alleged impossibility of evolution. I will refer the reader to Chapters 12 and 9 respectively for a treatment of these topics. Gish's next ploy was to apparently quote evolutionists themselves as disproving the theory. This is a marvelous idea indeed; what better than to use leading figures in your opponent's field to attack his arguments? But of course there are no leading biologists who refute evolution, so Gish had to fish for a couple of misfits – which you can find in any field given a large enough population – and for people long dead whose ideas he misrepresents. His first candidate in this series is Soren Lovtrup, a Swedish scientist who denies that evolution occurs by mutation and natural selection. He is instead an advocate of the so-called "hopeful monster" scenario, an idea proposed originally by Richard Goldschmidt (1940) in the 1940s and since completely abandoned by the scientific community. Goldschmidt suggested that "genomic revolutions" (similar to the equally non-existent "genetic storms" of Fred Hoyle; see Chapter 9), i.e., large rearrangements of the genetic material of an individual, instantaneously result in completely new types of organisms. Since these would be very different from whatever came before them (including their own parents, a point not lost on Gish's dry sense of humor), they would indeed be "monsters." The hopefulness comes because some of these monstrosities might be able to survive better than their own original type and therefore start a new evolutionary lineage. While Goldschmidt was a highly respectable geneticist and many of his ideas are still been considered today (Schlichting and Pigliucci 1998), hopeful monsters justly rest in the dustbin of science history. This does not mean that Goldschmidt was inept – even Einstein proposed unworkable ideas; indeed any good scientist is bound to make mistakes while carrying out frontier science. It does however raise some questions about the competence of good Dr. Lovtrup, who half a century after Goldschmidt should simply know better.

Gish then turned against mutations, those changes in the genetic material of organisms that provide the fuel for evolution to occur. He claimed that he has never seen a beneficial mutation, even though I had already invited him personally to my laboratory to check a few out for himself. There are plenty of misconceptions about mutations, one of which is that they are "errors" in the replication of DNA. The word "error" implies a context within which to judge the occurrence of a particular event. Mutations per se are neither good nor bad, therefore they are not errors; they are simply changes. It is the environment that provides the context and therefore the yardstick to measure the usefulness or detrimental effect of any given mutation. It has been established now for some time both on theoretical (Kimura 1983) and on empirical (Hey 1999) grounds that the majority of mutations are neither deleterious nor advantageous; they are neutral or quasi-neutral (i.e., they may carry a very slight advantage or disadvantage). Therefore, Gish's apocalyptic vision of zillions of genetic defects burdening natural populations is not a biological reality. More importantly, the effect of mutations depends on the environment in which the organism carrying them happens to be living. The classical example, that Gish knows very well and still chooses to misconstrue for his public, is the gene that causes sickle cell anemia. While in most human environments such mutation is deleterious because it causes anemia, in regions where malaria has a high incidence the gene is actually beneficial, because it modifies the shape of the red cells in a way that precludes the agent of malaria from replicating and infecting the whole body. Is the sickle cell gene "bad"? It depends on the environment. On one thing I do agree with Gish. Referring to evolution by mutation and natural selection he said: *"The worst process that one could think to create."* That is exactly why nobody actually *thought* of creating it; it happened naturally, and nature has an uncanny tendency to be messy.

The conclusion of Gish's opening statement had predictably nothing to do with science. As with Craig before him (Chapter 10), he completely abandoned any pretense of scientific or rational discourse and admonished people: *"Let me say this, as I said to you, either God is or God isn't."* In other words, if you accept evolution, you will go to Hell, make no mistake about it. This kinds of statement makes it extremely clear that, contrary to what most people seem to think, the creation-evolution controversy is not at all a scientific debate. It is about religion and ideology, about

Figure 11.5. Different types of eyes found among present-day organisms that show some of the possible intermediate stages of the evolution of a complex eye such as the vertebrate one.

Gastropods: *Patella*

Most groups; many
annelids and gastropods

Gastropods: *Helix*

Fish; squids; some gastropod
annelids and crustaceans

emotions and human psychology, about power and control over people. And a sprinkle of science here and there, of course.

Of eyes and whales

The first comeback of Gish after my rebuttal was typical of the creationist strategy: *"He says we cannot hid behind this 'well God did it'. The evolutionists hid behind this 'natural selection did it'."* It sounds fair enough. Is it not true that natural selection is just a hand wave, a *deus-ex-machina* invoked at the convenience of the scientist to explain away something he does not understand? And, consequently, is it not true that evolutionism is just a religion, or at least an ideology, disguised as science? Of course not. The difference is that if Gish is asked to put some meat on his claims, to come up with some more detailed explanations in place of his "God did it," he would be at a complete loss. By definition, nobody knows how God does things, and if we knew we would be gods ourselves. But if you ask a scientist to explain what she means by natural selection, she can provide you with plenty of graduate-level textbooks devoted to precise mathematical analyses of the phenomenon (Hartl and Clark 1989) or to a discussion of pertinent empirical studies (Endler 1986). Of course, this difference cannot come out in a debate format, because it requires quite a bit of time and effort to explain what the mathematical theory of evolution consists of, or what are the empirical data in its support. That is why debates can only be meant to stimulate someone's curiosity to devote some serious time to study the matter and educate oneself, a point that I always make during my presentations. Ignorance is easy, while knowledge requires a lot of effort. Once again, there is no shortcut to the truth.

In response to my argument that evolution is not random (because it is the result of a random process, mutation, and a non-random one, natural selection), Gish quoted Douglas Futuyma, one of the preeminent evolutionary biologists alive today as saying that *"by coupling undirected purposeless variation to the blind uncaring process of natural selection, Darwin made theological or spiritual explanations of life processes superfluous."* This is a great example of how subtle points can be lost on an audience and easy points can be scored in a debate. Futuyma said that selection is blind and uncaring, not that it is random. By blind he meant that there is no general direction, no higher purpose, to the doings of selective mechanisms; that is entirely clear if one actually reads the paragraph in the original context. Selection simply favors those organisms that, for whatever (quantifiable) reason, survive and produce more offspring. This is not at all a random process, but it is one that does not have a predetermined direction simply because the environment can change, and what was an advantage before may turn out to be a handicap now. Futuyma was also very careful in his statement about theological or spiritual explanations. Notice that he didn't say that they are not true, because that would be a philosophical, not a scientific conclusion. However, they are certainly superfluous, in the sense that we have a natural (and therefore simpler) explanation for the history and diversity of life on earth.

Gish then used the old argument from design (see Chapters 9 and 10), which I had brought up and criticized earlier in the debate. He quoted biochemist Michael Behe (1996) as saying that the eye is an "irreducibly complex" structure, and could not therefore have evolved by mutation and natural selection. That is very strange on the face of the evidence. First, we know of many intermediate stages in the evolution of a complex eye in animals that are still alive today, which clearly demonstrates that simpler eyes than ours can work quite well and therefore that the structure is not irreducibly complex, whatever that means. For example, gastropods (small invertebrates closely related to clams) of the genus *Patella* have an almost flat eye, while other gastropods of the genus *Helix* have almost round eyes, with a much more complex structure and better visual acuity. The respective nervous systems are also proportionally scaled to be able to handle the level of sensorial input. How would such observations be explained within the creationist mindset? I had previously remarked that in fact the human eye is less perfect than we might think, and in particular it is not "designed" as well as the eye of mollusks such as squids and octopuses. This is because of the fact that our eye has nervous termini and blood vessels located in front of the retina, which among other things causes blind spots Squids and octopuses have their termini and vessels where one would expect them to be, in the rear of the retina, and therefore suffer from no related inconvenience. My conclusion would be that either God cared more for squids than for humans, or that this result occurred by natural processes that are genuinely uncaring and "blind" (no pun intended) in the sense of Futuyma. Gish's response was that we cannot know that the squid's eyes are better designed than ours because we cannot implant them in a human to see how they would work. This is once again a gross caricature of science, which unfortunately resonates with at least part of the public. We don't *need* to do the transplant because we can carry out careful observations of the visual acuity and other characteristics of these animals; we can also produce sophisticated mathematical models of how the eye of any creature works from the point of view of optics and engineering. For the same reason, we don't need to have been on the surface of the sun to conclude that its temperature is about 6000°C; telescopes and spectrometers, together with the known laws of physics, tell us that. Science is a much more complex, beautiful, and effective enterprise than Gish makes it out to be.

Table 11.1 – A few cases of observed speciation.

Mechanism	Type of organism	Example
Polyploidy	Plant	Evening primrose: *Oenothera gigas* arose from *lamarckiana* (1905)
Polyploidy	Plant	Kew primrose: *Primula kewensis* observed to rise from *P. floribunda* in 1905, 1923, and 1926.
Hybridization	Plant	*Raphanobrassica* is obtained around 1927 from *Raphanus sativus* and *Brassica oleracea*
Reproductive isolation	Plant	*Stephanomeria malheurensis* originates *S. exigua* (1973)
Reproductive isolation	Insect	A new species of *Drosophila* originated from *D. paulistorum* in the laboratory between 1958 and 1963
Ecological speciation	Insect	Different populations of *Drosophila pseudoobscura* developed reproductive isolation as a byproduct of selection in different habitats (1989)
Reproductive isolation	Worm	A new species of polychaete worm emerged from *Nereis acuminata* over 20 years of breeding (1992)
Invasion of a new habitat	Mammal	A new species of house mouse evolved on Faeroe Island within 250 years from human introduction of the animals

In response to my invitation to come and see beneficial mutations in my laboratory, Gish said: *"I do not care what you start with, if you start with roses, you end up with roses. If you start with onions, you end up with onions, you start with corn, they got a lot better corn today, but it is still corn."* Notice once again the rhetorical device of shifting the target of the criticism: my invitation was meant to answer his claim that there are no beneficial mutations, but he turns around and asks me now to show him that I can synthesize new species in the laboratory. Of course, this has been done, too. The literature in the field of appearance of new species, either under laboratory or field conditions, is not extensive, partly because such events are rare on a human time scale, but it is nevertheless impressive. Geneticists have created all sorts of new plant species, for example, and have been able to recreate in the laboratory some new species that occur in the field; furthermore, some examples of speciation have actually been observed in recent times (Table 11.1). Gish may have been misinformed on the subject, since this is a rather technical field of inquiry within evolutionary biology. Then again, he is supposed to be a professional debater, so he should devote some time to library research.

The following attack by Gish is worth reporting in full, because it is so indicative of both mindset and strategy: *"He {Pigliucci} talked about the evolution of whales, examples of transitional forms and if I had time I would show some of these pictures. Notice what the ancestor was? A wolf! A wolf-like creature, do you really believe that anyone would really believe that a wolf would go into the water? I mean, it has all this great wonderful food on the land, abundant food supply. Do you mean to tell me that it would go into the water and fish around to try and get some clams and crack the clams with his teeth and stay around there long enough to evolve into a whale or something that was the ancestor of a whale? The very idea is ridiculous and they imagine that these things are intermediate."* The reference is to a slide I had shown that portrays the intermediate fossils linking terrestrial animals to modern whales (Thewissen et al. 1994). Never mind that the fossils are a fact that needs to be explained, regardless of Gish's denial, and that the most logical explanation is that indeed whales originated from land mammals around 50 million years ago. How does Gish know that the food supply of these ancestors was indeed plentiful? The struggle for limited resources is one of the most common themes in ecology, and in part one of the major drives behind evolutionary changes, so it is not at all inconceivable that competition for resources pushed whale's ancestors into the water, precisely in a reverse fashion to the push that got their much earlier ancestors to abandon water as fish and colonize the land as amphibians. The comic image conjured by Gish's explanation of how these terrestrial animals would have fed themselves cannot possibly beat the reality of watching a penguin, a sea lion or an hippopotamus doing the same today. If Gish wants to see intermediate forms, I suggest a fun trip to the zoo.

And speaking of intermediate forms, Gish felt compelled to attack our own fossil record as hominids, the real reason creationists get so upset with paleontologists. He quoted the work of Lord Zuckerman, who studied fossils of *Australopithecus*, one of the primates most closely related to *Homo* (our own genus) and rejected the idea that they belong to the same line of descent as humans. Naturally, Gish conveniently neglected to mention that Zuckerman's conclusions were based on very early fossil findings, and that they are now completely rejected by the paleontological community (more on Zuckerman below). That is simply the way science works, unless of course you prefer to think of international conspiracies being ran all the time to stifle the scientific insights of the minority.

Let me give the reader yet another example of Gish's strategy, again hovering right at the boundary between ignorance and deceit. He mentioned an episode concerning evolutionary biologist Richard Dawkins, one of the harshest critics of creationism: *"I wish he {Pigliucci} would invite Richard Dawkins {to see beneficial mutations in the lab}; he is a famous British evolutionist and he is a spokesman for evolution in England, I saw him on television. The person asked him, 'Dr. Dawkins, would you please describe some beneficial mutations for us?' And he looked up like this and then he looked up like this, and then he asked him to shut off the camera."* Sounds like somebody was caught red-handed and an embarrassment for the evolution community has finally been unmasked. The actual story is told in detail by Dawkins himself (1999b). What happened was that a television troupe from Australia showed up unannounced in Dawkins' office. He usually does not conduct interviews without an appointment, a normal precaution for a busy person. But the pleading of the troupe members that they had come from Australia expressly to interview him for a documentary on evolution did the trick. When the infamous question to which Gish referred was asked without the usual agreement that goes on in these matters (even experts have to have the time to brush up on their sources), Dawkins realized he had been duped by a group of creationists and was so angry that he asked to shut off the camera and for them to leave. He eventually agreed to continue the interview, but instead of reporting the actual interview, the crew thought that the initial emotional reaction would better serve their propaganda. So much for honesty in broadcasting.

Of flowering plants and going to Hell

A few minutes later, during his concluding remarks, Gish made a statement that at the time had not much consequence, but that will haunt him for the rest of his debates with me. He said: *"you know flowering plants just burst upon the scene fully formed; I think there are forty-three families of flowering plants that appear in the fossil record. This has been a great mystery ever since Darwin."* He was referring to what Darwin termed "the abominable mystery" of the origin of flowering plants. Indeed, until 1999 nobody had the faintest idea of where flowering plants came from. But to declare a scientific theory dead because it has not solved one problem, even one that has lasted for almost 140 years, is always dangerous. To use such failure as a cornerstone of your belief in God is foolish. Someone could publish a paper the following week and throw the anti-scientific position in disarray. That is exactly what happened toward the end of 1999, when three groups of scientists independently published papers containing the solution to Darwin's abominable mystery (Mathews and Donoghue 1999). It turns out that the most primitive angiosperms (the technical term for flowering plants) include water lilies. This work points to the conclusion that the first flowering plants were probably woody species, with the herbaceous habit evolving shortly thereafter and probably accounting for the massive radiation of species that has made it so difficult to solve the puzzle until now.

Gish eventually concluded with an interesting, and in my opinion self-contradictory statement: *"there are and there will always be many unanswered questions. That is why we have an Institute for Creation Research. That is why we have a Creation Research Society with more then 600 members. That is why we are doing so much research on all of these things, because there is so much that we need to know, so much that we will never know, but listen, there is enough information available today to know beyond doubt that evolution is false and God created this universe and its living organisms. It is such that through the things that God has made, we can discern easily the unseen attributes of God, so that no one has any excuse."* The first part is attempting to portray the Institute for Creation Research as a bunch of cutting edge, honest researchers who are not blinded by faith and ideology. Yet remember the statement of faith that these very same "scientists" have to sign every year to keep receiving their paychecks from ICR. Also recall that no such statement is signed by any tenure-track faculty at any public or private recognized research university. But it is the last part of that sentence that bothers me and should bother any intelligent member of the audience. It is not only an admission that the conclusion has already been arrived at (and therefore there is no need for further "research"), but more importantly it is a thinly veiled threat ("no one has any excuse") to the audience once again attempting to play on their emotions and fears rather than appealing to their intellect and rationality. I would be hard pressed trying to remember a single instance in which a colleague at a scientific meeting has made any statement even remotely comparable to this one. Once again, this is a debate about religion and ideology, not science.

Is Gish honest?

The skeptical community has been debating for some time now the question of Gish's personal beliefs. Is he honest about his understanding of science and evolution, in which case he is extremely naïve about it; or is he lying straight through his teeth and following Luther's suggestion that even lies are commendable if they further the "true faith"?[46] Even after having met Gish three times in formal debates and having talked to him off stage (though not much, since he doesn't like to mix socially with his opponents), it is really hard for me to say.

Duane Gish certainly sounds very convinced, and he can effectively convey his message to his audiences. On the other hand, there are clear times in which it is hard to shake the feeling that you are listening to a consummate politician or car salesman. In this essay I have pointed out several occasions in which giving him the benefit of the doubt was really pushing the envelope as far as it would go. For example, one of Gish's regular complaints is that the scientific community engages in an anti-creationist conspiracy that

---

[46] This is what Martin Luther said on the subject: "What harm would it do, if a man told a good strong lie for the sake of the good and for the Christian church … a lie out of necessity, a useful lie, a helpful lie, such lies would not be against God, he would accept them."

precludes him or any other creationist from ever publishing his ideas. Now, I know for sure that such complaint is not without foundation, given the contempt with which scientists see creationists. However, he was offered the opportunity to publish an article on the second principle of thermodynamics in a well respected journal several years ago, provided that the arguments were laid out in rigorous mathematical terms, as in any professional scientific publication (see Appendix to this chapter). He never took advantage of the offer, leading one to conclude that the bluff had been called and Gish had lost.

Gish's behavior has been at least questionable in a few other instances. For example, in *American Biology Teacher* of November 1976, p. 496, he refers to a book by Norman Macbeth entitled *Darwin Retried*, and says: "Macbeth, who is by no means a creationist, has flatly stated that 'Darwinism is not science.'" However, Macbeth *is* in fact a creationist who has published several books on the topic, and is not a scientist – as implied by Gish – but a lawyer. In his *Evolution: the Fossils Still Say No!*, Gish quotes paleontologist Stephen Gould as follows:

"The fossil record with its abrupt transitions offers no support for gradual change."

What Gould actually wrote, in *Natural History* volume 86, p. 22 in 1997 is:

"The fossil record with its abrupt transitions offers no support for gradual change, and the principle of natural selection does not require it – selection can operate rapidly."

The first part of the sentence taken alone implies that Gould is rejecting evolutionary theory, while it is clear from the whole sentence that he is doing no such thing. When asked about the curious omission, Gish said that he couldn't quote a whole article and had to stop somewhere. But surely the specific breaking point he chose is at least peculiar.

Joyce Arthur has spent considerable time examining Gish's writings and debates, and has published a detailed analyses of his questionable tactics (Arthur 1996). The following are some of the examples she discusses:

1. One of Gish's favorite arguments against the fossil record of human evolution is based on the assertions of Lord Solly Zuckerman about the interpretation of australopithecine fossils such as the famous Lucy. Gish says that Zuckerman carried out a thorough and careful 15-year study concluding that these creatures did not walk upright, contrary to common paleontological wisdom. What Gish does not say is that Zuckerman's conclusions were based on the analysis of a cast of only one half of a pelvis from only one specimen, that they were published *before* the discovery of Lucy, and that Zuckerman never studied Lucy's skeleton. Although corrected on several occasions, at least since a debate in 1982 in Lion's Head, Ontario against Chris McGowan, Gish never changed his story, and repeated it in a debate against me in 1998.

2. In one of his books, *Dinosaurs: Those Terrible Lizards* (1991), Gish claims that one of the most famous dinosaurs, *Triceratops*, appeared suddenly in the fossil record, with no ancestor whatsoever. Yet, he was confronted as far back as 1982 by Frederick Edwords in a debate and told that there are in fact earlier forms clearly antecedent to *Triceratops* known to paleontologists. Gish's reply was that such forms are actually found in the same strata as *Triceratops*, so they couldn't be ancestral. Edwords retorted that they are found between 10 and 45 million years earlier, plenty of time for the evolution of *Triceratops* from those animals to occur. Despite a similar correction to his views from Kenneth Miller, again during a 1982 debate, Gish went on presenting the same false picture of *Triceratops'* mystery to his audience up to at least 1995.

3. The bombardier beetle is a classic creationist battle horse, which Gish has used several times. The beetle is capable of combining two chemicals produced by its glands, hydrogen peroxide and hydroquinone, into a jet of noxious gas it expels when threatened by enemies. Gish has claimed that there is no way evolution can explain such a phenomenon, since the individual components (glands,

enzymes to make the gas, etc.) could not have evolved independently of each other. Biologists do not see any problem with this, since it is well known that the bombardier beetle is a member of a group of insects among which one can still observe various stages of the development of the beetle's formidable defense (furthermore, see Isaak 1997 for a detailed scenario of how the beetle might have evolved its defense mechanism). The important point here is that Gish made a prediction that represents a rare instance of falsifiable hypothesis advanced by a creationist. As a biochemist, he said that the beetle's mechanism could not have originated by natural means simply because mixing hydrogen peroxide and hydroquinone would cause an explosion that would kill the animal. In 1978, William M. Thwaites and Frank T. Awbrey, of San Diego State University, tested Gish's claim and demonstrated that the mixing does not result in any explosion, but simply in a brownish solution. After such a humiliating defeat for a biochemist, Gish still used the story of the bombardier beetle, this time simply adding that the mixture would explode "or decompose," as if that solved everything.

I could go on, but Arthur's article is more thorough and enjoyable than any mere repetition I could offer here. The point is that all these examples raise legitimate questions about Gish's tactics. I don't think anybody but Gish himself can answer the question of how much he really believes what he says; perhaps not even he can, as it is a well-known phenomenon that people can convince themselves of almost anything if they repeat it often enough and if it fits their most deeply held beliefs. However, the literature on Gish should make one thing clear to anybody who is not entirely blinded by ideology: not only his arguments are scientifically fundamentally flawed, but his oratorical tactics are in strident contrast with the kind of ethics that most of his audience sincerely espouses and that he claims guides his own efforts and life.

Appendix - A Friendly Challenge to the Creationists

The challenge below was issued to Dr. Gish at a debate with Dr. Edward Max in 1989. It represented an opportunity for "creation scientists" to refute the view that they are pseudoscientists, who direct their arguments exclusively to lay audiences ill equipped to evaluate them professionally. At the debate, Dr. Gish agreed to submit a response to the challenge. Although the deadline for response was indefinitely extended, creationists have never submitted a written response to this challenge. They continue to use the same thermodynamics arguments in debates. Are they pseudoscientists? Draw your own conclusion.

Whereas:

1. Creationists believe that their "creation science" arguments against the theory of evolution deserve to be taken seriously as critical challenges to the validity of evolution. They say that their views cannot receive a fair hearing through the normal route of publication in scientific journals because their submitted manuscripts would be rejected for publication by prejudicial journal referees.

2. Evolutionary scientists tend to view "creation science" as pseudoscience, i.e., an attempt to bolster invalid arguments by the inappropriate use of scientific terminology and scientific-sounding arguments. In this view, pseudoscientific arguments succeed in debates before lay audiences only because these audiences are not well enough trained in science to see through a false argument when it is phrased with impressive scientific terms that they don't fully understand.

Therefore:

We would like to offer a friendly challenge to help establish which of these two views of "creation science" is most correct. This challenge focuses on a particular example of a creationist argument that many scientists believe is pure pseudoscience: the creationist argument that the evolution model cannot be correct because it violates the Second Law of Thermodynamics. Is the creationists' Second Law argument based on a valid thermodynamics analysis, or is it simply a debating ploy that is effective with audiences who are not trained in thermodynamics?

We now invite Dr. Gish to demonstrate that the creationists' Second Law argument is not pseudoscience by publishing the scientific details of such calculations in a rigorous manner suitable for readers who are working scientists specializing in thermodynamics. Dr. Gish need not worry that biased journal referees will refuse to publish his analysis because at our request, Frederick Edwords, editor of the journal *Creation/Evolution*, has agreed to provide a forum for the creationists. He will publish this challenge and a creationist response of up to 15 typewritten double-spaced pages (limited exclusively to a technical analysis of the evolution model in light of thermodynamics) if the response is received before October 30, 1989. If no response is received, then this challenge will be published alone, and readers will be left to draw their own conclusions as to whether the creationist thermodynamics argument is science or pseudoscience.

We anticipate that the creationists will be eager to respond if they are able to rigorously support their Second Law claims and if they are sincere in their desire to advance their arguments beyond the parochial readership of creationist-sponsored publications. We hope that this challenge and the creationist response will be a step towards converting an often acrimonious battleground into a substantive exchange of ideas. If – as sometimes happens when mathematicians are forced to write out the technical details of what seemed to be a quite obvious proof – the creationists find that their Second Law argument against evolution cannot be rigorously and quantitatively supported, and if they therefore decline to respond to this challenge, we hope that they will refrain from using this argument in future debates.

Part V - Tales at the frontier of science

The last three essays of this book may appear to be a departure from the rest, but they do fit in a logical continuum. So far I have criticized and debunked irrational beliefs, and now I turn to criticize science itself. Far from being a contradictory stance, I think that critical thinking and skepticism should apply across the board, no matter what the object at hand. My criticism of science is not as far reaching as the one of pseudoscience. I am a practicing scientist and am convinced that science is indeed the best way to know about the world. But this does not of course put it beyond criticism. On the contrary, it is in the very nature of science to be continuously scrutinized and improved upon.

The first essay in this series focuses on one of the most important and difficult questions that science has ever asked: where do we come from? Despite much research on the origin of life, however, we still know very little about it. This is no cause to fall back into a supernatural "explanation" (notice that the latter is a contradiction in terms, since nobody knows how gods do what they allegedly do). Instead, it is a call to arms for young minds to attack this exceedingly difficult problem with all their might. The essay therefore discusses some sensible and not-so-sensible proposals for the origin of all living beings on Earth, while at the same time sounding a cautionary note concerning the limits of modern science.

Perhaps an equally compelling, and even more difficult, question regards the existence of other intelligent forms of life outside the planet Earth. In that essay I reconsider the famous Drake equation, which has been used for decades as a conceptual tool for discussions on extraterrestrial life forms, and in the process suggest a new formulation of this classic. I also briefly discuss the current and perhaps most ambitious effort to search for ET, and how everybody can participate with their own personal computers. In general, however, I am interested in involving the reader with questions concerning the very nature of such efforts: why is it that we look for extraterrestrial intelligence, why should we care, and what chances do we have of ever finding it? Again, this is yet another aspect of the general question of the meaning and purpose of science, as well as of its limits.

Finally, I turn to a much used, and a bit abused, relatively novel field of inquiry, generally including what are known as chaos theory, fractals, and complexity theory. This branch of nonlinear mathematics has leaped at the attention of the general public with the promise of soon solving an incredible variety of problems, from the origin of life to the behavior of the stock market. I think that nonlinear mathematics is indeed a very powerful tool for understanding many difficult questions, but that some of its practitioners have jumped the gun, leading to a flood of "applications" of chaos and complexity theories that have little to do with science. Such expansions of a legitimate scientific theory are not only often fruitless or downright nonsensical, but they may negatively affect the scientific reputation of the approach itself by casting a shadow of doubt on the integrity and competence of some of the researchers involved. This is an interesting case of a science at its inception, simultaneously characterized by the promise of a rapid expansion and by the threat of a premature collapse. It is a great opportunity for scientists, skeptics, and the public to follow and analyze the evolution and impact of a new discipline and its eventual consolidation into mainstream science.

Chapter 12 - Where do we come from?
We still have few clues to the origin of life[47]

"Life has to be given a meaning because of the obvious fact that it has no meaning." (Henry Miller, The Wisdom of the Heart)

Science is about answering our questions about the natural world in a rational manner. One of the fundamentals of the scientific method is the repeatability of the phenomena under investigation. Here lies perhaps the most difficult aspect of the endless quest for the origin of life on earth. It clearly is a question about the natural world, in fact perhaps one of the ultimate questions (together with the origin of the universe itself). Yet, the events we are attempting to investigate are by definition unique. Life may well have originated multiple times in the universe, including perhaps in our galactic neighborhood. But so far we only have one example to go by. Planet earth is the only place that we know for certain harbors life as we conceive it.

Before entering into a skeptical evaluation of the heart of the problem, let us consider an even more fundamental question: why do we care? Well, I can propose three reasons. First, definitely ascertaining that life originated by natural means would certainly have profound implications for any religious belief, further shrinking the role of any god in human affairs. Second, should we arrive at the conclusion that life originated elsewhere in the universe and was then somehow "imported" to earth, this would automatically imply the existence of life as a widespread phenomenon in the universe, and therefore the fact that living beings are not unique to our planet; it is hard to conceive of a more compelling blow to anthropocentrism since Copernicus and Galileo swept the earth away from the center of the universe a few centuries ago. Third, and perhaps most relevant, humankind would finally have a decent answer to the question "where did we

---

[47] This essay was originally published in *Skeptical Inquirer* vol. 23(5), pp. 21-27, 1999.

come from?" that, like it or not, has been vexing our philosophy, art, and science since the beginning of recorded history (and probably much earlier than that).

Couldn't we just look at the simplest organism?

Let me start by clearing from the field one important misconception: there is no such thing as a modern-day "primitive" organism that we can examine to tell what our earliest ancestors looked like. True, there are plenty of "simple" organisms around today, from viruses to bacteria to slime molds. But slime molds are in fact eukaryotes (albeit of taxonomically very uncertain position), i.e., their cellular structure and metabolism are basically not different from those of an animal or a plant (they actually look like fungi, though they are not even closely related to them). Way too complex for our purposes. Bacteria are prokaryotes, i.e., their cells are indeed simpler than most other living beings. Yet, bacteria have been around for more than three billion years, and they have become perfect reproductive machines, characterized by an incredibly efficient metabolism and ability to withstand environmental changes. After all, it is not by chance that they have proliferated for so long. So, no go there either. Finally, viruses are indeed among the simplest living creatures in existence, so simple in fact that some biologists even doubt that they really qualify as "living." However, evolutionarily speaking, viruses are late arrivals on the Darwinian stage. Viruses are short pieces of nucleic acids wrapped in a protein, they live only inside cells, they originated from pre-existing cells, and they entirely depend on the host's metabolism to reproduce. Quite obviously, since our problem is to understand how the first living organisms came about, we cannot use as a model something that cannot survive outside an already existing cell. No, we are looking for something simple, yes, but self-sufficient, and *really* primitive.

The alternative question: what about God?

No serious scientific discussion of any topic should include supernatural explanations, since the basic assumption of science is that the world can be explained entirely in physical terms, without recourse to god-like entities. However, skepticism has the flexibility of going beyond the strict scientific method – even though the two modes of inquiry are tightly connected (see Chapters 2 and 6). After all, as that fictional archetype of rationalism known as Sherlock Holmes said, "when you have eliminated the impossible, whatever remains, however improbable, must be the truth" (it is indeed ironic that Holmes' creator, Conan Doyle, believed in spirits and poltergeists, but that's another story: Polidoro 1998). So, should it turn out that we really do not have a clue about the origin of life, we must entertain other, more esoteric possibilities, however unpleasant they may sound to a skeptical ear. Furthermore, in the specific case of the origin of life, even some scientists of decent reputation, such as the British astrophysicist Fred Hoyle, have gone on record precisely suggesting a supernatural beginning to all life on earth (see Chapter 9 for some more on Hoyle). Hoyle, together with his colleague Chandra Wickramasinghe, suggested that a sort of silicon-chip creator actually goes around the universe sprinkling the seeds of life here and there, though for what purpose is not at all clear.

An entirely different, yet congruent, argument is the one advanced by creationists such as Duane Gish (Gish 1995, see Chapter 11). In Gish's case, of course, all we have is the classical God of the bible, who created the universe and humankind with a personal touch, and did so in the span of only six days.

There is one crucial problem with both Hoyle's and Gish's position, of course: there isn't a single shred of evidence supporting them. Furthermore, at least Gish's claims are falsifiable and have been verified to be false: one of the cardinal points of his theory is that the earth is only a few thousands years old, while geology has long ago demonstrated that the real time frame is measured in billions of years. Hoyle's proposition suffers from the hallmark of all non-scientific statements: it is not disprovable.

There isn't a single experiment that could reject the British physicist's hypothesis, which means that it lies by definition outside science's realm.

Should a skeptic then reject outright any possibility of special creation of life? Well, no. As much as it is implausible, it is still possible. There are two points that must be borne in mind, however, before going for a Hoyle-like explanation of the origin of us all. First, it has to be true that we really don't have a clue about how *on earth* life originated by natural means. As we will see, though the situation is messy, it is not that desperate. Second, the mere fact that we cannot currently (or even ever) explain something does not constitute *positive* evidence for a supernatural explanation. After all, for a long time we did not know what natural phenomena could cause lightning, but eventually the theory based on Zeus's anger did turn out to be wrong. Consequently, even if we had no better answer, it is still up to the "supernaturalists" to provide at least a sliver of positive evidence. Without that, the next best position to hold on to would simply be a provisional and salutary "I don't know."

Out of this world?

The next class of explanations about the ultimate provenance of life is that – as any good old-fashioned science fiction movie or magazine of the 1950s would have proclaimed – it is not of this world. Interestingly, Hoyle and Wickramasinghe have made their contribution in this realm too, by suggesting that life was brought on this planet courtesy of an interstellar cloud of gas and dust, or perhaps by a comet (Hoyle and Wickramasinghe 1978). Yet another British scientist (and also a trained physicist – but I'm sure this is a coincidence), the Nobel laureate Francis Crick, joined the ranks of the extraterrestrialists. Crick suggested a scenario that envisions extraterrestrials "seeding" the galaxy (Crick 1981), much in the same fashion of Hoyle's silicon-chip creator.

Contrary to the supernatural explanations, the Hoyle-Wickramasinghe theory (but not Crick's, for the same reasons seen above) is at least in principle open to experimental verification, in that it makes some relatively precise predictions. For one thing, we should find plenty of organic compounds in interstellar clouds and/or inside comets. Both these expectations have superficially been verified. I say superficially because the kind of compounds found by astronomers in these media are very simple, much too simple to provide any meaningful "seed" for the origin of carbon-based life forms on earth. Furthermore, extraterrestrial organic compounds have random chirality, unlike the organic compounds typical of living organisms. Chirality is a property of any chemical structure that deals with the three-dimensional arrangement of its atoms and molecules. For example, all amino acids, the building blocks of proteins, can in theory come in two versions – which are mirror images of each other. These are called "left-" and "right-" handed forms, and they are characterized by exactly the same chemical properties, so that there is no physical-chemical reason for one form to be more abundant than the other. Accordingly, the organic compounds (which is a general term for carbon-based chemicals and, contrary to the misleading name, does not necessarily imply the result of an organism's metabolism) found in space or in meteorites come in equal proportions of right and left handed forms.[48] Not so the compounds that are actually used by living organisms on earth, which are found only in one version. If indeed life had come from space, one would expect to find some sort of chiral asymmetry in space organic matter as well.

A second crucial objection to the life-from-space hypothesis is the solution of continuity problem. If comets and meteors brought us – literally – to earth a few billion years ago, why are they not doing it now? Meteors continue to bombard our planet and our neighbors in the solar system on a regular basis, yet so far not a single living organism or complex organic molecule has been found inside any of them. There is no reason to think that the primordial "shower of life" has ceased. Even though the conditions for the persistence of primordial life on our planet do not hold any longer (because of dramatic changes in the composition of the atmosphere, or because of competition from "resident aliens," i.e., from currently living organisms), presumably the space

---

[48] This particular statement may need to be modified because of recent research showing that cosmic radiation can in fact cause asymmetric chirality without the intervention of living organisms.

surrounding our solar system has not changed that much, leaving Hoyle, Crick and the like with a major hole in their argument.

Another thought about extraterrestrial theories of life's beginning is that at a minimum they violate one of the most venerable principles of natural philosophy, namely Ockham's razor (see Chapter 6). This is the idea that if two theories explain equally well a given problem, one should prefer the alternative that assumes the fewest number of entities (i.e., makes the fewest gratuitous hypotheses). Since all extraterrestrial theories still rely on organic chemistry, and since they require further assumptions, for example the fact that the "seeds" found a safe passage through the earth's atmosphere without burning into nothingness as it happens to most meteors, they violate Ockham's rule. On the other hand, there is no real guarantee that the universe behaves as Ockham suggested, so the razor can be invoked only as a provisional way of favoring simpler explanations, not as a definite argument against more complex or less likely alternatives.

Finally, it has to be realized that even if we do admit that life originated outside earth and was then imported here, we really would not have an answer to *how* life started. We would have simply shifted the question to a remote and very likely inaccessible location.

The chicken or the egg in the soup?

We are now getting to the crux of the debate. Having excluded – at least temporarily – gods and extraterrestrials, we are left with plain old biochemistry and biology to give us clues to the origin of life on our planet. The history of scientific research in this field is long and fascinating. It started in the 1920s with the Russian Alexander Oparin and his "coacervates," blobs of organic matter (mostly containing sugars and short polypeptides), supposedly the precursors of modern proteins. It was Oparin, together with the British biologist J.B.S. Haldane, who came up with the idea of a 'primordial soup' (Oparin 1938; Haldane 1985), that is the possibility that the ancient oceans on earth were filled with organic matter formed by the interaction between the atmospheric gases

Fig. 12.1. The basic idea behind Miller-type experiments is to investigate the production of organic molecules under conditions simulating the pre-biotic earth. The ball of gases represents the primordial atmosphere, while the electrodes provide energy such as could have been provided by lightning (or volcanic eruptions, or a variety of other possibilities). The boiling water provides moisture to create the "soup," which accumulates and is purified on the lower right part of the apparatus. These experiments are now so easy to replicate that the apparatus can be used for high school projects.

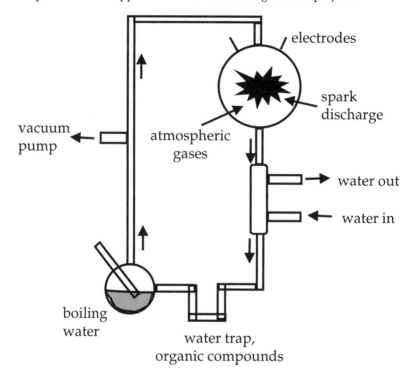

and energy provided by volcanic eruptions, powerful electric storms, and solar ultraviolet radiation.

We had to wait until the 1950s for Stanley Miller to actually attempt to experimentally reproduce the soup (Miller 1953). Miller started with a reasonable composition of the ancient atmosphere: mostly methane and ammonia, with no oxygen – since atmospheric oxygen, together with the ozone that blocks UV radiation, was in fact produced by the organic process of photosynthesis in blue-green algae much, much later than soup time (which is a fortunate coincidence, given that oxygen attacks and destroys – technically "oxidizes" – organic compounds at a very fast rate).[49] Miller put the whole thing in a ball, gave it some electric charge, and waited. He did find that amino acids and other fundamental complex organic molecules were accumulating at the bottom of his apparatus. His discovery gave a huge boost to the scientific investigation of the origin of life. Indeed, for some time it seemed like recreation of life in a test tube was within reach of experimental science. Unfortunately, Miller-type experiments have not progressed much further than their original prototype, leaving us with a sour aftertaste from the primordial soup.

Both Oparin and Miller, as well as other prominent researchers in the field up until the 1960s, thought that the problem was how to explain the appearance of proteins, since they must have caused the initial spark of life. (Another student of the problem who thought along similar lines was Sidney Fox, who discovered the possibility of forming "proteinoids," protein-like structures that can be obtained by heating up mixtures of amino acids in a dry state. All in all, a very distant cousin of actual biological proteins). Now, any student of introductory biology knows that there are *two* major players inside every living cell: proteins and nucleic acids (such as DNA and RNA). The problem is that the structure of DNA was discovered only in 1953 (in fact, the same year of Miller's experiment), and the nature of DNA as the information carrier of the cell was little appreciated before James Watson and Francis Crick unveiled the double-helix nature of this remarkable molecule.

The origin of life debate after the 1950s, however, became decidedly slanted in favor of nucleic acids preceding proteins. The new discipline of molecular biology was making spectacular progress, first uncovering the universal code by which the instructions for making proteins are embedded in the nucleic acids, then by finding ways to actually extract and compare that information from different and distantly related species, and finally with the spin-off of modern genetic engineering and the

---

[49] Recent research has questioned the notion of complete absence of oxygen from the primordial atmosphere, but the jury is still out on exactly how reducing or oxidizing the primordial conditions were. The alternative to the soup, the pizza proposed in the next section, would solve the problem by making the atmospheric conditions pretty much irrelevant.

ability to directly modify the genetic information, thereby transforming the characteristics of species more or less at will. Scientists such as Leslie Orgel, Walter Gilbert and others therefore proposed that the egg, so to speak, came before the chicken. Some sort of primitive nucleic acid had appeared first, followed only later by proteins.

Now, in today's biochemically sophisticated cells, proteins and nucleic acids play very distinct roles. In fact there are *four* fundamental activities that we need to discuss:

1. The DNA (deoxyribonucleic acid) encodes the information that eventually will give rise to proteins.

2. The 'messenger' RNA (or mRNA, ribonucleic acid, the same as DNA, but with an extra oxygen atom and a few other chemical differences) then carries the information to specialized structures known as ribosomes.

3. Inside the ribosomes (which, by the way, are made of *both* nucleic acids and proteins) the message gets translated into proteins by virtue of a second type of RNA, known as 'transfer' RNA (tRNA). The tRNA has the peculiar ability to attach itself to the mRNA on one side, and to amino acids (the blocks that make up proteins) on the other side. This way, you have a chain of mRNA that is paralleled by the forming chain of amino acids, which in turn will eventually result in the final protein.

4. The proteins, most of which (but not all) are enzymes, are actually the "doers" of the cellular world, in that they are both the building blocks of cell structures and membranes, and the builders themselves, in the form of enzymes capable of catalyzing all sorts of chemical reactions, including the replication of DNA and the transcription of its message into RNA – which, of course, closes the circle!

It should be clear from the above extremely concise description of what goes on in a cell that we are indeed facing a classical chicken-egg problem. If the proteins appeared first, so that they could eventually catalyze the formation of nucleic acids, how was the information necessary to produce the proteins themselves

Fig. 12.2. The most important functions of the basic constituents of life as we know it today inside a cell (large oval). The DNA template gets copied into messenger RNA (and from time to time copies of it are made to prepare for cell duplication). The mRNA transfers the information coding for proteins to the ribosomes, organelles made of nucleic acids and polypeptides which attract and align the correct transfer RNAs. The sequence of amino acids that results folds in three-dimensional space to yield a protein.

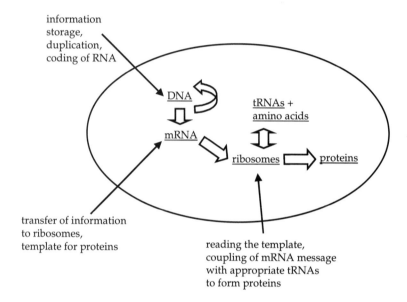

coded? On the other hand, if nucleic acids came first, thereby embodying the information necessary to obtain proteins, by which means where the acids replicated and translated into proteins? It seems clear that the answer, as much as it is still very much nebulous at the moment, must lie in the proverbial middle (Miller 1997). In fact, the existence of tRNAs points to the distinct possibility of dual structures, containing both RNA and amino acids. On a slightly different take, the discovery by Sydney Altman, Thomas Cech, and others that some RNAs are at least partially self-catalytic (i.e., they can catalyze chemical reactions onto themselves), lends support to the idea of a mixed origin of life in which the original molecules were both replicators and enzymes (Ertem and Ferris 1996), with the two functions slowly diverging through evolutionary time and eventually assigned to distinct classes of molecules. Most importantly, doesn't that appeal to your sense of aesthetics as well?

Primordial soup or primordial pizza?

There is one major problem with the Haldane-Oparin soup scenario: it could get too watery. Since the organic compounds would be freely bumping into each other within the ocean, unless their concentration was extremely large it is difficult to see how often dense enough pockets of organic molecules could have formed to allow some significant prebiotic chemistry to occur.

This is even more of a problem when we consider the question of the origin of the first metabolic pathways. Metabolism requires proto-enzymes to interact with their substrates so that a given reaction can take place. However, it was unlikely for enzymes and substrates to come close enough together in a three-dimensional space with no enclosing barriers (hence several hypotheses about the formation of proto-cells with a lipid membrane). Furthermore, most of the necessary reactions for prebiotic chemistry, such as the formation of polypeptides by aggregating individual amino acids, produce water. This kind of reaction is difficult to have in an aqueous environment because of thermodynamic considerations (it requires energy, and the products are unstable and can be hydrolyzed back to their component parts).

An alternative to the primordial soup has therefore been proposed, and it has become known as the "primordial pizza" (Maynard-Smith and Szathmary 1995). The idea is that early organic chemistry occurred on dry land, on the surface of minerals with physical properties conducive to accumulating and retaining organic molecules in place. Perhaps the best candidate for such a role is pyrite, fool's gold. On a two-dimensional surface, enzymes and substrates, or even simply different amino acids or nucleotides without enzymes, would find themselves constrained with much less freedom of movement which, of course, would increase the chance of reciprocal encounters. Furthermore, since the pyrite surface would have no water on it, the occurrence of water-producing reactions would be much facilitated. In fact, thermodynamic calculations show that these reactions would increase entropy, and would therefore occur spontaneously. Very little empirical research has been done on the concept of a primordial pizza, and other candidates are possible as material substrates besides pyrite, but the concept is appealing in its elegant solution of two major problems facing prebiotic chemistry. We should see some progress in this area in the next few years.

And then what? Hypercycles and emerging properties

I suggest that the problem of how complex organic compounds, the building blocks of life as we know it, might have formed on the primordial earth has been satisfactorily solved by Miller-type experiments or one of their variants. Furthermore, there are good reasons to believe that the initial complex molecules that underwent chemical evolution were some sort of nucleic acid-protein mix such as modern day tRNAs or autocatalytic RNAs. But what happened after that? There is still a very large gap between a semi-catalytic, semi-replicating nucleo-protein and the first living "organism," whatever that may have been.

Moreover, the uncertainty about what the original organisms looked like is an important part of the problem. What exactly *is* life? That question was asked precisely in such fashion by physicist Erwin Schrodinger (1947). While Schrodinger's thinking led him to predict some of the properties of DNA as a necessary component of a living organism, we still have only a vague notion of the boundary between life and inert matter. And so it should be, if we accept the idea that living organisms are made of inert matter that happens to acquire some "emergent properties" when it is assembled in particular manners. To put it into another fashion, living beings are not separated from the rest of the universe by some mysterious force or vital energy. At least, we have no reason to believe so.

How do we know, then, what is life from what is not? Well, we can come up with a list of attributes, some of which can be properties also of non-living systems, but the ensemble of which defines a living organism. Here is what I could put together:

- Ability to replicate, giving origin to similar kinds (reproduction)
- Ability to react to changes in the environment (behavior, not just limited to the special meaning that the word has in animals)
- Growth (i.e., reduction of internal entropy at the expense of environmental entropy – note that even single cells grow immediately after reproduction, so this is not a property restricted to multicellular life)
- Metabolism (i.e., capacity of maintaining lower internal entropy, including the ability of self-repair)

How did we get from a nucleo-protein to an entity capable of all of the above? And what did this entity (sometimes known as the "progenote") look like? There are very few even tentative answers to these questions, and this – I think – is wherein the real problem of the origin of life lies. The German Manfred Eigen has come up with one possible scenario that invokes what he called "hypercycles." You can think of a hypercycle as a primitive biochemical pathway, made up of self-replicating nucleic acids and semi-catalytic proteins that happen to be found together in pockets within the primordial soup or on the primitive pizza. It is possible to imagine that some of these hypercycles are made of elements that "cooperate" with each other, i.e., the product of a component of the cycle can be the substrate for another one. Different hypercycles could have coexisted before the origin of life, and they would have competed for the ever-decreasing resources within the soup or pizza (the resources were decreasing because the hypercycles were using up some organic compounds at a higher rate than they were formed by comparatively inefficient inorganic processes). Eventually, this competition would have favored more and more efficient hypercycles, where the "efficiency" would be measured by the ability of these entities to survive and reproduce, that is by the parameters of Darwinian evolution. Life as we know it (sort of) would have begun.

Eigen and modern followers of complexity theory also expect these systems to have become more complicated by addition of new components to the cycle. From time to time, the addition of one component would modify the whole system dramatically, giving it properties that the previous group did not possess (sort of like adding an atom of oxygen to two of hydrogen and suddenly getting something completely distinct and more complex: water, see Chapter 3). Complexity theorists such as Stuart Kauffman and Christopher Langton have indeed demonstrated on the basis of mathematical models that some self-replicating systems can display unexpectedly complex patterns of behavior (Farmer et al. 1986; Kauffman 1993). The textbook examples of this phenomenon are the so-called cellular automata, mathematical entities first imagined by John von Neumann in 1940 and that can now be studied at leisure by anybody who has a personal computer and a copy of a game aptly called "Life" (Langton 1986).

So, the general path leading to the origination of life seems to have been something like this:

=> **Primordial soup or pizza** (simple organic compounds formed by atmospheric gases and various sources of energy)

=> **Nucleo-proteins** (similar to modern tRNAs)

=> **Hypercycles** (primitive and inefficient biochemical pathways, emergent properties)

=> **Cellular hypercycles** (more complex cycles, eventually enclosed in a primitive cell made of lipids)

=> **Progenote** (first self-replicating, metabolizing cell, possibly made of RNA and proteins, with DNA entering the picture later on)

How plausible is all this? It is fairly conceivable, as far as modern biology can tell. The problem is that each step is really difficult to describe in detail from a theoretical standpoint, and so far (with the exception of the formation of organic molecules in the soup and of some simple hypercycles) has proven remarkably elusive from an empirical perspective. It looks like we have several clues, but the puzzle may very well prove one of the most difficult for scientific analysis to solve. The reason for such difficulty could be – as pointed out at the beginning – that after all we only have one example to go by. Or it may simply be that the events in question are so far remote in time that there is very little we can be certain about. Consider that the fossil record shows completely formed, "modern-looking" bacterial cells a few hundred million years after the formation of the earth – i.e., about 3.8 billion years ago. This tells us that whatever happened before that happened fast (on a geological time scale), but there is no record of it. Finally, it could very well be that we are missing something fundamental here. It may be that the origin of life field has not had its Einstein or Darwin just yet, and that things are going to change just around the corner, or maybe never.

From dust to dust...

Apparently, a contemporary discussion of the question of the origin of life cannot be complete without the inclusion of A.G. Cairns-Smith's theory of clay crystals (Cairn-Smith 1985; Maden 1995). Well, I hope this will not be the case for much longer (except as a footnote of historical value). Don't get me wrong; I am familiar with Cairns-Smith's research and writing, and I find it excellent. But everybody can make a mistake, and I think the clay theory clearly falls within the cracks of Cairns-Smith's career, as much as it is ingenious and at first glance enticing.

Briefly, the idea is that life did not originate with *either* nucleic acids *or* proteins (and for that matter, neither with a combination of the two). No, the original replicator-catalyzing agents were actually crystals to be found everywhere in the clay that laid around the primitive earth. The cardinal points of the Cairn-Smith hypothesis are four. First, crystals are structurally much simpler than any biologically relevant organic molecule. Second, crystals grow and reproduce (i.e., they can break because of mechanical forces, and each resulting part continues to "grow"). Third, crystals carry information and this information can be modified. A crystal is a highly regular structure, which tends to propagate itself (therefore it carries information). Furthermore, the crystal can incorporate impurities while growing. These impurities alter the crystal's structure and can be "inherited" when the original piece breaks (hence, the information can be modified). Fourth, crystals have some minimum capacity of catalyzing (i.e., accelerating) chemical reactions.

Cairns-Smith then proposed that these very primitive "organisms" started incorporating short polypeptides (proto-proteins) found in the environment – presumably in the soup or on the pizza – because they enhanced the crystals' catalyzing abilities. The road was then open for a gradual increase in the importance of proteins first, and then eventually of nucleic acids, until these two new arrivals on the evolutionary scene completely supplanted their 'low-tech' progenitor, and became the living organisms that we know today.

What is wrong with this picture? First of all, Cairns-Smith seems to completely ignore what a living organism actually is. For one thing, crystals don't really have a metabolism, at least not in a sense even remotely comparable to what we find in actual living organisms. This may have something to do with the fact that not only are crystals structurally much less complex than a protein or a nucleic acid, but also with their non-carbon-based chemistry, recognizably much simpler than the chemistry used by living organisms on earth. The lower complexity and simpler chemistry may be insurmountable "hardware" obstacles to the origination of a true metabolism in clay matter. Secondarily, crystals don't really react to their environment either, another hallmark of every known living creature. Notice that this is a property distinct from metabolism, in that metabolism can be entirely internal, with no reference to the outside (except for some flux of energy that must come into the organism to maintain its metabolism). On the other hand, living organisms universally actively respond to changes in external conditions, for example by seeking sources of energy or by avoiding dangers. Furthermore, an argument can be made that crystals are not actually capable of incorporating new information in their inherited "code," unlike what happens with mutations in living beings. True, they can assimilate impurities from the environment and 'transmit' such 'information' to their 'descendants' for some time; but these impurities do not get replicated, they need continually to be imported from the outside, and they do not become a permanent and heritable part of the crystal. Moreover, impurities do not create new types of crystals, the way mutations give eventually origin to entirely new kinds of animals and plants.

Another colossal hole in the clay theory is that we have no clue of how the "mutiny" of nucleic acids and proteins actually occurred, and in fact we are given only very faint hints about how a crystal could possibly co-opt a polypeptide to enhance its growth (which, by the way, should be something relatively easy to test in a modern biochemistry laboratory). It is true that the competing, more biologically traditional, hypotheses also are at a loss providing detailed scenarios; but in the case of Cairn-Smith's suggestions, we don't simply miss the details, we literally have no idea of how such a transition would come to pass. So, as much as creationists might like the flavor of a theory of the origin of life in which the first living beings came literally from dust (although Cairns-Smith is certainly no creationist), we are still left with ribonucleo-proteins as our best, albeit fuzzy, option. This is one question that skeptics and scientists will probably be pondering for some time to come.

Chapter 13 - Are we alone, and do we care?

*"Until they come to see us from their planet, I wait patiently.
I hear them saying: Don't call us, we'll call you."
(Marlene Dietrich, Marlene Dietrich's ABC)*

Next to the question "where do we come from?" (Chapter 12), undoubtedly the one investigating the possibility of someone else being "out there" is the most philosophically intriguing, and it certainly is even more frustrating for a mind inclined toward scientific inquiry. Possibly humans started asking this question since they looked up at the stars for the first time, but more likely we thought of ET only much later, after we realized that stars and planets were likely to be worlds like our own sun and earth. In Western society for a long period it was the church's dogma that the celestial spheres could not be inhabited by anything less perfect than angels, and many lost their lives at the stake for daring to question such an assumption, Giordano Bruno (1548-1600) being the most famous example. Fortunately, today not only scientists, but writers and movie directors can freely speculate on what life would be on another planet, what we would do in encountering another form of life, and how boldly we would go about the whole business.

The story of the modern SETI (search for extraterrestrial intelligence) has been recanted in several places (e.g., Casti 1989), and I will therefore not repeat here the details of the daring enterprise of Frank Drake, the radioastronomer who started *Project Ozma*, the first such attempt back in 1960; or how we came to send the only radio message ever consciously broadcast to potential extraterrestrial listeners from the Arecibo radiotelescope in 1974. Current, more sophisticated and faster searches are going on thanks mostly to private funding. Depending on their outcome, this whole discussion might be totally irrelevant any day, or perhaps remain forever as current as it is now (the secret wish of every writer, yet the nightmare of the scientist).

What I would like to focus on here instead are the following points: first, how do we approach the question of the existence of extraterrestrial life from a rational, scientific standpoint? Second, how is it that some parties involved in the debate take it as a given that the answer is positive, while others are equally unmovable from an uncompromisingly negative perspective? Third, does it make sense that we are mostly trying to listen, instead of broadcasting? And, are our feeble attempts at taking the initiative a realistic scientific enterprise, or little more than a good topic for party conversation? Fourth, is the whole endeavor worth our attention and, especially, money?

Is it a scientific problem? The omnipresent Drake equation

Is the pursuit of ET a scientific question, or should we leave it to philosophers, religious authorities, or better yet, the writers of *Star Trek* and *2001*? One of the cardinal points of the scientific method as expounded by Descartes (1637) is that any broad question such as this has first to be broken in several components. This process of atomization, or reductionism, has of course limits of its own (e.g., Brandon 1996). Yet, it has been incredibly successful in all realms of modern science and technology, and it is still our best bet to attack any complex problem. However, how does one partition the search for extraterrestrial intelligence into digestible bites? There is a lot of contention about this point, but any serious discussion of the topic just cannot avoid considering in detail the famous (some would say infamous) "Drake equation." This equation was proposed by the same Frank Drake who initiated the experimental approach to the problem of SETI, as a way to pin down the difficulties of considering the question from a theoretical viewpoint. So, here it goes:

$$N = R * f_p * n_e * f_l * f_i * f_c * L \qquad \text{(eq. 1)}$$

where: N is the number of advanced communicating civilizations in our galaxy; R is the per year rate of formation of stars in the Milky Way; f_p is the proportion of those stars that have planetary systems; n_e is the number of planets in a given system having conditions suitable for the origin of life; f_l is the probability of life actually originating on one of these planets; f_i is the probability that that life will evolve to the status of "intelligent"; f_c is the likelihood that that intelligent life will also be able to communicate outside its solar system; and L is the time in years that ET actually spends trying to communicate. As Casti pointed out (1989), all major scientific disciplines are involved or called into action by the equation, from physics and astronomy, to geology and biology, to technology and the social sciences.

Before we can briefly discuss what do we actually know, or can guess, about each term in the Drake equation, let me raise one very serious criticism to its current form. The multiplication signs interspersed among the quantities are equivalent to one powerful and very dubious assumption: that each term is independent of the others. In probability theory, the only time one is allowed to multiply two fractions or likelihood estimates is when the two events to which they refer happen independently of each other. For example, if you flip a coin twice, the probability to get "head" at the first attempt is half, i.e., 0.50. The probability to get "head" the second time is still 0.50, because the coin doesn't have a "memory" of what happened in the previous trial. In other words, the second outcome is not influenced by the first one in any manner. Therefore, the two events are independent, and we can simply multiply their probabilities to obtain the joint likelihood that the ensemble of the two trials will yield "head" in both cases: $P = 0.5 * 0.5 = 0.25$. But what if the two events are not independent? What if the outcome of the first one somehow influences the result of the second one? For example, let us assume that we are dealing a hand of poker. The probability that the first card handed out will be an ace is four out of 52 (because there are four aces in a deck of 52 cards). Now, what is the probability that the *second* card is also an ace? It is 3/51, because there are 51 cards left, and only three of them are aces. In order to determine the probability of the second event, however, we had to know what the first one was. If, for

Fig. 13.1 Frank Drake, the initiator of the original Search for Extra Terrestrial Intelligence in 1960, and one of the most energetic proponents of this unusual quest at the limits of science.

example, the first card had been a five, then the probability of getting an ace as a second card would have been higher, 4/51 to be precise. This is because there would still be 51 cards left in the deck, but now *four*, not three of them would be aces. It is clear that the probability of the second event depends on the outcome of the first one; in statistical terms, we are dealing with *conditional* probabilities.

Now, it is conceivable that some of the terms in the Drake equation are indeed independent from each other. For example, the galaxy-wide rate of formation of new stars and the likelihood for a given star to have a planetary system are probably not connected to each other. On the other hand, the number of planets suitable to host life and the likelihood that life actually originates on one of these planets must be intimately connected, since they both depend on the parameters of the planet's orbit in relation to the type of star it orbits around (but they are not one and the same, because the fact that a planet *could* host life does not necessarily imply that it will). Therefore, the Drake equation should be rewritten accounting for the lack of independence of some of its terms:

$$N' = (f_c | f_i | f_l | n_e | f_p) * R * L \qquad \text{(eq. 2)}$$

This particular version embodies a different set of assumptions from Drake's. Namely, the terms f_c through f_p are assumed to be hierarchically nested within each other (the | indicates conditional probability), with the likelihood of the next term being dependent on the previous one. R and L, on the other hand, are considered independent of each other and of the nested set of conditional probabilities. Obviously, one could come up with yet another model, embedding a distinct set of assumptions. My point is that this source of variation (and discussion) in the Drake equation has not being extensively explored.

Now we can turn to the discussion of each single term, with the understanding that its actual value may in fact be directly connected to the value of other terms as exemplified in equation 2. I shall not attempt to actually attach numbers, or even ranges, to these variables. Few people have tried, and the variation in the guesses is so vast that the particular numbers proposed become meaningless. What is important, on the other hand, is to arrive at least to a qualitative judgment of the order of magnitude of these parameters. If any of these terms turns out to be too small, the final product of the Drake equation would be a number very close to zero (although we know that it has to be at least one, since *we* exist!). Also notice that in the following discussion I will refer to a kind of life similar to our own, that is based on carbon, or at most on silicon under the proper temperature/pressure conditions. There may be something out there that "it is life, Jim, but not as we know it," as Mr. Spock would have pointed out in *Star Trek*, but we are in no position to speculate scientifically about it, and such a possibility is best left to pure science fiction, at least at the moment.

f_p, *the probability that a given star forms a planetary system.* This used to be pretty much an unknown quantity in astrophysics, simply because the only star with an actual planetary system we knew about was our own sun. It is true that theoretical models of the formation of planetary systems have been devised (e.g., Wuchterl 1991), and that they can be used to define theoretical boundaries for the actual number. But to a skeptic, convincing empirical evidence is a must, and the first experimental confirmation of the existence of other planetary bodies outside our own solar system came only very recently. However, now we know for sure of the existence of several extrasolar planets (Bennett 1999; Svitil 2000), there is no doubt that this term of the equation is far from being zero.

All these planets have been identified in the proximity of our own star, because current telescopes are not powerful enough to reveal any at all at greater distances, even if they existed. This is good news for SETI, since it implies that planets may indeed be abundant in our galaxy (or at least, in our corner of the galaxy). The downside of these recent discoveries is that all the planets so far confirmed orbiting nearby stars are giants, often larger than "our" gaseous big planets, Jupiter and Saturn. In fact, some of them are so large that certain astronomers have questioned if the concept of planet can reasonably be stretched that far. Then again, the reason we uncovered only the largest among interstellar planets is once more because of the limited power of our telescopes, and does not imply that smaller, earth-like and presumably more life-friendly planets do not exist. Also, the recent discovery of conditions that may be suitable to the development of life on the largest satellites of the solar giant planets (Hiscox 1999) is certainly another reason for optimism. All things considered, I would be willing to bet that f_p is indeed not so minuscule to endanger the credibility of SETI projects.

n_e, *the number of planets in a given system characterized by an environment capable of sustaining life.* Here – as for several other terms in the equation – we really have only a sample size of one to go by. Even though we know of other planets in different star systems, and even though we know something about the physical characteristics of the stars they orbit around (temperature, chemical composition, mass), we still have no way to know how likely it is that the candidate planets will be of the right type and at the right distance from the central star.

As far as we can tell from our knowledge of biology and physiology, an earth-like life form is more likely to develop on a solid than on a gaseous planet, and it requires an atmosphere and a fairly limited range of temperatures. But these are vague conditions which can be fulfilled not just by a planet like the earth or Mars, but by satellites around giant planets, such as some of the Medicean satellites orbiting around Jupiter, or perhaps by Titan around Saturn (see above). The argument has been made that there is a fairly restricted "belt" around a star within which a planet will be at a safe distance so not too be too hot, while at the same time receiving enough energy not to freeze. In our solar system, Venus is clearly outside such a belt, being too close to the sun, while the jury is still out about Mars. In any case, the space between Venus and Mars (with the earth in between) is certainly not... astronomical, thereby casting doubts on the likelihood of this set of circumstances happening frequently in the galaxy. But the distance and amplitude of the safe zone depends entirely on the type of star, its mass, and its age, so it is not that simple to generalize from our very limited direct experience. Furthermore, if indeed satellites of larger planets outside the belt can also be considered likely candidates to host life, then the argument becomes less cogent and the likelihood of this parameter being much larger than zero increases considerably. All in all, I think that even if n_e is relatively small, the astounding number of star systems in our galaxy will probably make it large enough not to nullify the product of the Drake equation.

f_l, *the likelihood that life will originate on a given planet.* Again, we run here into the problem that our empirical evidence is limited to a unitary sample size, our own case. The origin of life on earth is in itself largely a mystery, still only scratched at the surface by modern science; therefore, attempting to generalize from a single case that we understand very little is hazardous to say the least. The only point we can make is that our fossil record here on earth indicates that life did originate very early, soon after the planet's crust was cold enough to allow any complex chemical compound to exist in a semi-stable form. So, when given the opportunity, life apparently sprang out of the primordial soup or pizza with little hesitation (although we have only vague ideas about *how* this happened, see Chapter 12). And this is the best we can estimate would happen anywhere else, since there is no particular reason to think otherwise.

f_i, *the probability that life will evolve intelligence.* Of course, what constitutes intelligence is in and of itself a very controversial question. And how much intelligence do we need from ET, anyway? Once more, one can point to the only example we have available directly, that is evolution of "intelligent" life on earth. If we define intelligence in a broad sense, as a general problem-solving ability, we have several independent examples of its evolution on our planet. Cephalopods (squids, octopuses), for example have evolved a very complex central nervous system that makes them capable of refined movements and of solving simple tasks. That ability clearly evolved independently of the type of intelligence that we find in vertebrates, and in fact, the evolution of birds, mammals, dinosaurs, and reptiles, although these are groups that are phylogenetically connected to some extent, shows the independent or repeated appearance of several features that we consider hallmarks of "higher" intelligence. In general, intelligence seems to be associated to a predatory life style, probably because of the necessity that such a life style carries for a large brain capable of coordinating the multifaceted information sources and appropriate responses involved in successfully capturing a prey (Futuyma 1998). My sense is that a variety of evolutionary scenarios may favor the occurrence of intelligent life forms as a generalized strategy to enhance Darwinian fitness, and that therefore the magnitude of f_i may be moderate, but not dangerously small.

f_c, the likelihood that an intelligent life form will become technological and be able to communicate over interstellar distances. Currently, there is no reasonable way to even estimate the order of magnitude of this entry in the equation. Obviously, there is only one species that has reached technological levels and is actually able to communicate with creatures from other star systems that we know of, good old *Homo sapiens*. But this may have been the result of historical accidents, or because we are so competitive and destructive that other primates simply didn't have a chance (Tattersall 2000). As a cautionary statement, on the other hand, it did take more than

Fig. 13.2 An area of the Lagoon Nebula where new stars and solar systems are forming, beautifully captured by the Hubble Space Telescope.

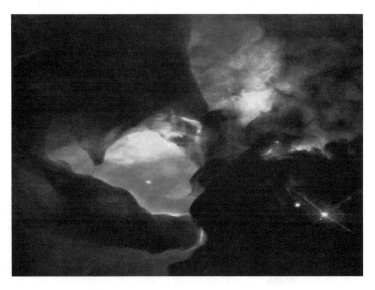

three and half billion years for natural selection to produce the atomic bomb as an epiphenomenon of human evolution, not exactly a fast track for technologically-bent intelligence (unless someone is willing to submit the idea that that's the *real* reason for the extinction of the dinosaurs...). This is the first of the terms in the Drake equation that may really be vanishingly small, and that certainly requires completely new approaches to be presented. Any bright idea, anyone?

R, the rate of formation of stars in the Milky Way. It is a large galaxy (more than 200 billion stars), and astronomers know of several places, such as the Orion Nebula, in which stars are being formed as we speak. The Hubble telescope is providing fascinating new insights into the process of stellar formation, and I do not see anything in the astronomical literature to indicate that we should be pessimistic about the value of R.

L, the time during which a technological culture tries to communicate with the external world. This is the second term of the equation that we simply have to label with a question mark. Judging from our own example (see below), L would be incredibly small, at least up until now. But the situation may change even for us, and we literally just started to play the galactic game. A technological society has to have not just the means, but also the curiosity and will to do it. We, for example, do have the technology to reach the nearest stars (contrary to popular belief). But it would take so much energy and investment of resources, both material and in terms of commitment, that it simply is not happening. And we certainly cannot bet that an alien psychology will be driven by the same sense of innate curiosity which is one of the best characteristics of at least some human beings. Nevertheless, as in the case of f_c, this is bound to be philosophical speculation, if not down right science fiction, at least for now.

Overall, it seems to me that most of the terms of the Drake equation can be reasonably assumed to be either large or moderate, and certainly not minuscule. The exceptions are represented by the two terms dealing with the characteristics of technological societies, of which our science knows the least, and that should be the focus of renewed investigation.

In discussing the Drake equation, it is often said that the best guess we can make is to assume that whatever happened on earth is typical of the rest of the galaxy. This has been somewhat scornfully nicknamed the "principle of mediocrity" by John Casti (1989). However, Casti himself gives the best rationale for it. If we consider the problem from a statistical standpoint (after all, the terms in the equation are probabilities), basic statistics teaches us that with a sample size of n=1, the best estimate of the mean of the population at large is exactly that single value. True, with a larger sample size we may find that our first observation was an atypical outlier, but the farthest an outlier is from the true mean, the less likely it is to occur at all, and therefore the less probable it is that it will occur in your sample, however small. (The statistically savvy reader will have noticed that I am assuming a normal, bell-shaped distribution of the parameters in the Drake equation. This may in itself not be true, but normal distributions are remarkably... normal in nature!)

There is another good reason to trust the principle of mediocrity, at least provisionally: history. Every time humans have thought and seriously believed that they were something absolutely special and out of the ordinary, they have set themselves up for sore disillusionment. Copernicus (1543) was the one who wiped us out of the center of the universe, and Darwin (1859) inflicted another blow by directly linking us by descent to every other form of life on the planet, including bacteria and amoebae. I really don't see any reason to think that we are any more special than the guy next door, wherever "next door" will turn out to be.

Given the uncertainties outlined above, is there a point in the Drake equation? Well, yes and no. No, in the sense that it isn't really an "equation" in the usual scientific sense of the term. Currently, we cannot solve the equation even to an approximate degree, either by empirical or by computer simulation methods. Yes, in the sense that it is a formidable tool for getting a grip on this overwhelming problem. At least, it is a way to fix our ideas on a concrete, albeit incredibly difficult, subset of questions related to our general quest for ET. It seems to me that the answer to our preliminary question, is SETI a scientifically legitimate problem, is a qualified "yes." It is indeed a problem that can be broken down in smaller parts, and there is a possibility for us to experiment or otherwise gain knowledge on all of these parts. But we're still in the very preliminary rounds of the game.

Why do scientists disagree on SETI?

This question deals more with scientists' attitudes and characters than with science *per se*. But we all know that science is to some extent a social enterprise, affected by the vagaries of human nature (Kuhn 1970). Therefore, it makes sense to ask why is it that we encounter a full spectrum of reactions and positions about the SETI enterprise among scientists.

First of all, most practicing scientists simply do not devote any professional time to the problem. This is very likely not a reflection of the *importance* of the question, but rather a result of the difficulty in making any headway. The best quality of a scientist is curiosity, but a close second is pragmatism. Especially in this modern era of competitive universities, costly laboratories, and ever decreasing public funding for science, the first thing that graduate students learn from their advisors is not to pick a topic for their dissertation that will not surely give them publishable results within the following few years. This publish or perish attitude is arguably a major plague of the modern scientific enterprise, and it certainly is worth a separate discussion in and of itself. Its main result may be a huge amount of practical or focused knowledge, but a dearth of wide-ranging studies that, after all, are those that entice any curious mind to become a scientist in the first place. As for SETI, I think this is the main reason so little effort and money is being spent on it. It certainly is not a matter of lack of potential payoff; whoever will get the first positive evidence of intelligent life outside our planet can count on an immediate Nobel prize, as well as to claim a place in the pantheon of people who shaped our cultural history, right next to Galileo, Newton, or Einstein.

Among the scientists who have pronounced themselves on the subject, two extreme views prevail. On the one hand we have the ultraconservatives, who claim that the likely answer to the question of how many civilizations exist in the Milky Way is: just one, and no need to look further than your mirror. At the opposite end of the spectrum are the overly liberal, the people who think that the galaxy swarms with other cultures and that we are just about to enter the galactic yellow pages, more or less *a la Star Trek*.

Certainly Drake, as well as Carl Sagan, belong to this latter category. Their enthusiasm is as contagious as it is tenuously founded (see our discussion above). The best that can be said about these pro-ET scientists is that they keep the dream alive, which is not a small feat in this dreamless age.

On the other hand, I think the negativists really have little redeeming qualities. From a strict scientific viewpoint they are probably as naive (or at least, they have as little basis for their opinions) as their optimistic counterparts. And as far as curiosity goes, they would gladly shut down the whole enterprise so to have a few more cents to spend on sequencing one more genome or on smashing atoms into ever smaller pieces. The best (or worst) example of this sort is a scientist for whom I otherwise have the utmost respect: the Italian Enrico Fermi. The story goes that Fermi was asked about SETI in 1950, at a lunch at Los Alamos National Labs. One of the people present at the gathering apparently claimed that ET must exist in some form or another. Fermi's laconic reply was "then where are they?" This anecdote has ever since been celebrated as "Fermi's paradox." Let's analyze this supposed mortal blow to the quest for extraterrestrial intelligence.

The core (and in fact, the whole) of the paradox rests on the observation that – so far – we have not been visited by ETs. *Ergo*, ET does not exist. By the same token, of course, if you have not suffered from a deadly disease, the virus that causes it does not exist! Or, since the Aztecs weren't aware of the existence of Spaniards for most of their history, they shouldn't have had to be afraid of being suddenly slaughtered... Fermi's paradox is one of the most silly manifestations of anthropocentrism that I have ever come across. It amounts to saying that if anything important is going on in the galaxy, we're bound to know about it! Moreover, by applying the same logic, anybody else out there can safely conclude that there is no such thing as the human race, because *they* have not been visited by *us*. I hope the logical fallacy of the argument is plainly evident at this point, so that we can dismiss one of the few blunders of Fermi's career.[50]

---

[50] Incidentally, I took a biophysics course with the late Dr. Mario Ageno, one of Fermi's students. He told us an amusing story which occurred when Ageno was taking one of Fermi's classes. Fermi submitted to his students that every scientist publishes something of which he will later be ashamed. One of the

If everybody is listening, is anybody transmitting?

Ever since I got interested in SETI I wondered about a simple fact: we are spending quite a bit of energy, time, and finances to listen to possible extraterrestrial signals. But we only broadcast *one* such message from Arecibo in 1974. And the occasion was simply the celebration of the completion of that giant of radiotelescopes, i.e., more of a cute publicity stunt than a serious scientific attempt.

Furthermore, the Arecibo signal was probably sent on the wrong frequency, directed at the wrong target, as well as only sent once. That is, we violated every single precept of our own guidelines for uncovering ETs. As far as the frequency is concerned, the Arecibo signal was transmitted at 2380 MHz, probably because of convenience factors related to the available hardware (which was not designed for SETI). But according to a famous article by Morrison and Cocconi (1959), the "ideal" frequency is actually much lower, centered around 1420 MHz. This is known as the "waterhole," a low background noise region of the spectrum between the frequencies of interstellar hydrogen (H) and hydroxyl radical (OH) (whence the name, H + OH produce H_2O, that is water). Morrison and Cocconi's reasoning was that such a choice would come "naturally" for most civilizations (even those whose evolution has not been linked with water) simply because of the extreme convenience of that band, and because of its association with the frequency of the most abundant element in the universe, namely, hydrogen. Yet, when it came down to take the initiative and actually put into practice what Cocconi and Morrison suggested, mere convenience got the best of our logical arguments (no surprise there, eh?).

What about the target? Bad choice indeed. By the reasoning we put forth when we discussed the Drake equation, and by general acceptance in the SETI community, we should target sun-like stars. It is not that we know for sure that other types of stars cannot harbor planetary systems carrying life, but we do know for sure that at least in one case this kind of star *is* associated with life.

---

attendees then asked where did Fermi publish *his* questionable material. To which the physicist replied that he was being honest, but not *stupid*, and that it would be up to the student to find the paper in question.

Fig. 13.3 The famous plaque, designed by Carl Sagan and Frank Drake, that left Earth on board the spacecraft Pioneer 10 on 2 March 1972 and which is now well beyond the confines of the solar system. The plaque is one of the few attempts humans have made at communicating with extra-terrestrial intelligences. Only one of these attempts, from the Arecibo radiotelescope, was via radio.

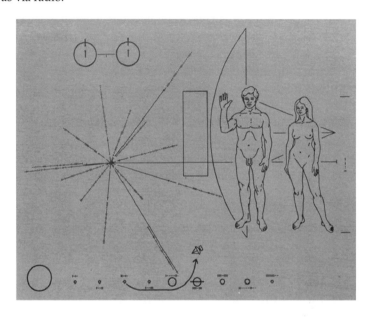

Well, the chosen target of the Arecibo message was a very dense globular star cluster known as M13, in the constellation of Hercules. Even though numerically it may have seemed a good choice (M13 is made of 300,000 stars), the distance and type of stars make it a good bet that we won't get any answer at all. First, M13 is about 25,000 light-years from earth, which means that the Arecibo signal will be there in the year 26,974 (and we would have to wait until at least the year 51,974 for an answer, assuming the ETs are prompt). Second, most stars in M13 are *not* of solar type. Furthermore, these stars are so densely packed in a relatively small amount of space that they must exert an incredibly strong gravitational attraction onto each other, with the likely result that any planetary system either never had a chance to form, or has by now been crushed in a chaotic (in the sense of Chapter 14) gravitational game.

Finally, we only sent the Arecibo message once. This is again contrary to any rational thinking. If we received a message, even one that can hardly qualify as "natural," but we got only one instance of it with no repetition, we would have to relegate it to the ocean of scientific curiosities. In fact, a similar event has occurred. I am referring to the "Wow" signal received in 1977 at Ohio State University. The signal was received on all 50 channels then being scanned, and its intensity was so far above background radiation to immediately qualify it as a very good SETI candidate. Except, the signal never repeated itself, it was never observed by any independent observatory, and it is now part of the SETI folklore, not of the annals of great scientific discoveries. It may indeed be an inevitable limitation of the scientific method that scientists can deal effectively only with repeatable phenomena, but that we ourselves would consciously play such an ignominious trick on the poor inhabitants of M13 is beyond excuse.

With all its defects (and notice that I haven't even gotten into the details of *how* the message was in fact put together), the Arecibo signal is nevertheless the only attempt at radio contact ever purposely enacted by human beings. It seems that the prevalent reasoning in the SETI community is that it is more "cost effective" to listen than to broadcast. I suspect that this is yet another situation in which good old selfish human nature emerges. After all, should we get some, any, information from outer space, we would benefit immensely – if not from a practical standpoint, certainly from a scientific and philosophical one. But what's the advantage to us of broadcasting our knowledge or existence to the rest of the universe? Of course, we can only hope that that particular human trait is not widespread throughout the galaxy, or we may be in a crowded galaxy and never hear a fly go by.

Is the bang worth our buck?

The ultimate question about any scientific enterprise is: is it worth it? Now, unlike in many other realms of human experience, "worth" in science is not measured only in terms of vile hard cash. Don't get me wrong, especially in the latter part of the 20th century and at the beginning of the 21st scientists are very much aware of the difficulty of raising funds for anything, and they therefore have to look uncomfortably closely to what their chronically meager purse can afford. Nevertheless, scientific worth is a compound measure in which several quantities weigh together. First and foremost, scientists have to agree that the question to be pursued is indeed a scientific question. Mind you, not just an interesting question, but one that can – at least potentially – be answered using a scientific approach. There are plenty of fascinating questions out there, but many simply do not lend themselves to the rigors of the scientific method (for example, what was there before the Big Bang? Or, what where Neanderthal people's feeling after the death of one of their own?). Second, even if the question is answerable in principle, is it likely that a significant contribution can be made within a few years to a few decades? This is important because most research grants do not last more than five years, which is also the life span of a graduate student's tenure in a university. As I pointed out above, modern scientific research proceeds by tackling "bite-size" questions, which constitute the best material for a PhD thesis or a grant proposal. Alas, few scientists today could afford a lifetime project such as the one that brought Darwin to formulate the theory of evolution by natural selection, or which finally brought us the solution to the infamous Fermat's theorem (Cipra 1993). Third, assuming that the question is addressable in a relatively short period of time, what do we gain by doing so? To put it into another fashion, how would the solution of this particular riddle further our intellectual growth, or even merely augment our material welfare?

I think the answer to the first question is a definite yes, as I have tried to show at the beginning of this essay. SETI is indeed a scientific enterprise. It is no different in kind from the search for a new subatomic particle, or the attempts to detect black holes. Sure, it is in theory possible that there is no ET, or that we do not have the means to find them, but that sort of uncertainty is a normal component of scientific discoveries. The only science that proceeds with the certainty of positive results is rather boring and trivial (though often not devoid of practical value, like the purification of a new antibiotic, contrasted with the *discovery* of antibiotics). We do have good reasons to think that extraterrestrial civilizations are out there, and we do have a variety of tools to investigate their presence.

Is ET a bite that can be chewed by a graduate student or a tenure-track faculty? Clearly not. Unfortunately, no scientific journal would accept a paper that reported that, well, after five years of searching at 1420 MHz we found no intelligent communication from the Andromeda galaxy. Is there a way around this difficulty? Piggybacking, of course: the key is to set up SETI programs that can produce side results worth paying for. For example, a search around the "water hole" frequency could yield a detailed map of the distribution of interstellar hydrogen and hydroxyl radicals in selected regions of space. This information would be simultaneously valuable for astro-chemists while potentially leading to our first interplanetary "hello!" This example is not that far-fetched. Many scientists (including me) actually use this strategy every day: get funding for projects that are "reasonable" (i.e., they have some kind of short-term outcome), while diverting some of the money and energy to more high risk enterprises. Why? Because if one of these enterprises should turn into a home run, its payoff would be much greater than the minor investment one has made on it (sort of like winning the lottery while buying a low cost ticket once in a while – you don't plan to buy your next home or immortality for your soul with it, see Chapter 4 – but if it happens...).

A very clever example of how SETI can proceed with little spending is provided by the current incarnation of it at the University of California Berkeley, known as SETI@home (http://setiathome.ssl.berkeley.edu/). Not only are they using data that are being collected by the Arecibo radiotelescope for other purposes and scanning them for signs of extraterrestrial intelligence, but they are making millions of personal computers worldwide perform the complex and endless task of analyzing such data! The problem is very difficult and the solution brilliant: the data incoming from the telescope constitute an endless stream, and the analyses to be carried out to accurately search for non-natural signals are very elaborate. The computer time required for such task would be prohibitive even for a highly funded scientific enterprise. Therefore, the scientists at SETI@home have designed a program that works like a screen saver on your personal computer and that anybody can download from the project's web site. But the program is much more than a screen saver: whenever your computer is idle, it starts a set of calculations on small packages of data that from time to time the program itself down- and up-loads from the SETI server. At the time I am writing my computer has already performed more than 13,000 hours of calculations for SETI. The inducement to PC users all over the world is the thrill of participating in one of the potentially most far-reaching enterprises of modern science, and of course the (astronomically small) probability of actually finding the right signal.

All of the above notwithstanding, what would the payoff of a positive SETI program actually be? Well, let me start by stating what it probably would *not* be. ET will probably not solve humanity's problems, will not cure cancer or AIDS, nor tell us how to stop wars or avoid environmental suicide. Why should they, and how could they? Probably several of our problems are just that: ours. It is very unlikely that what we experience as cancer and AIDS would exist in a different part of the galaxy, where the local life forms would have evolved for billions of years under different circumstances from those prevalent on earth. What about possibly more universal questions such as the threat of global environmental collapse (which possibly, but not surely, a technological society would sooner or later have to face)? For one thing, the problem may be universal, but the solution would probably turn out to be contingent on the particular resources, as well as on idiosyncratic sociological and psychological factors. Furthermore, if our own efforts at interstellar communication are any guide, the most likely kind of message we may hope to receive is just an elaborate "hello there!" It would simply be very costly to send a much longer, information-rich message. And what purpose would it serve from the ET's perspective? Finally, since the possibility of a radio dialogue is basically nil because of the vast interstellar distances and the finite speed of radio signals, there would be no point in hoping for a prolonged Q&A session across the galaxy. (Of course, all this assumes that the actual contact would occur along lines foreseen by current SETI researchers. There is always the remote possibility that we will find a completely new medium which could overcome some of these difficulties)

What we would get out of the knowledge that ET is really out there is, however, far from negligible. First of all, we would have the answer to a fundamental biological question: is life a unique, or a relatively common phenomenon in the universe? This would constitute a giant leap forward for biology, together with offering new clues about the origin of life itself, perhaps one of the most persistent and involving questions of modern science. Second, ET would bring a fatal blow to that perversion of modern cosmology known as the "anthropic principle," that is the idea that the universe is custom-made to allow for the evolution of humans (for a detailed critique see: Stenger 1996; 1999). If ET exists we would be forced to conclude that others share the dubious distinction of having zillions of galaxies and stars brought into existence just to make sense of their everyday ramblings about the universe. Thirdly, the discovery of ET would be one of those once-in-a-long-while scientific results capable of influencing a larger portion of the human experience, including philosophy, religion, and our perception of humankind's place in the universe. Whoever will confirm the existence of extraterrestrial intelligences will demolish any remnants of irrational pride that *Homo sapiens* may still harbor. We would know that the same mindless process that originated us has also produced other similar creatures, possibly in turn deluded about some central role they played in the universe. At least up to the moment they received an unnatural signal from a small planet orbiting a perfectly average star at the periphery of a rather ordinary galaxy. As the immortal Monty Python song (from *The Meaning of Life*) goes:

> Just remember that you're standing on
>   a planet that's evolving
> and revolving at 900 miles an hour,
> that's orbiting at 19 miles a second, so it's reckoned,
> a sun that is the source of all our power.
> The sun and you and me and all the stars that we can see,
> are moving at a million miles a day
> in an outer spiral arm, at 40,000 miles an hour,
> of the galaxy we call the Milky Way
> ...
> So remember when you're feeling very small and insecure
> how amazingly unlikely is your birth
> and pray that there's intelligent life somewhere up in space
> because there's bugger all down here on earth.

Chapter 14 - Chaos, fractals, complexity, and the limits of science[51]

"Chaos is a name for any order that produces confusion in our minds."
(George Santayana, Dominations and Powers)

The birth of modern science has been attributed to a variety of circumstances, events, and people (Lindberg 1992), but unquestionably one of the key figures in its development was René Descartes, the French philosopher who first articulated the fundamentals of the modern scientific method of inquiry (Descartes 1637). A major tenet of Descartes' approach was the idea that complex systems can be analyzed one part at a time to be understood, and then put back together to yield a comprehensive picture. This reductionism has been at the core of some of the most spectacular successes of the scientific endeavor, from particle physics to molecular biology. But what if some natural phenomena simply cannot be so conveniently partitioned to facilitate human comprehension? What if breaking the components apart alters their properties so much that what we learn from the separate pieces of the puzzle gives us a different and misleading idea of the whole picture? In other words, how can a reductionist science study emergent properties, by definition the result of complex interactions?

The first matter to deal with in this context is a coherent definition of emergent property. There has been much talk of emergent properties, especially in describing the complexity of biological development and evolution. Yet, it is hard to put a finger on what even sophisticated researchers mean when they say, for example, that human consciousness is an emergent property of the physical structure of the brain and of its interactions with the environment. Perhaps the simplest way to understand emergent properties is to consider the relationship between hydrogen, oxygen, and water (see Chapter 3, Figure 3.4). Although the

---

[51] This essay is currently in press for *Skeptic* magazine.

combination of two atoms of hydrogen and one of oxygen yields water, the complex properties of the resulting substance (e.g., the temperatures at which it undergoes state transitions) are not readily derivable from the individual properties of hydrogen and oxygen. In other words, knowing all we know about the structure and behavior of the atoms composing water, we can predict the structure but not the behavior of water. This, of course, does not mean that the formation of water is a magic feat outside the investigative powers of science. But it does mean that complexity comes with new properties that are specific of the new level of organization (in this case, molecular vs. atomic) and that are due not to the sum, but to the *interaction* of the component parts. This, it would seem, is enough to stop the Cartesian research program dead in its tracks.

Scientists of several disciplines, from astronomy to meteorology, from evolutionary biology to the social sciences, have been struggling with interactions and emergent properties, without a good paradigm to adopt to make headway. That is, until chaos theory and its more recent derivative, complexity theory, appeared on the scene. As we shall see, these novel conceptual and mathematical approaches to the study of complex systems carry the astounding promise of providing a way out of the thickets of emergent properties. Science, it seems, has finally cracked the next level of analysis, one that will replace the Cartesian approach and substitute a new, scientific holism for the old reductionism. More than 35 years after the publication of the first study on chaos, with an entire institute devoted to the study of complexity, (The Santa Fe Institute at http://www.santafe.edu/), and with technical journals and thousands of papers published on both theories, it is time for a general evaluation of the new holism. Has chaos/complexity delivered on its promises? Or has it fallen much shorter than its original goals? Does it provide a truly new set of tools and answers, or is it just a passing fashion in the academic world?

What do you mean, chaos?

What is chaos? In the vernacular, the word is a synonym for randomness, a completely non-deterministic and irregular phenomenon. The term usually comes with a negative connotation attached to it – a chaotic situation is one that we would like to avoid. In mathematical theory, however, chaos refers to a *deterministic* (i.e., nonrandom) phenomenon characterized by special properties that make the predictability of the outcomes very much reduced.[52] In fact, a chaotic behavior is such that even though it does not happen randomly, it looks like a series of random occurrences. As an example, compare the two upper graphs in Figure 14.1. While they both look random at first sight, only the one on the left is really non-deterministic. The other one is a time series generated by a set of equations describing a mathematical object called the Henon attractor; this series is chaotic, not random. The lower graphs in the figure help discriminate between the two kinds of behavior. These representations are obtained by plotting the status of the system at time *t* against the status of the same system at time *t+1*. Also known as phase plots, they reveal an orderly structure in the case of the Henon attractor (Fig. 1d) but not in the case of the random sequence (Fig. 1c).

Chaotic dynamics are usually, but not always (Altenberg 1991) the property of nonlinear systems, i.e., of systems whose behavior can be described by sets of nonlinear equations. However, the converse is not true: not all (in fact not many) nonlinear dynamics generate chaotic behaviors (Gulick 1992). Typically, a given system of equations can produce both non-chaotic and chaotic outcomes, depending on the range of values assumed by the parameters entering into the equations. In fact, in many systems one can increase the value of a key parameter and obtain a progression of outcomes from a steady equilibrium state to regular oscillations with two equilibria, to more complex cycles with multiple equilibria, finally bringing about the chaotic condition. Since the latter can be thought of as an ensemble of an infinite number of equilibrium points (the so-called "strange

---

[52] For a general introduction to and history of chaos theory see Gleick (1987).

attractor"), this process is sometime termed the "doubling route" to chaos (Gulick 1992).

Another phenomenon typically associated with chaos is the so-called "butterfly effect." The term came from a famous analogy proposed by Edward Lorenz, the discoverer of the first formal system of equations that yields chaotic behavior (Lorenz 1963). Lorenz said that chaos is analogous to a situation in which the flapping of a butterfly's wings in Brazil ends up starting a cascade of events that results in a tornado in Texas. The technical term for this phenomenon is *sensitivity to initial conditions*, and it means that a small perturbation of a system can cause a series of effects that

Figure 14.1. Time series and phase plots. The two upper graphs show two time series (a plot of the value of a variable against time): the one to the left is random, the other one is chaotic. The lower graphs are phase plots, that is plots of the value of the variable at time *t* vs. the value of the same variable at time *t+1*. These plots help distinguish the random series from the chaotic one, which describes what is know as the Henon attractor.

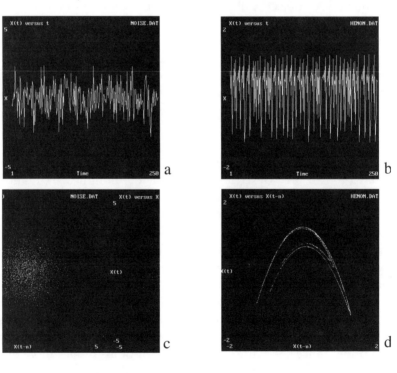

eventually lead to macroscopic consequences later on in the time sequence. Had that perturbation been of a different nature, an entirely different series of events would have unfolded.[53] There is a very important qualification to be made about sensitivity to initial conditions: it may happen only in some circumstances. For example, while it is conceivable that the tiny movement of air caused by flapping a butterfly's wings may indeed initiate a causal chain that affects macroscopic weather patterns, most of the times millions of butterfly wings flapping around will not alter the weather forecasts a tiny bit! If that is the case, the system (in this case the weather) will actually behave as chaotic at some moments in time, but as predictable or random at others.

A more rigorous way to put the butterfly effect is to state that the predictability of the system decreases exponentially with time. That is, our predictions of where the system will be are relatively good for the immediate future, but lose accuracy for slightly longer intervals of time, and pretty soon they are completely useless. However, the system will still be found within the strange attractor, if viewed in phase space. We are now ready to consider the formal definition of chaos which, as we shall see, makes the application of chaos theory to several fields unwarranted, or at best haphazard. A chaotic system is one whose mathematical function is characterized by at least one of the following (Gulick 1992):

i.   It has a positive Lyapunov exponent at each point in its domain that is not eventually periodic.
ii.   It has sensitive dependence on initial conditions on its domain.

A Lyapunov exponent is a convenient measure of how fast the trajectories of the system diverge in phase space. If the exponent is negative, the system actually converges at an equilibrium point; if the exponent is near zero the system behaves with periodic regularity; and if the exponent is positive the system is either

---

[53] Science fiction authors have had a field day with the consequences of the butterfly effect well before Lorenz formally discovered it. A precious example is the short story entitled "What if," by Isaac Asimov, originally published in 1952 (Asimov 1990).

chaotic or – for very high exponents – random (it makes sense that a random series diverges more rapidly than a chaotic one; in fact the first one should diverge infinitely fast).

The last question that remains to be addressed before getting to complexity theory, of which chaos theory can be considered a subset, is: how do we know if a system is chaotic? This is a crucial point, because we will see later that wild claims of the presence of chaos are made without even approximating the rigor required within mathematics and science. Essentially, there are two ways to demonstrate chaos. One follows a theoretical approach; the other one is empirical. The theoretical approach consists in analyzing the set of equations describing the system and determining the presence of a positive Lyapunov exponent. Of course, the problem is that in many (real or alleged) applications of chaos theory we do not know what set of equations actually describes the system; all we have are empirical observations. Not to worry. There are several methods that make possible to estimate Lyapunov exponents from an empirical time series (Wolf et al. 1985; Wolf and Bessoir 1991; Ellner and Turchin 1995). Very good software called "Chaos Data Analyzer," is also readily available (at http://www.aip.org/pas/pashome.html). All this has lead to what Mandelbrot (in Peitgen et al. 1992) calls somewhat oxymoronically "experimental mathematics."[54]

Here is where things get tricky, however. Suppose we are trying to determine if an empirical time series is chaotic, random, or periodic. As we have seen, a simple plot of X vs. t will not suffice, and we need a phase plot to look for orderly structures. Except that these will emerge only after we plot hundreds, possibly thousands, of points. If we plot only a few points, both diagrams will seem random, because the chaotic system jumps from one point on the attractor to another in no systematic sequence. The problem is that in many alleged applications of chaos theory we simply don't have enough data points to clearly see the attractor, if it is indeed there. While this is an empirical, not a conceptual problem, it is a major hindrance to the application of chaos theory to non-physical sciences such as biology or geophysics, where often the accumulated data sets are much shorter than required to

---

[54] I am not referring here to the wide fields of statistical analysis or applied mathematics.

demonstrate chaos (Pool 1989; Morris 1990; Hastings et al. 1993; Stone 1994). Things become desperate when it comes to the social sciences (Shermer 1993, 1995, 1997c), and border on ridiculous for applications in the humanities, such as literary criticism (Horgan 1995; Boon 1997).

What has this got to do with fractals?

A topic that is usually brought up in conjunction with chaos theory is that of fractal geometry. And for good reasons, because there is indeed an intimate mathematical relationship between the two. Geometrically speaking, fractals are those often beautiful and always intricate geometric forms that arise by the infinite iteration of some mathematical function. Mathematician Benoit Mandelbrot proposed the term and it captured the imagination of scientists as well as of the public. Mathematically, fractals have non-integer dimension when this is calculated using one of a series of alternative definitions of dimension (Gulick 1992), hence the name.

It turns out that strange attractors are geometrical shapes characterized by fractal dimension, i.e. strange attractors are in fact fractals. The implication is that if one observes a spatial structure that is fractal, one can reasonably infer that the temporal dynamics generating that structure were chaotic. In a sense, fractals are the fingerprints left by chaotic phenomena.

Enter complexity

If fractals are a component of chaos theory, chaos theory itself is a component of a larger, albeit less well-defined, theoretical framework known as complexity theory. An excellent history of complexity theory is provided by Waldrop (1992), and a comprehensive treatment can be found in Kauffman (1993). Complexity theory deals, well, with complexity. But what is complexity? The answer to this deceptively simple question is far from clear. In biology, for example, there has been an almost incessant talk about the evolution of complexity, yet when the term is dissected more closely it turns out to mean many different things depending on the author that is addressing it (McShea 1991, 1996). Essentially, we can think of complexity theory as an attempt to study systems that satisfy two conditions: 1) they are made of many interacting parts, and 2) the interactions result in emergent properties that are not immediately reducible to a simple sum of the properties of the individual components. This has been the goal, for example, of developmental evolutionary biology throughout the 20th century, and only very recently have researchers started to gain some new significant insights into the problem (Schlichting and Pigliucci 1998).

Complexity theory essentially uses nonlinear dynamical modeling to account for the behavior of orderly complex systems. The dynamics manifested by a given system depend fundamentally on two parameters (Kauffman and Levin 1987; Bak and Chen 1991): the number of parts that compose the system, N, and the average number of connections among parts within the system, K. So-called NK systems then fall into three categories, depending on the relationship between K and N:

I.   Systems in which the number of connections is very small compared to the total number of parts. In this case each part behaves pretty much independently of the others, and the properties of the system are the simple sum of the properties of its individual parts. These systems tend to be static or reach simple dynamic equilibria and are sometimes called "sub-critical."

II.   When K increases compared to N, the dynamics becomes more complex and emergent properties appear. Local changes propagate to distant parts of the system because of the connectivity, but do not usually cause global changes since the ratio of N to K is still relatively small. These systems are said to be at the "edge of chaos" situations, also referred to as "critical" systems.

III.   As K approaches N most components of the system are connected to almost every other component. This creates the deterministic but unstable "super-critical" systems described by chaos theory.

Incidentally, the Lyapunov exponent introduced above is also a good guide to distinguish among *NK* systems, since sub-critical systems have a negative Lyapunov exponent, critical systems have an exponent near zero, and chaotic systems are characterized by a positive exponent (Solé et al. 1999). Most classical mathematics, physics, and biology, deal with type I systems, chaos theory and fractal geometry study type III systems, and complexity theory focuses on type II systems and on the transitions between classes.

Examples of systems at the edge of chaos (type II) allegedly include the evolution of natural populations, the developmental biology of plants and animals, the stock market, the global economy, and the dynamics of clusters of galaxies, to name but a few. You can see why complexity theory is a field of inquiry of potentially all-encompassing importance. But is this taking on too much all at once? Will the positive insights of chaos and complexity eventually be lost if the whole discipline tumbles down on its own eagerness to become a theory of everything?

Chaos and complexity in science: when it works, and when it doesn't

Although I take here a skeptical position toward chaos and complexity theory, let me make clear that I think these are genuine contributions to modern science and to our understanding of the world. The rest of this chapter is simply a cautionary statement against the overuse of these theories within science, as well as of their abuse outside of science if and where the application has wandered far from rigorous intellectual exercise, or into downright nonsense.

Let me start by highlighting what I think have been some of the legitimate accomplishments and applications of chaos and complexity. First of all, both chaos and *NK* systems are indubitable mathematical realities. While the phrase "mathematical reality" may seem oxymoronic, what I mean is that certain classes of nonlinear equations originate chaotic dynamics and certain *NK* systems, such as cellular automata (Wolfram 1984; Langton 1986) do display emergent properties. Therefore, the effort of chaos and complexity scientists cannot be dismissed out of hand.

Second, chaos – and to a lesser extent complexity – has certainly yielded applications in the empirical sciences. Chief among the disciplines that have benefited from chaos theory is perhaps physics, for two main reasons. On one hand, theoretical physics is much more advanced than any other theory in any other branch of science, partially because physics deals with the simplest objects in the universe (compare the complexity of an atom with that of the human brain, for example). On the other hand, in physics it is relatively easy to accumulate the long temporal series of observations that are necessary to empirically study nonlinear dynamical systems. For example, complexity theory adequately and elegantly explains the relatively complex physics of sand piles (Bak and Chen 1991). Other advances have been made by the use of chaos and complexity theory in the study of celestial movements (the three-body problem), the onset of turbulence in fluids, and the use of echoes by dolphins (Howlett 1997), to name but a few.

Moving beyond physics, there is a whole series of proposed applications of chaos/complexity that are perfectly legitimate in theory, but have run against empirical limitations. For example, ecologists have been flirting with chaos for a long time (Pool 1989; Hastings and Powell 1991; Hastings et al. 1993; McCann and Yodzis 1994). However, claims of chaotic dynamics found in food webs or population fluctuations are dubious because of the problem of short available time series mentioned above. This, of course, does not mean that at least some of these applications will not eventually turn out to be genuine. But the jury is still out, and it may be perennially hung if the limitations intrinsic in short empirical data series are not overcome.

There are also situations in which the new theories can be applied, but the results are entirely sterile. A well-known technique in chaos theory and fractal geometry is the so-called "chaos game" (Gulick 1992). The game consists in the iteration of some simple geometrical construction that, depending on the conditions used, results in a fractal. The chaos game algorithm has been used to uncover regularity in DNA sequences (Jeffrey 1990; Hill et al. 1992). However, the results are a simple function of the frequencies of nucleotides (the letters of the genetic code) in the DNA of a given organism and the chaos game does not add anything at all to our understanding of these patterns (Golman 1993).

In other cases, complexity theorists have been accused of reinventing the wheel. For example, while computer scientists have rightly been enthusiastic about the development of the so-called "genetic algorithms" (literally, evolving computer programs), evolutionary biologists and population geneticists have been much more cool about the hype that this has generated. After all, the twin principles of mutation and selection used to develop genetic algorithms and neural networks are exactly how biologists have explained the action of natural selection since the beginning of the 20th century (Provine 1971). Even one of the major conceptual tools of complexity theory applied to evolutionary biology, the "rugged adaptive landscape"[55] (Kauffman and Smith 1986) is a refinement of ideas proposed much earlier by biologists throughout the 20th century (Wright 1932; van Valen 1973; Lewontin 1978). Scientists from the fields of evolutionary biology and populations genetics (including me) are amused and somewhat pleased that their tools and concepts are being applied to new fields such as the development of computer software. This, however, points toward contributions of Darwinian theory to complexity more than the other way around. Again, this is not to say that complexity theory has not or cannot improve our understanding of evolutionary problems (e.g., Niklas 1997). My point is simply that it would be best to make reasonable claims, to acknowledge the roots and intellectual development of ideas, and to work in interdisciplinary cooperation rather than isolation.

In the literature one can also find much more dubious connections between empirical science and chaos/complexity, for example articles that have simply suggested a vague parallel between the concepts of complexity theory and difficult to quantify natural phenomena such as biological evolution (Ferriere and Clobert 1991; Green 1991; Doebeli 1993). The problem seems to be that these authors have no idea of exactly *how* chaos and complexity can be used to further our understanding of evolution. We see here a shift from a rigorous dialectic between mathematical

---

[55] An adaptive landscape is an imaginary space in which the frequencies of genes contributing to a certain phenotype are plotted against the fitness of individuals having those genes. Such landscapes can have adaptive "peaks," toward which natural selection will push a population, and "valleys," which selection will avoid and where a population could go extinct.

theory and empirical science to the use of chaos/complexity terminology as a metaphor. But metaphors, while undoubtedly useful for human thinking, do not make science, and are open to the endless problems generated by an imprecise and sometimes downright sloppy usage of language. As we shall see in the next two sections, metaphors and analogies tend to be the main conceptual tools of complexity theorists in the social sciences and humanities, which makes these endeavors highly questionable from an intellectual and scientific standpoint.

Chaos in economics, history, and the social sciences

Economics is perhaps one of the quasi-scientific disciplines that come closer to the application of scientific methodology, especially when we consider the heavy use of statistics and of mathematical modeling. Nonetheless, my example of chaotic pseudoscience in this area concerns a major and potentially most lucrative target of study, the stock market. Furthermore, the culprit is none other than Benoit Mandelbrot, the "father" of fractals.

Mandelbrot published a provocative article in *Scientific American* entitled "A multifractal walk down Wall Street" (Mandelbrot 1999). The article's bold premise is that "the geometry that describes the shape of coastlines and the pattern of galaxies {i.e., fractals} also elucidates how stock prices soar and plummet." Well, you can't get any more interdisciplinary than this, can you? Unfortunately, Mandelbrot's delivery falls far short of his promise, so much so that had such a tumble been experienced on Wall Street we would have all lost our shirts. Mandelbrot starts by criticizing standard econometric models on the basis that the optimality assumptions on which such models are constructed do not hold. People don't behave as perfect rational agents, and major shifts in the market are therefore unaccountable by classical economics. All of this is reasonably true, though not necessarily a fatal flaw.[56]

---

[56] A similar situation arises whenever we model a complex system, as for example in population genetics (Hartl and Clark 1989). The process of modeling should actually be seen as a continuous interaction between simple mathematically tractable hypotheses and the complexity of reality. The goal is

But just criticizing the existing body of work is obviously not enough, and Mandelbrot proposes fractals (or, more exactly, the more complex version known as multi-fractals) as a better alternative. A fractal "simulating" the stock market can be generated by simply drawing an *arbitrary* line characterized, say, by an upward trend, followed by a downward one, followed by another upward section. The axes of the plot are time on the abscissa and price of imaginary shares on the ordinates. Each segment is then considered in turn, and a curve identical to the original one, but smaller, is interpolated within that segment. By repeating this process ad infinitum one generates a fractal. But Mandelbrot goes much further, stating that such a fractal "increasingly resembles market price oscillations." Oh? Remember that the starting curve was drawn arbitrarily. How can an arbitrary curve repeated for a high number of iterations yield something that simulates a real phenomenon in any meaningful sense of the word?

The only reason we are led to believe that Mandelbrot's fractal in *Scientific American* simulates the stock market is because he wrote "time" and "price" on the two axes. Had he written "time" and "population size" would this be an accurate rendition of the dynamics of populations of voles? But that is exactly the point, say the enthusiasts of chaos theory: completely different phenomena show an uncanny similarity of patterns. If they *look* the

Figure 14.2. A time series and phase plot (right) of data from the S&P 500 Index. The series seems random and no orderly structure emerges from the phase plot.

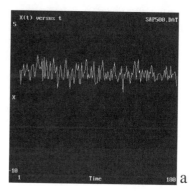
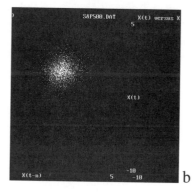

a   b

same, there must be something there. Perhaps, but then what are we to make of the fact that the process of formation of RNA from DNA looks like a Christmas tree when observed through an electron microscope? I doubt that anyone would seriously suggest that we can gain insights into molecular biology by opening gifts on December 24th.[57] Furthermore, it is a well-known fact in science that similarity of patterns by no means guarantees, or even necessarily indicates, similarity of causes. This is because the same patterns can be caused by entirely different phenomena, while the same phenomena – when the circumstances are varied a little – may originate entirely different patterns.

All that Mandelbrot really can offer is a graph in which a series of multifractals looks superficially similar to two real series of data obtained from the stock exchange. There is no theory explaining why this should be regarded as anything more than a superficial similarity. This is science by analogy, as the alchemists and astrologers did before Descartes. But it certainly does not enlighten us on the mechanistic basis of stock market fluctuations and I still don't see what this has to do with either coastlines or galaxies. Incidentally, so many people have tried (and failed) to "crack" the stock market using chaos theory that the thing has become a simple exercise in classes on nonlinear dynamics. For example, figure 14.2 shows a real sequence of economic data, the Standard and Poor's 500 Index prior to the drop of October 19, 1987. The time series (left) looks random, and indeed a phase plot does not reveal any hidden attractor (right). The truth can sometimes be sorely disappointing.

History, like economics, also does not fall under the strict definition of science, and yet valiant and successful attempts to bring the rigor and usefulness of the scientific method to this traditionally humanistic discipline have been published (Sulloway 1997) and have received wide attention. The search for patterns connecting historical events in a non-random fashion is the Holy Grail of the historian. As Michael Shermer puts it: "Is history one damn thing after another, or is it the damn same thing over and over?" (Shermer 1997c). In a series of articles, Shermer (1993, 1995,

---

[57] Actually, a biologist named Lima de Faria did propose just that during a seminar at the University of Rome in the mid'80s, but as I recall he was laughed out of the room. Perhaps he was far ahead of his time, and still is!

1997c) proposes that the complexity of history can best be understood in terms of chaos, thinking of pivotal historical events as bifurcations leading to rapidly divergent paths (historical sequences). Sensitivity to initial conditions, the hallmark of chaos, is to be found at crucial junctures in history, when minor and apparently inconsequential changes in one direction may have shifted the entire course of events onto a different track.

Shermer's proposal is intriguing, and he certainly does not see chaos everywhere. He points out that the same minute change in conditions, should it happen at a different moment, would have no long term consequences whatsoever. Furthermore, he thinks that once an historical sequence (however defined) has been put in motion and has abandoned the area of sensitivity from initial conditions, events unfold in a potentially very predictable way (though hindsight, as we know, is always 20/20). Shermer's reasoning is compelling, and his metaphors have the potential to really yield new insights into the problem, though if he is right history would best be represented as a system at the edge of chaos in the sense discussed above. Additionally, he presents actual concrete examples where the historian could start to look for the signatures of chaos: from the evolution of Auschwitz into an extermination camp during World War II, to the consequences of the battle of Antietam during the U.S. Civil War, to the witch craze in New England from 1560 to 1620.

Table 14.1. Five statistics describing Shermer's series on the witch craze compared to three known time series: one generated by random noise, one typical of the Henon chaotic attractor, and one tracking a periodic phenomenon, the sine trigonometric function. It is difficult to tell if Shermer's series is random or chaotic.

Characteristic	Witch craze	Random noise	Henon attractor	Sine function
Sample size	47 (detrended)	2000	2000	2000
Probability distribution	One sharp peak	Broad (bell shaped)	Broad (almost flat)	Two sharp peaks
Power spectrum	Broad	Broad	Broad	One dominant peak
Correlation dimension	6.291 +/- 1.108	4.555 +/- 0.031	1.239 +/- 0.080	0.894 +/- 0.624
Deviation from randomness	-1.525	-11.789	0.371	0.063
Lyapunov exponent	0.455 +/- 0.334	0.780 +/- 0.034	0.597 +/- 0.033	-0.001 +/- 0.026

The devil, in this case, is in the details, or lack thereof. Shermer does not go much further than providing a series of suggestive examples, mostly using verbal arguments and providing reasonable but ad hoc scenaria. The one case in which we see quantitative data is his study of the witch craze (Shermer 1995). His graph shows the number of cases of accusation of witchcraft and sorcery per year as a time series diagram (Figure 14.3a). But there is no phase plot, no strange attractor, and no calculation of Lyapunov exponents. For all we know, the sequence might be entirely random. I re-analyzed Shermer's data with the Chaos Data Analyzer software as an exercise for this chapter. Notice that a serious study cannot be performed due to the fact that the time sequence is too short (48 points), so what follows must be considered only illustrative of the approach.

First, it is clear that the original data set follows a simple trend: the number of cases of denunciation of witches rises from an initial zero value to a climax where peaks alternate rapidly. The whole phenomenon then withers away toward the end of the craze. When faced with this kind of data, one needs to "detrend" them, that is, to eliminate the trivial source of predictability and see if there is any underlying complex dynamic in the system. Figure 14.3b shows such detrended data, in which each data point now represents an increase or decrease in denunciations, not their

Figure 14. 3. Shermer's data on the witch craze in New England between 1560 and 1620. The graph on the left shows the original data. The central plot shows the detrended data, that is the graph of *variation* in the number of cases instead of the absolute numbers themselves. The rightmost diagram shows a phase plot of the detrended data. Because of the shortness of the time series, it is impossible to tell if the phase plot depicts a random or a chaotic series.

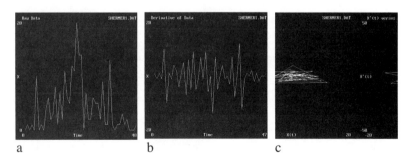

a   b   c

absolute number. The phase plot (Figure 14.3c) does not help much, showing no clear structure, again probably because of the paucity of data points. Table 14.1 then summarizes a series of statistics characterizing Shermer's data and comparing them to three well known data sets: random noise, the chaotic Henon attractor (Figure 14.1c,d), and a sine function representing periodic behavior. The probability distributions of these data (not plotted) show some differences: randomness and chaos are associated with a broad distribution with no peaks, while the periodic function generates two peaks. Shermer's data are characterized by one peak, thereby suggesting some sort of simple periodicity. However, a more powerful test based on the power spectrum of the data (an analysis looking for regularities based on fast Fourier transforms) likens the witch craze to either a chaotic or a random sequence, not to a periodic one. The third test was based on the calculation of the correlation dimension, an index of the complexity of the data. Here the historical series definitely looks random, with a correlation dimension even higher than the one characterizing random noise. I then calculated a measure of deviation from randomness for the four data sets: the witch craze falls in the negative domain, indicating a pretty random series. Finally, the Lyapunov exponent (a measure of sensitivity to initial conditions) for the witch craze is indeed positive and smaller than the one of the Henon attractor, suggesting chaos rather than randomness. All in all, one (weak) indicator points toward regularity, one toward chaos, one excludes regularity, and two go for randomness. My hunch would be that the series is probably random, but it could be chaotic. Again, the problem is in the paucity of data. The point of the exercise is to show that we cannot stop at suggestions and reasonable verbal arguments. History may very well be chaotic, but the burden of proof is on the historian to uncover the hidden strange attractor.

Another interesting case in the realm of quasi-scientific disciplines is presented by psychology. It also uses all the tools of quantitative science, but so far it has fallen short of full science status for the same reason that limits history and – perhaps to a lesser extent – economics: there is no successful (i.e., predictive) theory unifying the field and guiding its research, no overarching paradigm. Sociology, history, and in part economics do not have their equivalent of quantum theory or of evolution. Within psychology, psychoanalysis is perhaps in an even worse shape, still marred by decidedly unscientific theories proposed by Freud (MacDonald 1996) and by some of its disciples and later opponents, such as Jung.

Chaos theory does not seem to be helping psychoanalysis, despite the attempts of at least one of its modern exponents, Jeffrey Goldstein of Adelphi University (Horgan 1995). Goldstein thinks that the point of chaos in his discipline is "to provide therapists with new metaphors and analogies rather than with ways to make their mental models more mathematically rigorous." It would be hard to find a more telling illustration of where the problem lies!

In 1995 Goldstein got about 30 therapists together to participate in a conference dedicated to "the self-organizing psyche," despite the fact that no one knows what a psyche is to begin with, let alone how it self-organizes. One of the attendees provided a rare moment of lucidity when he reminded his colleagues of Ludwig Wittgenstein's warning that language is a double-edged sword: it can illuminate a subject, but it can also obscure it to the utmost degree. Not surprisingly, another participant seriously asked Goldstein if the term attractor that he was using so generously in his presentation referred to some kind of sexual attraction. Freud would have probably answered that sometimes a cigar is just a cigar, but the episode is a quintessential example of one of the most crucial problems undermining the widespread talk about chaos: most people who incorporate it in their speeches literally do not know what they are talking about.

It gets worse. One of the participants to the conference, Alan Stein, suggested that "the lesson of nonlinear science is that no one can ever really 'know' anyone else, because the mind constantly shifts between different states." Besides the obvious nihilistic consequences of such a statement (what, then, is the point of having a psychotherapeutic session? Somebody should have told Woody Allen long ago), Stein conveniently neglected to specify how these shifts occur or what the states consist of. The comical, but perfectly logical, consequence of Stein's presentation was that another therapist asked – again in all seriousness – if it wouldn't be best to do absolutely nothing to a patient, receiving a nod of approval from the speaker! Yet another participant went so far as recalling an instance in which a patient started to improve once she decided to spend her therapy time sitting in her car instead of going to the practitioner's office. I think this doesn't require any further comments.

Chaotic humanities and literary criticism

The humanities, and especially literary criticism and deconstructionism, don't get much of kind treatment in skeptical writings (e.g., Haack 1997). Alas, this chapter is not going to be an exception. While the examples below are taken from one specific book, they are particularly illuminating in that the author draws on a variety of sources spanning the gamut of the humanities, thereby opening a window onto the nonsense that at times characterizes the other side of the divide between the two cultures.

The otherwise fascinating book by Kevin Boon, *Chaos Theory and the Interpretation of Literary Texts: the Case of Kurt Vonnegut* (Boon 1997) is perhaps one of the best examples of how the unwarranted application of chaos theory can quickly lead to nonsense. Don't get me wrong, Kurt Vonnegut is one of my favorite contemporary authors, and I enjoyed reading through Boon's book because he does provide many perceptive comments on Vonnegut's writings. However, and contrary to the main theme of the book, these insights don't have anything to do with chaos theory at all. Perhaps the crux of the problem is summarized by Boon himself when he writes:

"In this study, I employ 'Chaos' as a metaphor in the Aristotelian sense that through its use 'we can best get hold of something fresh.' Chaos as a metaphor, then, occupies a space between its more rigid scientific application and its more liberal ideational application." (p. 38)

It is this more liberal and less rigid application that should turn on the skeptical radar, and the blips, as we shall see, just keep coming. The best I can do is to yield again to the writing of Boon, which – I hope – will require very little commentary on my part. On mythology, he says:

(Interpreting author Barbara G. Walker) "Chaos is presented as a state of flux between solid worlds, an indeterminate margin between two determinate systems. Her definition ... prefigures contemporary views on chaos ... as does the Sumerian myth of the netherworld where opposites are shaped from the dirt of the abyss into life only to eventually ... become one again 'in the pit of darkness.'" (p. 41)

It is hard to even fathom exactly what this passage means. Furthermore, I'm quite sure that we can credit the Sumerians for a lot of things, but certainly not for anticipating the modern mathematical theory of chaos.

On philosophy, Boon comments, referring to Hegel:

"The structure of his method forces an important opening in philosophical thought relevant to contemporary views on chaos. If ... every assertion carries with it its own negation, then every assertion carries with it the seeds of its own change." (p. 46)

This is saying that Hegel's philosophy of dialectics has direct correspondence with self-similar chaotic systems. But the only correspondence is in the misleading metaphor that Boon proposes; it is superficial, and it does not illuminate either chaos theory or Hegel's philosophy.

Boon then plunges in an almost comical list of quotations by thinkers from disparate fields, from literary criticism to psychology, one more preposterous than the other. Here are a couple of excerpts:

Quoting H. Skinner: "Perhaps we should borrow the metaphor of fractional dimension, and consider that the effective dimensionality of alcohol or drug dependence will vary according to different populations." (p. 69)

Quoting J.R. Van Eenwyk: "Jung's archetype corresponds with unstable saddle points, homoclinic orbits and bifurcations ... archetypes break up the linear flow of consciousness, infusing it with a chaotic/non-linear flow." (p. 69)

And so on. What do all these passages have in common? First, it's clear that the authors quoted have no actual understanding of chaos theory in the legitimate sense of a mathematical theory describing the behavior of certain physical systems. Second, there is a lot of jargon being thrown around, so that the reader can be duly impressed and his mind conveniently obfuscated. Third, in all cases the best one can say is, again, that chaos is being used as a metaphor, with no possibility of actually testing any hypothesis or insight one might derive from it. At best, this is what Dawkins (1998) refers to as bad scientific poetry in his *Unweaving the Rainbow*. There is nothing wrong with using metaphors or poetic images. Scientists do it all the time to either understand something or teach it to somebody else. But good metaphors bring understanding. The ones I listed above simply bring, well, chaos. However, if one takes the view of John Casti (1989), incidentally a complexity theorist, the above symptoms are common to all forms of pseudoscience, and this is how we should treat chaos theory within the humanities – at least for now.

What about Vonnegut, the reader may rightly ask, does he use the word "chaos" in his novels? Of course, but very clearly (as Boon himself freely acknowledges) he means total disorder – chaos in the vernacular sense – not at all what chaos theory is about. In *Galapagos* Vonnegut notices that big brains cause desperation in people, so – one of his characters asks – why not shrink them? The irony and sophistication of this question is certainly superior to Boon's literal interpretation: "Without big brains we do not perceive chaos."

The ridiculous: chaos for gullible people

Naturally, if you really want to experience how silly chaos theory can become, you have only to surf the Internet. I do not have enough space to get into much detail here, and the topic might deserve a separate book, but here are some entries (in random, not chaotic, order) that anyone can uncover in an hour by using one of the major search engines available online.

- Naturally, chaos theory can yield an "alchemic computer assemblage of thought, sound and image" where you can find "Orphism, a feminine psychedelic worldview based on the deities of chaos, Gaia and Eros"(http://www.slip.net /~richgaik/chaos.html)
- I always suspected that war was chaotic and that soldiers' brains were unreliable, but you can learn about the details (without encumbering your own brain with mathematics) at http://www.au.af.mil/au/database/research/ay1997/acsc/9 7-0229.htm
- Even though we wish we could, how can we possibly ignore the fundamental contribution of postmodernism to science and human welfare in general? At http://uiah.fi/bookshop /isea_proc/nextgen/14.html you'll learn that chaos imagery is "a postmodernist metaphor in the worst sense, of a refusal of bodily scale and the historical situation." What we really need is an "aesthetic critique of chaos theory."
- The School of Sacred Geometry & Coherent Emotion (http://www.danwinter.com/) tells us that a "perfect nesting or embedding or phillotaxis was called the Priori de Scion" and that "Scion meant to branch perfectly." At this site you'll also learn about the "ringing piezoelectric DNA," as well as when "waves and cells and memories became unsustainable."
- Last, but not least, a "learning consultancy" agency reveals to web surfers that "chaos theory teaches us to work with tendencies instead of with specifics ... Words like 'suggest' and 'imply' are indicators of the awareness of chaos theory" (http://bertschco.sunset.net/)

Needless to say, *none* of the above sites contains any real practical application of the mathematical theory of chaos as understood in the sciences. But such is the (often misleading) power of metaphors.

The good, the bad and the ugly of chaos theory: understanding the limits of science

Are scientists working on chaos and complexity in any way responsible for the widespread misunderstanding and inappropriate use of their own theories? Or is this simply another case of naïve non-scientists, pseudoscientists and true believers usurping one more achievement of modern science, as happens frequently with quantum theory (Mole 1998)? I believe that chaos theorists, unlike quantum physicists, do bear part of the responsibility for the inflation that threatens their field of inquiry. When practitioners of a science publicly trumpet a new theory as the best thing since sliced bread (if not better) and make every effort to popularize its very preliminary results, often bypassing the peer review process and going straight to the general public, something is bound to go awry in the popular imagination.

As I have tried to document, even some serious scientists like Kauffman and Mandelbrot have abandoned themselves to wild claims about the usefulness of what they do (Lewin 1992; Waldrop 1992). Or, more precisely, of what they *could* do if only they were not so busy advertising the potentials of their science and, in several cases, profiting from it by forming premature partnerships with private companies.

This is not just bad science, it is ugly education for the public, already surrounded by so many alleged magic bullets offered for all sorts of problems and coated with a thin patina of science. It is no wonder that science itself is losing credibility compared to pseudoscience: how can you choose if you can't tell the difference?

But chaos has a positive story to tell, too, though not one that favors the traditional view of science. It is clear that chaos and complexity are not only mathematically interesting phenomena, they actually occur in the real world. They can certainly be found in physics (Gulick 1992), very likely in biology (Olsen et al. 1988; Goldberger et al. 1990; Allen 1991; Turchin 1993; McCann and Yodzis 1994), and perhaps in economics, history, and psychology. But the lesson that we learn as scientists from the existence of deterministic chaos (the correct technical term for what we have been talking about) is that science, at least in some cases, cannot be predictive. At least, not in the sense traditionally attached to the term. If a chaotic attractor describes weather patterns, we can predict that the system will stay within that attractor, which we can visualize in a particular phase space. But *by definition* we will be unable to predict a specific temporal series of weather changes more than a few days long. This is the inevitable consequence of sensitivity to initial conditions and the ensuing rapid decay in information content.

There is no need to despair and give up on understanding complex systems. But the very nature of our understanding might be different from what Cartesian science has grown comfortable with. This is perhaps the most important legacy of chaos and complexity theory, and one that future generations of scientists and the public will need to reckon with.

Finale: Goethe's "active doubt" and the meaning of skepticism

Skeptics have a bad reputation. The word is usually interpreted as a synonym of cynicism, conjuring up the image of an old curmudgeon who complains about everything and doesn't believe in anything. I was once with skeptic Michael Shermer on the Halerin Hill radio talk show in Knoxville, TN, and our host commented that Shermer didn't look like a skeptic because he was smiling too much! I get a similar response from the audience of some of my talks and debates. This is rather peculiar and needs to be corrected.

Skepticism is not a philosophy of life, and it is far from being a philosophical position of total denial of any evidence. Instead, skepticism is one of the components of the epistemology of critical or analytical thinking. As fellow freethinker David Schaefer pointed out, critical thinking is founded on three ways of knowing: empiricism, rationalism, and skepticism. The differences among these and other "isms" are discussed in Chapter 1, but it's worth summarizing them again here in relation to the particular problem to be analyzed. *Empiricism* is the idea that knowledge must come in part from actual data about the world that surrounds us. Our senses are the most obvious source of these data, although modern science relies on a number of technical enhancements and specific methods to systematically collect information about what's out there. *Rationalism* is the use of rational and logical thought to reach reliable conclusions about the nature of the world that we get to know through empirical means. In modern science, empiricism and rationalism – once philosophical foes – are two essential players of the scientific method, continuously informing each other in an endless dialectical interaction. *Skepticism* is the third component, the attitude of caution that is required in evaluating any claim before reaching a tentative conclusion. Skepticism is what keeps the scientist, and the sensible person, from committing too many type I errors – accepting a false hypothesis (see Chapter 4). However, too much skepticism is not good either, as it increases the likelihood of type II errors – rejecting true hypotheses and ultimately leading to Hume's absurd denial of cause and effect and eventually to nihilism. A reasonable person, therefore, will approach *any* problem, not just scientific ones, with a healthy dose of empiricism (you want to know the facts), rationalism (you want to think about such facts in a logical way), and skepticism (you want to avoid being too gullible).

Perhaps the best way to think about skepticism was summarized in the first review of Darwin's *Origins of Species*, which appeared in 1860 in the London *Times*. The reviewer pointed out that Mr. Darwin's theory was certainly to be taken with caution due to its novelty and revolutionary content. However, such skepticism should be along the lines of what Goethe termed *Thatige Skepsis*, or "active doubt." The idea is that skepticism should not simply be a negative position, but one of active investigation: a true skeptic is someone who does not believe until the evidence is favorable enough, but who actively searches for such evidence before rejecting a new idea.

Are modern skeptics following Goethe's precept, or are they simply debunkers who pay lip service to the ideal of free inquiry? I know examples of both, of course. Skeptics are first of all human beings, and as such they are subject to all the idiosyncrasies and limitations intrinsic of being human. But that does not mean that the philosophical position is not a good one. Even religionists would argue that they defend the *ideal* of their religion, not necessarily the particular incarnation of such idea in any single individual. The reason I am a skeptic rather than a religionist is because I think the idea of skepticism is immeasurably healthier and closer to the truth than the ideas proposed by any religion, regardless of human fallibility in both camps.

Perhaps the most important consequence of skepticism is that it enlarges the scope of scientific inquiry to any topic amenable to logical discussion and empirical investigation. As we have seen in Chapter 6, science proper focuses on a more restricted set of problems, and can only reach firm conclusions within such limits. But there is so much more that, while not directly within the realm of science, can nevertheless be approached in a rational way, with an eye toward the evidence, and with a healthy dose of skepticism. In fact, since skepticism, empiricism, and rationalism are the three epistemological components of critical thinking, and since critical thinking can be applied to any problem we encounter in our lives, skepticism really can reach far and wide.

The crucial message of skepticism for our society is that each and every conclusion should be tentative, and that therefore we should be tolerant of novel ideas, since they may turn out to be correct. There are no authorities that are the final repositories of truth, and we should therefore not delegate important decisions affecting our lives to people who cannot make a cogent argument in their favor. Our educational system should accordingly strive to create a society of skeptics. This would not be a place where everybody is in a bad mood, never smiles, and doesn't believe in anything. To the contrary, it would be a much more sensible, fair, and therefore happy place to live in. Something for every human being to work towards for an entire lifetime.

References

Adams, D. (1986) *The More Than Complete Hitchhiker's Guide to the Galaxy.* Longmeadow Press, Stamford, CT.

Allen, J.C. (1991) Chaos and coevolution: evolutionary warfare in a chaotic predatory-prey system. Florida Entomologist 74:50-59.

Allen, S. (1999) Two mind-sets. Skeptical Inquirer 23 4, July/August, pp. 47-49.

Al-Najjar, Z. (1998) Organic evolution – Islamic view. The Frontier Post (accessed: 10/1999), web page, frontierpost.com.pk/art1sep-11.html.

Altenberg, L. (1991) Chaos from linear frequency-dependent selection. American Naturalist 138:51-68.

Arthur, J. (1996) Creationism: bad science or immoral pseudoscience? Skeptic 4-4:88-107.

Asimov, I. (1990) *The Complete Stories - Vol. 1.* Doubleday, New York, NY.

Bacon, F. (1825) *The Works of Francis Bacon, Lord Chancellor of England.* W. Pickering, London.

Bak, P. and Chen, K. (1991) Self-organized criticality. Scientific American January:46-53.

Barrow, J.D. and Tipler, F.J. (1986) *The Anthropic Cosmological Principle.* Oxford University Press, Oxford, England.

Behe, M.J. (1996) *Darwin's Black Box. The Biochemical Challenge to Evolution.* Free Press, New York.

Bennett, D.P., Rhie, S.H., Becker, A.C., Butler, N., Dann, J., Kaspi, S., Leibowitz, E.M., Lipkin, Y., Maoz, D., Mendelson, H., Peterson, B.A., Quinn, J., Shemmer, O., S, S.T. and Turner, S.E. (1999) Discovery of a planet orbiting a binary star system from gravitational microlensing. Nature 402:57-59.

Beyestein, B.L. (1997) Why bogus therapies seem to work. Skeptical Inquirer 21-5:29-34.

Boon, K.A. (1997) *Chaos Theory and Interpretation of Literary Texts: the Case of Kurt Vonnegut.* Edwin Mellen Press, Lewiston, NY.

Boxhorn, J. (1995) Observed instances of speciation. Talk.Origins (accessed: 12/29/99), web page, www.talkorigins.org.

Brakefield, P.M., Gates, J., Keys, D., Kesbeke, F., Wijngaarden, P.J., Monteiro, A., French, V. and Carroll, S.B. (1996) Development, plasticity and evolution of butterfly eyespot patterns. Nature 384:236-242.

Brandon, R.N. (1996) *Concepts and Methods in Evolutionary Biology.* Cambridge University Press, New York.

Brown, W.A. (1998) The placebo effect. Scientific American January, pp. 90-95.

Cairn-Smith, A.G. (1985) *Seven Clues to the Origin of Life.* Cambridge University Press, Cambridge, England.

Casti, J.L. (1989) *Paradigms Lost.* Avon Books, New York.

Cipra, B. (1993) Fermat's last theorem finally yields. Science 261:32-33.

Collins, H. and Pinch, T. (1998) *The Golem: What You Should Know About Science*. Cambridge University Press, Cambridge, England.

Copernicus, N. (1543) *De Revolutionibus Orbium Coelestium*. Johns Hopkins University Press {1978}, Baltimore, MD.

Crick, F. (1981) *Life Itself*. Simon and Schuster, New York, NY.

Dalrymple, G.B. (1991) *The Age of the Earth*. Stanford University Press, Stanford, CA.

Damasio, A. (1999) *The Feeling of What Happens: Body and Emotion in the Making of Consciousness*. Harcourt Brace & Co., New York, NY.

Darwin, C. (1859) *The Origin of Species by Means of Natural Selection: or, the Preservation of Favored Races in the Struggle for Life*. A.L. Burt (1910), New York, NY.

Darwin, C. (1890) *The Expression of the Emotions in Man and Animals*. J. Murray, London, England.

Davies, P. (1993) *The Mind of God: The Scientific Basis for a Rational World*. Simon and Schuster, New York, NY.

Dawkins, R. (1996) *The Blind Watchmaker: Why the Evidence of Evolution Reveals a Universe Without Design*. W.W. Norton & Co., New York, NY.

Dawkins, R. (1998) *Unweaving the rainbow: science, delusion and the appetite for wonder*. Houghton Mifflin Co., Boston.

Dawkins, R. (1999) You can't have it both ways: irreconcilable differences? Skeptical Inquirer 23 4, July/August, pp. 62-64.

Dawkins, R. (1999b) The "information challenge": how evolution increases information in the genome. Skeptic 7 2, pp. 64-69.

de Waal, F. (1996) *Good Natured: the Origins of Right and Wrong in Humans and Other Animals*. Harvard University Press, Cambridge, MA.

Dembski, W.A. (1998) *The Design Inference*. Cambridge University Press, Cambridge, UK.

Descartes, R. (1637) *Discourse on Method*. Open Court Classics {1989}, La Salle, IL.

Doebeli, M. (1993) The evolutionary advantage of controlled chaos. Proceedings of the Royal Society of London B254:281-285.

Doolittle, W.F. (2000) Uprooting the tree of life. Scientific American 282(2):90-95, February.

Edmunson, M. (1997) On the uses of a liberal education. I. As lite entertainment for bored college students. Harper's Magazine September:39-49.

Edwards, P. (1967) Atheism. *The Encyclopedia of Philosophy*, pp. 174-189. Macmillan Publishing Co., New York, NY.

Eldredge, N. and Gould, S.J. (1972) Punctuated equilibria: an alternative to phyletic gradualism. In: T.J.M. Schopf (eds.) *Models in paleobiology*, pp. 82-115. Freeman, Cooper and Co., San Francisco.

Ellner, S. and Turchin, P. (1995) Chaos in a noisy world: new methods and evidence from time-series analysis. American Naturalist 145:343-375.

Endler, J.A. (1986) *Natural Selection in the Wild*. Princeton University Press, Princeton, NJ.

Ertem, G. and Ferris, J.P. (1996) Synthesis of RNA oligomers on heterogeneous templates. Nature 379:238-240.

Fagan, P.F. (1996) Why religion matters: the impact of religious practice on social stability. The Backgrounder 1064:1-29.

Farmer, J.D., Kauffman, S.A. and Packard, N.H. (1986) Autocatalytic replication of polymers. Physica 22D:50-67.

Ferriere, R. and Clobert, J. (1991) Chaos as an evolutionary stable dynamic. Acat Oecologica 12:697-700.

Feyerabend, P. (1975) *Against Method: Outlines of an Anarchistic Theory of Knowledge*. New Left Press, London, England.

Fisher, R.A. (1930) *The Genetical Theory of Natural Selection*. Clarendon, Oxford.

Futuyma, D. (1998) *Evolutionary Biology*. Sinauer, Sunderland, MA.

Galilei, G. (1632) *Dialogo Sopra i Due Massimi Sistemi del Mondo*. Rizzoli {1952}, Milano, Italy.

Gardner, M. (1997) Intelligent design and Phillip Johnson. Skeptical Inquirer 21:17-20.

Gaustad, E.S. (1987) *Faith of Our Fathers: Religion and the New Nation*. Harper & Row, San Francisco, p. 61.

Gazzaniga, M.S. (1998) The split brain revisited. Scientific American 279 1, July, pp. 50-55.

Genoni, T.C. jr. (1997) Religious belief among scientists stable for eighty years. Skeptical Inquirer 21(5):13.

Gish, D.T. (1991) *Dinosaurs: Those Terrible Lizards*. Institute for Creation Research, North Santee, CA.

Gish, D.T. (1995) *Evolution: The Fossils Still Say No!* Institute for Creation Research, North Santee, CA.

Gleick, J. (1987) *Chaos: Making a New Science*. Penguin, New York, NY.

Goldberger, A.L., Rigney, D.R. and West, B.J. (1990) Chaos and fractals in human physiology. Scientific American February:43-49.

Goldschmidt, R. (1940) *The Material Basis of Evolution*. Yale University Press, New Haven, CT.

Golman, N. (1993) Nucleotide, dinucleotide and trinucleotide frequencies explain patterns observed in chaos game representations of DNA sequences. Nucleic Acid Research 21:2487-2491.

Gould, S.J. (1996) *Full House: the Spread of Excellence from Plato to Darwin*. Harmony, New York, NY.

Gould, S.J. (1996) *The Mismeasure of Man*. W.W. Norton & Co., New York.

Gould, S.J. (1997) Nonoverlapping magisteria. Natural History March, pp. 16-22.

Gould, S.J. (1999) *Rocks of Ages*. Ballantine, New York.

Gould, S.J. and Eldredge, N. (1993) Punctuated equilibrium come of age. Nature 366:223-227.

Green, D.M. (1991) Chaos, fractals and nonlinear dynamics in evolution and phylogeny. Trends in Ecology and Evolution 6:333-336.

Green, R.H. (1999) *The Born Again Skeptic's Guide to the Bible*. FFRF, Madison, WI.

Greene, B. (1999) *The Elegant Universe: Superstrings, Hidden Dimensions, and the Quest for the Ultimate Theory.* Norton & Co., New York, NY.

Gulick, D. (1992) *Encounters with Chaos.* McGraw-Hill, New York, NY.

Haack, S. (1997) Science, scientism, and anti-science in the age of preposterism. Skeptical Inquirer 21(6):37-42.

Haldane, J.B.S. (1985) The origin of life. In: (eds.) *On Being the Right Size and Other Essays,* pp. Oxford University Press, Oxford, England.

Ham, K. (1998) *The Lie: Evolution.* Answers in Genesis, Florence, KY.

Ham, K. (1998) *The Lie: Evolution.* Answers in Genesis, Florence, KY.

Harris, W.S., Gowda, M., Kolb, J.W., Strychacz, C.P., Vacek, J.L., Jones, P.G., Forker, A., O'Keefe, J.H. and McCallister, B.D. (1999) A randomized, controlled trial of the effects of remote, intercessory prayer on outcomes in patients admitted to the coronary care unit. Archives of Internal Medicine 159:2273-2278.

Hartl, D.L. and Clark, A.G. (1989) *Principle of Population Genetics.* Sinauer, Sunderland, MA.

Hastings, A. and Powell, T. (1991) Chaos in a three-species food chain. Ecology 72:896-903.

Hastings, A., Hom, C.L., Ellner, S., Turchin, P. and Godfray, H.C.J. (1993) Chaos in ecology: is mother nature a strange attractor? Annual Review of Ecology and Systematics 24:1-33.

Haught, J.A. (1990) *Holy Horrors: an Illustrated History of Religious Murder and Madness.* Prometheus, Amherst, NY.

Haught, J.A. (1993) The beast in the shadows behind religion. Free Inquiry Summer, pp. 10-11.

Hawking, S. (1993) *Black Holes and Baby Universes.* Bantam Doubleday, New York, NY.

Hey, J. (1999) The neutralist, the fly and the selectionist. Trends in Ecology and Evolution 14:35-37.

Hill, K.A., Schisler, N.J. and Singh, S.M. (1992) Chaos game representation of coding regions of human globin genes and alcohol dehydrogenase genes of phylogenetically divergent species. Journal of Molecular Evolution 35:261-269.

Hiscox, J. (1999) The Jovian system: the last outpost for life? Astronomy & Geophysics 40:22-26.

Holden, C. (1999) Subjecting belief to the scientific method. Science 284:1257-1259.

Horgan, J. (1995) Complexifying Freud. Scientific American September, pp. 28-29.

Howlett, R. (1997) Flipper's secret. New Scientist 28 June, pp. 34-39.

Hoyle, F. (1999) *Mathematics of Evolution.* Acorn, Memphis, TN.

Hoyle, F. and Wickramasinghe, C. (1978) *Lifecloud.* Harper and Row, London, England.

Hume, D. (1740) *A Treatise of Human Nature.* Clarendon press {1896}, Oxford.

Hume, D. (1779) *Dialogues Concerning Natural Religion.* Gilbert Elliot, Edinburgh.

Hume, D. (1992) Hume's maxim. Skeptic 1(2):13.

Humphrey, N. (1996) *Leaps of Faith*. Basic Books, New York, NY.

Isaak, M. (1997) Bombardier beetle and the argument of design. Talk.Origins (accessed: 1/23/00), web page, www.talkorigins.org.

Jaeger, W.W. (1947) *The Theology of the Early Greek Philosophers*. Clarendon Press, Oxford, England.

Jeffrey, H.J. (1990) Chaos game representation of gene structure. Nucleic Acid Research 18:2163-2170.

Jennings Bryan, W. (1996) The most powerful argument against evolution ever made. Skeptic 4(2):90-100.

John Paul II (1997) Message to the Pontifical Academy of Sciences. Quarterly Review of Biology 72:381-383.

Johnson, P. (1997) *Defeating Darwinism by Opening Minds*. InterVarsity Press, Downers Grove, IL.

Kant, I. (1781) *Critique of Pure Reason*. Modern Library {1958}, New York.

Kauffman, S.A. (1993) *The Origins of Order*. Oxford University Press, New York.

Kauffman, S.A. and Levin, S. (1987) Towards a general theory of adaptive walks on rugged landscapes. Journal of Theoretical Biology 128:11-45.

Kauffman, S.A. and Smith, R.G. (1986) Adaptive automata based on Darwinian selection. Physica 22D:68-82.

Kimura, M. (1983) *The Neutral Theory of Molecular Evolution*. Cambridge University Press, Cambridge.

Kitty, A. (1998) Objectivity in journalism: should we be skeptical? Skeptic 6 1, pp. 54-61.

Kosko, B. (1993) *Fuzzy Thinking : the New Science of Fuzzy Logic*. Hyperion, New York, NY.

Kuhn, T. (1970) *The Structure of Scientific Revolutions*. University of Chicago Press, Chicago.

Kurtz, P. (1999) Should skeptical inquiry be applied to religion? Skeptical Inquirer 23 4, July/August, pp. 24-28.

Lakatos, I. (1974) Falsification and the methodology of scientific research programmes. In: I. Lakatos and A. Musgrave (eds.) *Criticism and the Growth of Knowledge*, Cambridge University Press, Cambridge, England.

Langton, C.G. (1986) Studying artificial life with cellular automata. Physica 22D:120-149.

Larson, E.J. (1997) *Summer for the Gods*. BasicBooks, New York.

Larson, E.J. and Witham, L. (1997) Scientists are still keeping the faith. Nature 386:435-436.

Larson, E.J. and Witham, L. (1998) Leading scientists still reject God. Nature 394:313.

Larson, E.J. and Witham, L. (1999) Scientists and religion in America. Scientific American September, pp. 86-93.

Ledo, M. (1997) *Bible Bloopers: Evidence that Demands a Verdict, too! A Skeptic Answers Josh McDowell*. Atlanta Freethought Society, Atlanta, GA.

Leff, G. (1975) *William of Ockham : the Metamorphosis of Scholastic Discourse.* Manchester University Press, Manchester.

Leikind, B.J. (1997) Do recent discoveries in science offer evidence for the existence of God? Skeptic 5(2):66-69.

Lewin, R. (1992) *Complexity: Life at the Edge of Chaos.* Macmillan, New York, NY.

Lewontin, R.C. (1978) Adaptation. Scientific American 213-230.

Lindberg, D.C. (1992) *The Beginnings of Western Science.* University of Chicago Press, Chicago.

Locke, J. (1959) *An Assay Concerning Human Understanding.* Dover Publications, New York.

Lorenz, E.N. (1963) Deterministic nonperiodic flow. Journal of Atmospheric Sciences 20:130-141.

Lynch, M. (1999) The age and relationships of the major animal phyla. Evolution 53:319-325.

MacDonald, K. (1996) Freud's follies. Skeptic 4(3):94-109.

Maden, B.E.H. (1995) No soup for starters? Autotrophy and the origins of metabolism. Trends in Biochemistry 20:337-341.

Madigan, T.J. (1993) Can illusions be mentally healthy? Free Inquiry Summer, pp. 11-12.

Mandelbrot, B.B. (1999) A multifractal walk down Wall Street. Scientific American February, pp. 70-73.

Mathews, S. and Donoghue, M.J. (1999) The root of Angiosperm phylogeny inferred from duplicate phytochrome genes. Science 286:947-950.

Maynard-Smith, J. and Szathmary, E. (1995) *The Major Transitions in Evolution.* Oxford University Press, Oxford, England.

Mayr, E. (1999) The concerns of science. Skeptical Inquirer 23 4, July/August, pp. 65.

Mayr, E. and Provine, W.B. (1980) *The evolutionary synthesis. Perspectives on the unification of biology.* Harvard University Press, Cambridge, MA.

McCann, K. and Yodzis, P. (1994) Biological conditions for chaos in a three-species food chain. Ecology 75:561-564.

McIver, T. (1996) A walk through Earth history: all eight thousand years. Skeptic 4-1:32-41.

McShea, D.W. (1991) Complexity and evolution: what everybody knows. Biology and Philosophy 6:303-324.

McShea, D.W. (1996) Metazoan complexity and evolution: is there a trend? Evolution 50:477-492.

Miele, F. (1996) The (Im)moral animal. Skeptic 4-1:42-49.

Miller, S.L. (1953) A production of amino acids under possible primitive earth conditions. Science 117:528-529.

Miller, S.L. (1997) Peptide nucleic acids and prebiotic chemistry. Natural Structural Biology 4:167.

Mole, P. (1998) Deepak's dangerous dogmas. Skeptic 6 2, pp. 38-45.

Monod, J. (1971) *Chance and Necessity; an Essay on the Natural Philosophy of Modern Biology.* Knopf, New York, NY.

Moore, G.E. (1903) *Principia Ethica*. Cambridge University Press, Cambridge, England.

Morris, S.C. (1998) *The Crucible of Creation: the Burgess Shale and the Rise of Animals*. Oxford University Press, Oxford, UK.

Morris, W.F. (1990) Problems in detecting chaotic behavior in natural populations by fitting simple discrete models. Ecology 71:1849-1862.

Morrison, P. and Cocconi, G. (1959) Searching for interstellar communications. Nature 184:844-846.

NAS (1998) *Teaching About Evolution and the Nature of Science*. National Academy of Science, Washington, DC.

Nijhout, H.F. (1996) Focus on butterfly eyespot development. Nature 384:209-210.

Niklas, K.J. (1997) Adaptive walks through fitness landscapes for early vascular land plants. American Journal of Botany 84:16-25.

Novella, S. and Bloomberg, D. (1999) Scientific skepticism, CSICOP, and the local groups. Skeptical Inquirer 23 4, July/August, pp. 44-46.

Olsen, L.F., Truty, G.L. and Schaffer, W.M. (1988) Oscillations and chaos in epidemics: a nonlinear study of six childhood diseases in Copenhagen, Denmark. Theoretical Population Biology 33:344-370.

Oparin, A.I. (1938) *The Origin of Life on Earth*. Macmillan, New York, NY.

Palevitz, B.A. (1999) Science and the versus of religion. Skeptical Inquirer 23 4, July/August, pp. 32-36.

Palevitz, B.A. and Lewis, R. (1999) Short shrift to evolution? The Scientist 2/1, pp. 11.

Paley, W. (1831) *Natural theology: or, Evidences of the Existence and Attributes of the Deity, Collected from the Appearances of Nature*. Gould, Kendall, and Lincoln, Boston, MA.

Pazameta, Z. (1999) Science vs. religion. Skeptical Inquirer 23 4, July/August, pp. 37-39.

Peitgen, H.-O., Jurgens, H. and Saupe, D. (1992) *Fractals for the Classroom. I. Introduction to Fractals and Chaos*. Springer-Verlag, New York, NY.

Pickett, F.B. and Meeks-Wagner, D.R. (1995) Seeing double: appreciating genetic redundancy. The Plant Cell 7:1347-1356.

Pigliucci, M. (1998) A case against god: science and the falsifiability question in theology. Skeptic 6 2, pp. 66-73.

Pigliucci, M. (1998b) "Science, religion, and all that jazz" (a review of E.J. Larson's *Summer for the Gods*). BioScience May, pp.

Pigliucci, M. (1999) Gould's separate "Magisteria": two views. A review of *Rocks of Ages: Science and Religion in the Fullness of Life* by S.J. Gould, Ballantine, 1999. Skeptical Inquirer 23 6, November/December, pp. 53-56.

Pigliucci, M. (2000) Chance, necessity, and the new holy war against science. A review of W.A. Dembski's *The Design Inference*. BioScience 50, pp. 79-81.

Pigliucci, M. (in press) *Beyond Nature vs. Nurture: the Genetics, Ecology and Evolution of Genotype-Environment Interactions*. Johns Hopkins University Press, Baltimore, MD.

Pinker, S. (1999) Whence religious belief? Skeptical Inquirer 23 4, July/August, pp. 53-54.

Polidoro, M. (1998) Houdini and Conan Doyle, the story of a strange friendship. Skeptical Inquirer 22(2):40-46.

Pool, R. (1989) Ecologists flirt with chaos. Science 243:310-313.

Popper, K. (1968) *Conjectures and Refutations: the Growth of Scientific Knowledge.* Harper & Row, New York, NY.

Provine, W.B. (1971) Population genetics: the synthesis of Mendelism, Darwinism, and Biometry. In: (eds.) *The origin of theoretical population genetics*, pp. 130-178. Chicago University Press, Chicago.

Provine, W.B. (1988) Scientists, face it! Science and religion are incompatible. The Scientist 9/5:10.

Raff, R.A. (1996) *The Shape of Life.* Chicago University Press, Chicago.

Raff, R.A., Marshall, C.R. and Turbeville, J.M. (1994) Using DNA sequences to unravel the Cambrian radiation of the animal phyla. Annual Review of Ecology and Systematics 25:351-375.

Ramachandran, V.S. and Blakeslee, S. (1998) *Phantoms in the Brain: Probing the Mysteries of the Human Mind.* William Morrow, New York, NY.

Raymo, C. (1998) *Skeptics and True Believers: the Exhilarating Connection Between Science and Religion.* Walker and Co., New York, NY.

Raymo, C. (1999) Celebrating creation. Skeptical Inquirer 23 4, July/August, pp. 21-23.

Richardson, M.K., Hanken, J., Selwood, L., Wright, G.M., Richards, R.J. and Pieau, C. (1998) Haeckel, embryos, and evolution. Science 280:983-984.

Rothman, T. (1989) *Science a la mode.* Princeton University Press, Princeton, NJ.

Ruse, M. (in press) A review of *Rock of Ages* by Stephen Jay Gould. Skeptic

Russell, B. (1957) *Why I Am Not a Christian.* Simon & Schuster, New York.

Schlichting, C.D. and Pigliucci, M. (1998) *Phenotypic Evolution, a Reaction Norm Perspective.* Sinauer, Sunderland, MA.

Schrodinger, E. (1947) *What is Life?* Macmillan, New York, NY.

Schwartz, B. (1987) *George Washington: the Making of an American Symbol.* The Free Press, New York, NY, p. 173.

Scott, E.C. (1999) The 'science and religion movement'. Skeptical Inquirer 23 4, July/August, pp. 29-31.

Shanks, N. and Joplin, K.H. (1999) Redundant complexity: a critical analysis of intelligent design in biochemistry. Philosophy of Science 66:268-282.

Shermer, M. (1993) The chaos of history: on a chaotic model that represents the role of contingency and necessity in historical sequences. Nonlinear Science Today 2:1-13.

Shermer, M. (1995) Exorcising Laplace's demon: chaos and antichaos, history and metahistory. History and Theory 34:59-83.

Shermer, M. (1997) *How to Debate a Creationist.* Millennium Press, Altadena, CA.

Shermer, M. (1997b) The myth of the beautiful people. Skeptic 5-1:72-79.

Shermer, M. (1997c) The crooked timber of history. Complexity 2:23-29.

Shermer, M. (1998) Is God dead? Why Nietzsche and Time Magazine were wrong. Skeptic 6 3, pp. 80-87.

Shermer, M. (1999) *How We Believe: the Search for God in an Age of Science.* Freeman & Co., New York, NY.

Shorris, E. (1997) On the uses of a liberal education. II. As a weapon in the hands of the restless poor. Harper's Magazine September:50-59.

Simpson, G.G. (1944) *Tempo and Mode in Evolution.* Columbia University Press, New York, NY.

Slijper, E.J. (1942) Biologic-anatomical investigations on the bipedal gait and upright posture in mammals, with special reference to a little goat, born without forelegs. Proc. Koninkl. Ned. Akad. Wetensch. 45:288-295 and 407-415.

Sloan, R.P., Bagiella, E. and Powell, T. (1999) Religion, spirituality, and medicine. Lancet 353:664-667.

Smith, G.H. (1991) *Atheism, Ayn Rand, and Other Heresies.* Prometheus Books, New York.

Smith, H. (1991) *The World's Religions.* Harper, San Francisco.

Snelson, J.S. (1992) The ideological immune system: resistance to new ideas in science. Skeptic 1, 4:44-55.

Sole`, R.V., Manrubia, S.C., Benton, M., Kauffman, S. and Bak, P. (1999) Criticality and scaling in evolutionary ecology. Trends in Ecology & Evolution 14:156-160.

Stassen, C., Meritt, J., Lilje, A. and Davis, L.D. (1992) Some more observed speciation events. Talk Origins (accessed: 12/29/99), web page, www.talkorigins.org.

Stenger, V.J. (1996) Cosmythology: was the universe designed to produce us? Skeptic 4(2):36-41.

Stenger, V.J. (1999) Anthropic design. Skeptical Inquirer 23 4, July/August, pp. 40-43.

Stevenson, J. (1998) *The Complete Idiot's Guide to Philosophy.* Alpha Books, New York.

Stone, L. (1994) Ecological chaos. Nature 367:418.

Sulloway, F.J. (1997) *Born to Rebel: Birth Order, Family Dynamics, and Creative Lives.* Vintage Books, New York, NY.

Svitil, K.A. (2000) Field guide to new planets. Discover March, pp. 48-55.

Tattersall, I. (2000) Once we were not alone. Scientific American 282 1, January, pp. 56-67.

Taylor, A.E. (1953) *Socrates.* Doubleday, Garden City, NY.

Tessman, I. And J. Tessman (2000) Efficacy of prayer: a criticial examination of claims. Skeptical Inquirer 24:31-33.

Thewissen, J.G.M., Hussain, S.T. and Arif, M. (1994) Fossil evidence for the origin of aquatic locomotion in Archeocete whales. Science 263:210-212.

Tipler, F.J. (1995) *The Physics of Immortality: Modern Cosmology, God and the Resurrection of the Dead.* Doubleday, New York, NY.

Trott, R. (1994) Debating the ICR's Duane Gish. talk.origins (accessed: 1/16/98), web page, www.talkorigins.org/faqs/debating/gish.html.

Turchin, P. (1993) Chaos and stability in rodent population dynamics: evidence from non-linear time-series analysis. Oikos 68:167-172.

van Valen, L. (1973) A new evolutionary law. Evolutionary Theory 1:1-30.

Voltaire, F.M.A. (1759) *Candide*. St. Martin's Press {1963}, New York, NY.

Voltaire, F.M.A. (1949) *The Portable Voltaire*. Viking Press, New York.

Waddington, C.H. (1961) Genetic assimilation. Advances in Genetics 10:257-290.

Waldrop, M.M. (1992) *Complexity: the Emerging Science at the Edge of Order and Chaos*. Simon & Schuster, New York, NY.

Webb, G.E. (1997) "Theory" and the public understanding of science: reflections on the evolution controversy in America. Journal of the Tennessee Academy of Science 72:37-41.

West-Eberhard, M.J. (1989) Phenotypic plasticity and the origins of diversity. Annual Review of Ecology and Systematics 20:249-278.

Wilson, E.O. (1998) *Consilience: the Unity of Knowledge*. Knopf : Distributed by Random House, New York, NY.

Wisdom, B. (1997) Skepticism and credulity. Skeptic 5(2):96-100.

Wise, D.U. (1998) Creationism's geologic time scale. American Scientist 86 March-April, pp. 160-173.

Witmer, J. and Zimmerman, M. (1991) Intercessory prayer as medical treatment? Skeptical Inquirer 15 Winter, pp. 177-180.

Wolf, A. and Bessoir, T. (1991) Diagnosing chaos in the space circle. Physica D50:239-258.

Wolf, A., Swift, J.B., Swinney, H.L. and Vastano, J.A. (1985) Determining Lyapunov exponents from a time series. Physica 16D:285-317.

Wolfram, S. (1984) Cellular automata as models of complexity. Nature 311:419-424.

Wright, S. (1932) Evolution in Mendelian populations. Genetics 16:97-159.

Wuchterl, G. (1991) Hydrodynamics of giant planet formation. 2 . Model-equations and critical mass. Icarus 91:39-52.

Yahya, H. (1999) *The Evolution Deceit: the Scientific Collapse of Darwinism and its Ideological Background*. Okur, Instanbul, Turkey.

Index

Figure credits

Fig. 1.1, Rene` Descartes, Perry-Castaneda Library, University of Texas Austin

Fig. 1.2, Leonardo da Vinci, Perry-Castaneda Library, University of Texas Austin

Fig. 3.1, Nicholas Copernicus, Perry-Castaneda Library, University of Texas Austin

Fig. 3.2, Charles Darwin, Perry-Castaneda Library, University of Texas Austin

Fig. 4.1, Blaise Pascal, University of Waterloo Philosophers' Gallery

Fig. 5.1, Comparison of levels of belief among scientists, adapted from Larson and Whitam (1997)

Fig. 5.2, Galileo Galilei, Perry-Castaneda Library, University of Texas Austin

Fig. 6.1, Michael Shermer, with permission by M. Shermer

Fig. 8.1, Bertrand Russell, University of Waterloo Philosophers' Gallery

Fig. 9.1, William Dembski, with permission by W. Dembski

Fig. 10.1, William Craig, with permission by W. Craig

Fig. 11.1, Duane Gish, with permission by D. Gish

Fig. 11.2, Developmental biology of butterflies, Paul Brakefield, Leiden University

Fig. 11.3, Crania of *Homo abilis* and *H. sapiens*, with permission by W.W. Norton

Fig. 11.4, Cranium of *Homo erectus*, with permission by W.W. Norton

Fig. 11.5, The evolution of the eye, redrawn from Futuyma (1998)

Fig. 13.1, Frank Drake, with permission by F. Drake, photo by Seth Shostak, SETI Institute

Fig. 13.2, The Lagoon Nebula, NASA Image Exchange

Fig. 13.3, The Pioneer 10 plaque, NASA Image Exchange

All other figures: drawings by Massimo Pigliucci